Current Issues in International Tourism Development

Edited by
Elizabeth M. Ineson

Business Education Publishers Limited

© David Battersby Paul Connellan Crispin Dale Catherine Feeney John Fenby
John Hunter-Jones Philippa Hunter-Jones Jarmila Indrová Christopher Mitchell
Gianfranco Nobis Zdenka Petrů Neil Robinson Neil Symon 2005

ISBN 1 901888 48 7

First published 2005

Cover Design by Tim Murphy Creative Solutions
Cover from an original painting by John Ineson

Published in Great Britain by
Business Education Publishers Limited
The Teleport
Doxford International
Sunderland
SR3 3XD

Tel: 0191 5252410
Fax: 0191 5201815

British Cataloguing-in-Publications Data
A catalogue record for this book is available from the British Library

The publisher has made every effort to obtain permission to reproduce material in this book from the appropriate source. If there are any errors or omissions please contact the publisher who will make suitable acknowledgement in the reprint.

Printed in Great Britain by the Alden Group, Oxford.

Elaine Crichton
August 2005

Contents

Introduction
Raising your Game
David Battersby OBE MSc FHCIMA   1

Chapter One
The Role of Food Culture in Tourism Development
Christopher Mitchell   7

Chapter Two
The Development of Wine Tourism
Neil Symon   29

Chapter Three
Accommodation Development: focusing on a case study of Eastern Europe
Neil Robinson   43

Chapter Four
Hotel Classification and Grading: towards the development of a unified system
John Fenby   61

Chapter Five
Developing and Managing an Event
Catherine Feeney   75

Chapter Six
The Development of Tourist Attractions and Entertainment
Crispin Dale and Neil Robinson   101

Chapter Seven
Health Tourism: new opportunities for destination development
Philippa Hunter-Jones   117

Chapter Eight
Developing Sustainable Tourism
Jarmila Indrová and Zdenka Petnů   127

Chapter Nine
Risks and Responsibilities
John Hunter-Jones and Philippa Hunter-Jones   157

Chapter Ten
Perspectives on the Economic Impact of Tourism
Paul Connellan

171

Chapter Eleven
Cultural Factors in Tourism Development
Gianfranco Nobis

187

Index

203

List of Contributors

Elizabeth M. Ineson lectures in Methods of Enquiry and Consultancy at Manchester Metropolitan University and tutors postgraduate students at the University Centre César Ritz in Switzerland; her PhD is in management education. Since 1988, she has conducted seminars for educators and industrialists in Central and Eastern Europe focusing on course development, research methods, experiential education and action learning, in particular promoting the development of industry/education links. Liz is a Fellow of the Hotel and Catering International Management Association and the Institute of Travel and Tourism; in 1999; she won the EuroCHRIE HCIMA/AHMA award for outstanding achievement.

David Battersby OBE, MSc, FHCIMA. Since January 1990, David has been Director of Hospitality and Leisure Manpower, the London based consulting group. He was previously Director of Training the Hotel and Catering Training Board, the industry's National Training Organisation. David has over 30 years experience of work at a strategic level in the tourism and hospitality industry. He works closely with government; major employers; employer associations; professional bodies; tourist boards; trade unions and educationists.

David is the past President of the Hotel and Catering International Management Association, a Vice-President of the European Catering Association, a Director of the Academy of Food and Wine Service, a Fellow of the Tourism Society, and a past Trustee of the Savoy Educational Trust. In 1998 David was made an Officer of the Order of the British Empire in the New Year's Honours for services to the Tourism Industry, and in 1999 was made a Fellow of the Royal Society of Arts.

Currently David is managing the Tourism Industry's "Best Practice Forum" for the Department for Culture, Media and Sport, and DTI as part of the Government's Tourism Strategy to increase competitiveness within the sector.

Paul Connellan is a Consultant specialising in Aviation and Tourism. His particular interest is Customer Service and he speaks regularly at conferences across the world on that subject. He is also a visiting university lecturer in marketing and customer service. He has worked in most areas of the tourism and aviation industry including time in Germany, the USA and the Middle East. His first degree was in Sociology and his postgraduate studies were at the London Business School on the Sloan Fellowship Programme.

Crispin Dale is a Principal Lecturer for Technology Supported Learning and the Course Leader for the MA Tourism Management in the School of Sport, Performing Arts and Leisure at the University of Wolverhampton. His current research interests focus on strategic management in tourism and hospitality and the use of virtual learning environments to support learning in leisure, tourism and hospitality education. He has also recently led the University of Wolverhampton's tourism team in a European Funded Tempus Tacis project to develop a tourism curriculum with the Bishkek Academy of Economy and Finance in Kyrgyzstan.

Catherine Feeney has been a Senior Lecturer at Manchester Metropolitan University since 1992 and is currently the Event Management Programme Leader. Having worked in the United Kingdom, Germany, Australia, Kingdom of Saudi Arabia and other areas of the Middle East in hospitality she has continued to this day, with her practice of managing large prestigious corporate events. These have ranged from Commonwealth Games in Manchester (2002), British Grand Prix, Ascot, Henley Regatta, various international sports tournaments and royal events.

John Fenby has taught at Manchester Metropolitan University for 14 years. He is Section Leader for all of the undergraduate degree and HND programmes in Hospitality and Events Management in the School of Food, Consumer, Hospitality and Tourism Management. His subject area is hospitality and events facilities management and specifically the design and planning of hospitality facilities. He is also an experienced interior and buildings designer and he has also been involved in facilities case study research in the context of a number of major UK hospitality companies.

John Hunter-Jones is the Course Director and a Lecturer on the Management and Leisure Degree at the University of Manchester. His teaching is focused on legal studies for the leisure and teaching professions, in particular matters relating to the health and safety of outdoor activities. His research focuses on health and safety issues in the leisure and education sectors. He is currently undertaking a PhD researching the validity and effectiveness of the current law in providing a legal framework for school trips. He has past experience working in the public and private sectors within the tourism industry.

Philippa Hunter-Jones is a Senior Lecturer in Tourism Management at Manchester Metropolitan University. She is the programme leader for the MSc Tourism Management and MSc Hospitality Management and is involved in teaching at both undergraduate and postgraduate level. Her research interests focus upon the relationship between holiday-taking and health. She is particularly interested in work exploring the circumstances of those who travel with pre-existing medical conditions and completed her PhD in this area in 2001.

Doc. Ing. Jarmila Indrová is the Head of the Tourism Department at the University of Economics, Prague, a member of Scientific Board of the Faculty of International Relationship, a member of the editing Committee of Economic Review (Slovakia, Banská Bystrica) and a member of the Nutrition Society. She graduated at the University of Economics in Prague with a PhD in Economic Sciences and is now a Senior Lecturer in Tourism. She is the leader of the postgraduate and undergraduate Tourism and Tourism and Regional Development programmes and also specialises in Hotel and Catering Management. She has many close industrial contacts and represents the Department of Tourism in the Professional Association HO-RE-KA and in the Association of Historical Cities in Bohemia, Moravia and Silesia. She is an author and co-author of numerous tourism textbooks and books.

Christopher Mitchell is a Senior Lecturer for Hospitality Management with Tourism at the School of Food, Consumer, Tourism and Hospitality Management at Manchester Metropolitan University. Since 2000 he has lectured in food and beverage production, service skills and licensed retail industry areas. Chris has also consulted on the European Regional Development Funds up-skilling project in the North West of England in 2001, developing training schedules for the delivery of NVQs in SMEs within the hospitality Industry. Research interests include Food and beverage, licensing issues (UK) and up-skilling. He is currently working towards a Doctorate in Education with a focus on on-line learning development.

Gianfranco Nobis is Senior Consultant to the Fondation pour La formation Hôtelière of Geneva. He is an experienced practitioner, academic and researcher having carried out several projects on behalf of government agencies in the UK and abroad. He lectured for 30 years until 1993 and completed his educational career in the UK as Head of Department at Bournemouth University. He is the co-author of 7 textbooks and has written a number of articles. In 1993 he founded Nobis Consultancy Ltd. Since 1990 he has lectured extensively in West and Eastern Europe, the Middle East, Africa and the Caribbean. He has served on several advisory committees on education and training in different countries.

Ing. Zdenka Petrů is a Lecturer at the Tourism Department at the University of Economics Prague. She graduated at the University of Economics in Prague and has worked for an in-bound Travel Agency as the Marketing and Sales Manager for seven years. In the last decade, she was awarded scholarships to study in Great Britain at Manchester Metropolitan University and in the U.S.A at Rochester Institute of Technology. She specialises in Travel Agency and Tour Operations, cooperates closely with the Industry in her work and was a member of the working group Czech Republic experts in CEN (Comité Européen de Normalisation), specialising in Travel Agency Services; currently she is a member of the working group for Language Study Tours. Zdenka is an author and co-author of many tourism textbooks.

Neil Robinson is a Senior Lecturer in Consumer Marketing at Manchester Metropolitan University with research interests in service sector management, small business development, consumerism and IT. He has worked overseas in the Far East delivering management development programmes and has been responsible for the creation of bespoke operational training systems for a number of large multinational companies including Panda Hotels (Hong Kong) and British Airways. On an academic front Neil has held various academic positions within the higher education sector in the UK, including The University of Central Lancashire, Liverpool John Moores University and The University of Bolton, teaching at both undergraduate and postgraduate level. From a research perspective Neil has published in several key academic journals including the Journal of Vacation Marketing, The Hospitality Review and the prestigious International Journal of Contemporary Hospitality Management. Neil is currently registered for a PhD, researching the impact of ICT on service sector SMEs.

Neil Symon has been with Manchester Metropolitan University since 2000 and is the Programme Leader for International Hospitality Management. He teaches finance, facilities management and business planning on Hospitality programmes. He lectures on wine tourism to all the Tourism programmes. His previous career has included teaching specialist wines and spirits courses to the wine trade. He holds an MSc in Hotel Management and the Wine and Spirit Education Trust Diploma.

Preface

This text examines a series of issues which impact on the potential for domestic and cross border tourism development, focusing on the utilisation of local resources in order to promote national economies. The introduction summarises research into International Best Practice. There then follows a series of chapters which examine international tourism issues from a developmental perspective. The focus in Chapters 1-6 is on specific sectors, that is food and beverage, wine, accommodation and hotel grading, events, attractions/entertainment and health, in the tourism industry. In Chapters 7-11, tourism developments are examined in an environmental context, that is, with respect to sustainability, risks and responsibilities, economic impacts and cultural perspectives. Although other books have been written on tourism development, their authors' fundamental approaches are different: they tend to focus on local areas, countries or economic issues as opposed to tourism development per se.

Throughout, basic academic theories are examined, and their applicability is demonstrated and assessed, through mini case studies, practical academic research employing the specialist knowledge and experiences of the contributors. Furthermore the theories are exemplified by international practices, mostly with a strong focus on Central and Eastern Europe. The practices and lessons learned from countries whose doors have opened up over the last 10 years, with consequently soaring numbers of international visitors, can provide valuable learning experiences for the future of international tourism development. In turn, academic theory and examples from relatively developed countries provide a framework within which countries whose tourism industry is less developed can move forward.

One of the principles behind the production of this text book was to provide access to materials for readers, perhaps located in less-developed countries, who may have neither the facility of a well-stocked local library close at hand nor access to on-line libraries. Therefore, many of the references and examples are accessible via the internet so that they can be of value globally for both face-to-face interactive and distance learning. Although every effort has been made to provide up-to-date material at the time of publication, there is a downside to researching and learning via the internet in that some of the websites are not maintained continuously and others may have their addresses changed or even be removed over time. However, the up-side is that many sites are updated daily with research information and increasing numbers of new and potentially useful sites continue to appear. A recommended good website at which to start is http://europa.eu.int/ where there is an initial choice of 20 languages via 'Gateway to the European Union' (EU). Within this site is the EU Bookshop which offers an online service giving access to publications from the EU institutions, agencies and other bodies and an online catalogue and archive of all EU publications. The EU Bookshop allows users to search for EU publications (some of which are available in up to five European languages) order them and where possible, download copies, almost invariably free of charge.

Acknowledgements

The editor would like to thank: *La fondation pour la formation hôtelière* and the *Fondation Nestlé Pro Gastronomia* (especially Prof. Gianfranco Nobis and Mr Otmar Sorgenfrei) for their continued generous support and interest in this project; *the contributors* for their expertise, patience and tenacity; the reviewers; and *the A-team* (Douglas, Jack, Jen and John) for their first class assistance.

We are grateful to the following for permission to reproduce copyright material:

Reprinted/adapted from:

International Journal of Wine Marketing, Vol. 11, No. 2, Dodd, T. Attracting Repeat Customers to Wineries, pp. 18-28, (1999), with permission from Barmarick Publications.

Managing Visitor Attractions: New directions, A. Fyall, B. Garrod, and A. Leask. The Nature and Purpose of Visitor Attractions, Leask, A. (2003), with permission from Elsevier.

The Development and Management of Visitor Attractions, Swarbrooke, J. (2000), with permission from Elsevier.

Managing Visitor Attractions: New directions, A. Fyall, B. Garrod, and A. Leask. Interpreting the Development of the Visitor Attraction Product, Wanhill, S. (2003a), with permission from Elsevier.

Events' Management, Bowdin, G., McDonnell, I., Allen, J. and O'Toole, W. (2003), with permission from Elsevier.

Thai and Other Emerging Ethnic Foods-UK (2003a), with permission from Mintel International Group Limited.

UK Outbound-2003, with permission from Mintel International Group Limited.

Tourism, an Introduction, Youell, R. (1998), with permission from Pearson Education Limited.

Wine Tourism, Parfitt, N. The Southern Downs Visitor Survey: Research Findings, (2003), with permission from Tourism Queensland.

International Travel and Health, World Health Organisation (WHO) (2005), with permission from the World Health Organisation.

Current Issues in International Tourism Development

Introduction

Raising your Game

David Battersby, OBE, MSc, FHCIMA

Tourism, Hospitality and Leisure is Europe's biggest growth industry. Principally, it is comprised of over three million small hotels and guest houses, restaurants and catering operations, leisure and visitor attractions, pubs and licensed retail outlets. Whilst 85% of these establishments employ fewer than 25 staff, nevertheless they have accounted for one in six of all new jobs created in the last 10 years and employ over 7% of Europe's workforce. The industry employs eight million people, 5% of Europe's workforce, and contributes 5.5% to Gross Domestic Product (GDP) (European Commission, 2002) and is Europe's largest invisible exporter. As an industry sector it is larger than the aerospace and the automotive industries combined.

Yet the tourism, hospitality and leisure industry is facing particular challenges as it strives to maintain its competitive edge at a time when competing destinations are investing heavily in product development and marketing. Many overseas destinations are better able to deliver 'world class' standards of Service Excellence at lower cost than Europe which is generally a high cost economy. To be competitive on a world stage, employers in the industry need increasingly to be driven by price, quality and value. Declining standards, rising prices and decreasing value, are of increasing concern. Europe needs to become a high quality, high value, tourist product. Billions of pounds are being invested in new hotels and upgraded facilities but they do not reflect public perceptions about Europe as a visitor destination. Good establishments are being dragged down by others which have a poor reputation. Job seekers, equally, do not rate the sector highly because of its perceived poor conditions of employment.

More resources need to be invested in quality. To do so, operating costs need to be cut through higher productivity. At a time when skilled labour is in short supply, the industry needs to be continually innovative and search for new ways to make better use of people: to help staff to work smarter, not harder. Yet across the industry as a whole, and within hotels in particular, productivity levels are half of those in the USA, and market growth in many overseas countries is twice that of the growth levels experienced in Europe.

It was in response to these challenges that the Best Practice Forum (launched in September 2001, http://www.bestpracticeforum.org) recently completed a major international study into Best Practice with a 12 strong research team led in the United Kingdom by Prof. Peter Jones of the University of Surrey. The Forum is seeking to improve the competitiveness of the tourism, hospitality and leisure industry. It is a direct response to the UK government's Competitiveness

White Paper (1998, http://www.dti.gov.uk/comp/competitive/main.htm) and aims to raise levels of quality, productivity and business performance, particularly amongst small businesses.

Over the first five years of the Forum's work the following improvements in business performance are being sought: sales per employee up by 15%; reject deliveries down by 7.5%; value added per employee up by 10%; capital employed up by 2.5%; average length of stay per employee up by 20%; new business from new markets up by 12.5%.

As the principal trade association for the hospitality industry, the British Hospitality Association (British Hospitality Association (BHA) http://www.bha-online.org.uk) has created the Forum and is leading its work in a strategic alliance with seven key industry associations, together with other national and regional partners, so that the benefits of its work can be felt across all industry sectors.

The research, the most comprehensive international study of its kind, sought principally to answer the question: "What is it that successful, winning companies do to achieve, and continually improve, 'world class' standards of service and business excellence?" The results were quite eye-opening: for example, the bottom 25% of companies are achieving profit levels one-tenth of those achieved by the top 25%. Moreover, the top 25% require three times less overhead than the bottom 25%, need three times fewer indirect staff and require half the number of managers.

Most successful businesses seek constantly to improve performance and productivity – that is the ultimate secret of their success. Tempting though it is to accept the status quo, particularly if it believes it is successful, a business will not grow – nor become more efficient – if it does not recognise the need to improve performance through innovation and continuous development. By regularly examining the way it operates and by bringing in new ideas and new methods of working, a business generates additional turnover, becomes more productive, and creates more profit.

What practical steps can a business take to become more productive? What are the key elements of any performance improvement programme? Research on behalf of the Best Practice Forum by the University of Surrey suggests that better productivity (that is, more output for correspondingly less input) is powered by five key drivers:

➢ Increasing customer spend

➢ Building customer volume

➢ Controlling material costs

➢ Controlling labour costs

➢ Improving the way we work

Whilst it could be convenient to attribute low productivity in the sector to a lack of capital investment, little use of new technology or inadequate government support, research findings suggest that the greatest impact on levels of productivity rests with improved management and supervision of the workforce. High operating costs and productivity losses are in the main attributable to an absence of operational management techniques such as planning, scheduling, resource co-ordination, communications and flexing to match demand. Organisation design also impacts on productivity.

Increasing Customer Spend

Increasing customer spend, while maintaining current staff levels, will make a significant contribution to the bottom line primarily because it involves little or no additional cost. However, there normally needs to be some investment in staff training, typically in sales and marketing expenditure, including point-of-sale merchandising. Increasing customer spend depends on upselling products and services so that existing customers are encouraged to buy more, or to buy more expensive items on which there are higher profit margins.

Building Customer Volume

Large companies are adept at building customer volume and use a wide variety of sales and marketing tools, including advertising, sales promotion techniques and, increasingly, electronic and web-based marketing. These activities demand expertise and, frequently, the use of specialist staff or agencies. Small and medium sized businesses may rely relatively heavily on word-of-mouth advertising. This technique can be even more effective than any other one; although its impact will not be so immediate, it may have more permanent benefits. Building up repeat custom in this way is one of the most effective ways of growing a business.

Operators can build customer volume in a variety of other ways: by training staff to provide outstanding customer service, thus giving added value which also encourages word-of-mouth advertising; by the owner taking advantage of local networking opportunities so raising his profile in the local community and building local custom; and by the owner and staff talking to customers regularly and generating customer loyalty. Again, these methods are doubly effective because they add little, if any, cost to the enterprise.

Controlling Material Costs

Material costs (that is, all costs other than labour) will represent in the region of 70% of the total costs of most businesses in the industry. These costs include rent and rates, food and beverage, energy, telecommunication, maintenance and other areas such as laundry, equipment rental, print and stationery. Controlling these items better may yield considerable savings for some businesses; examining energy usage, in particular, is especially beneficial. At the same time, taking advantage of group buying schemes (for example, through purchasing consortia) can be highly cost-efficient. However, this is an area in which many operators believe that their control procedures are totally effective; but without benchmarking, they cannot check this fact and they may be missing out on these savings.

Controlling Labour Costs

Labour is a major cost for most businesses in the tourism, hospitality and leisure industry, except for micro businesses where nearly all the work is done by the owners themselves. In the hotel industry, the labour cost ratio (the cost of labour as a percentage of total turnover) has been rising steadily in the last few years – from 23.7% in 1998 to 29.1% in 2002 (British Hospitality Association, 2003).

Anecdotal evidence suggests that, in some cases, labour costs are as high as 35%. There is no doubt that other sectors of the industry are also under pressure in this area, which will continue to increase as long as we have a relatively buoyant economy and full employment. The need to control labour costs is one of the most important objectives of any business.

It is often assumed that further labour cost increases are inevitable. They certainly are if no action is taken to control them. However, action can be taken – through better job scheduling, better induction and training, the introduction of multi-skilling and the employment of more skilled human resources management generally. Slicing a couple of percentage points off these costs, while maintaining revenue and customer service standards, will bring about savings that go straight to the bottom line.

Changing the Way we Work

Businesses tend to grow on an *ad hoc* basis and their methods of work grow in the same way, without examining closely how new ways of working could improve performance and productivity. All too frequently they still practice methods that were introduced 30 years ago. Of course, work methods may change on a trial and error basis, and they may be modified by new staff, who have different ways of doing things. However, changes take place more often by reacting to events and pressures than by any planned organisation.

Because work in a service industry is often less formalised than in manufacturing, it is also commonly assumed that methods of work cannot be improved. In manufacturing, however, production lines are highly systemised and structured; can some of the techniques used in manufacturing be adapted to tourism, hospitality or leisure? Certainly, staff and systems have to be flexible to meet the changing needs of customers and changing levels of demand, which make it difficult to lay down rigid patterns of work, but this does not mean that service industries cannot learn from manufacturing. The most important objective is to eliminate waste – in material costs, in labour costs and in effort:

➢ Doing too much

➢ Waiting

➢ Transporting

➢ Too much inflexibility in the approach to work

➢ Unnecessary stocks

➢ Unnecessary motions

➢ Defects

Each of these areas applies as much to businesses in the tourism, hospitality and leisure industry as it does to manufacturing. Recent evidence in two sectors of the industry– hotels and flight catering - suggests that significant gains can be made if waste is eliminated and new methods of work are introduced. For example, research in a hotel chain (Jones, 2003) showed a 20% reduction in labour cost by scheduling housekeeping staff more effectively, while improvements in the implementation of the 'just-in-time' philosophy in flight catering operations (Jones, 2003) are leading to a 30% reduction in labour costs.

Not every business will achieve savings of this magnitude (on the other hand, some will achieve more) but it is likely that any business that positively, and continually, addresses this area will achieve results that increase productivity, reduce costs and boost profits.

Jones (2003) suggests that very few, if any, businesses have adopted and implemented all five drivers of productivity, nor have they looked at all the different ways in which they can improve their ways of working. Good Practice is not common practice. Some have, however, introduced a selection of policies and procedures that are right for them, although these vary according to different sectors of the industry. For example, multi-skilling (one way of reducing labour costs) is already a practice widespread in the licensed trade but less commonly found in hotels and restaurants; material costs are an important element in the restaurant business but less so for visitor attractions. Hotel management are often very good at forecasting room sales, but not very good at forecasting food and beverage sales.

What action should a business take to implement these five drivers? It can take a number of steps to create the conditions in which the drivers will be successful:

> ➤ Partnering and networking with other operators

> ➤ Making sure standards are set and achieved

> ➤ Developing good internal and external communication

> ➤ Regularly measuring and evaluating business performance through benchmarking

> ➤ Encouraging employee retention through better employment practices and training

> ➤ Planning the development of the business and controlling it better

> ➤ Adding value to products and services

The final and most crucial 'enabler' is:

> ➤ The quality of leadership in the business

It is unlikely that taking a piecemeal approach is the most effective way for a business to tackle performance improvement because it ignores the complex relationship between each of these elements. For example, the need for good communication is an element that runs through almost all the ways of improving the way we work, the way we employ and retain staff, and the way in which we build customer relationships. Strategically managing the workforce – ensuring that staff are scheduled correctly and have the skills and commitment to undertake their allotted tasks – is the central element of successful performance management. This, again, is a feature of all the drivers and 'enablers'. Furthermore, any attempt to set standards without proper training, good communication and constant supervision is doomed to failure. Consequently, it is important that the whole picture is considered if a performance improvement programme is to be implemented successfully.

There is one further condition. If a business wants to improve its performance, and to measure its success in doing this, it needs to know from where it is starting. How successful is it already? What does it want to achieve? The only way it can define its level of efficiency and productivity is to measure its current performance against that of others. It can then measure its on-going success at regular intervals.

Benchmarking is thus an essential pre-requisite in any move to improve performance. The Best Practice Forum's Profit Through Productivity programme (http://www.bestpracticeforum.org) which gives all participants an initial 'health check' by means of a benchmarking exercise, is the ideal starting point. With the help of a business adviser, an action plan is then drawn up to build up the strengths of the business and to address its weaknesses – the first step on its journey to excellence.

The Best Practice Forum has published a series of case studies and research reports that examine in detail how these drivers and enablers of productivity can be harnessed to improve performance. Please access http://www.bestpracticeforum.org/ or contact Hospitality and Leisure Manpower (00-44-(0)-20-8977-4419) for further details. Further information on the Forum's Profit Through Productivity programme and its benchmarking system is also available on the website.

References

Best Practice Forum (2001). [on line] available from: http://www.bestpracticeforum.org/, [accessed February 24th 2004].

British Hospitality Association (2003). *Trends and Statistics,* British Hospitality Association, August, [on line] available from: http://www.bha-online.org.uk [accessed February 24th 2004].

Competitiveness White Paper (1998). [on line] available from:
http://www.dti.gov.uk/comp/competitive/main.htm [accessed February 24th 2004].

European Commission (2002). *Tourism and the European Union.* Directorate-General Enterprise, Tourism Unit, Brussels [on line] available from:
http://europa.eu.int/comm/enterprise/services/tourism/tourismeu.htm [accessed February 24th 2004].

Jones, P. (2003). *Enablers and Drivers of Productivity in Hospitality Tourism, and Leisure,* Best Practice Forum, University of Surrey.

Chapter One

The Role of Food Culture in Tourism Development

Christopher Mitchell

Overview

This chapter examines the nature and diversity of food culture and tourists' food preferences. Following a sharp decline in its popularity, it has been necessary for the fast food industry to develop and reposition itself in order to combat increasing consumer awareness of issues relating to food scares, obesity and healthy eating. In contrast, the philosophy of the slow food movement, which emerged in Italy and has opposed the unhealthy aspects of fast food, has underpinned the recognition placed on the passion and the concept of cuisine that is predominantly regional and cooked traditionally, particularly in parts of Europe such as France and the United Kingdom (UK). The case of Manchester, a UK city of culinary delight, is used to exemplify diversity in food culture which, it is acknowledged, is evident in most westernised countries. Finally, issues of access to information on dining out are reviewed. The need for hospitality personnel to appreciate cultural differences and to develop a diverse range of knowledge and skills to meet the evolving knowledge and meal experience is emphasised, acknowledging that consumers today have increasing opportunities to experience international food due to their exposure to such a vast array of differing food cultures.

Introduction

Food is an important component of cultural and heritage tourism (Bessière, 1998; Cusack, 2000). It has a strong role to play in social groups and societies in many cultures (Valentine, 1999) and it can be used to portray symbols of cultural identity (Frochot, 2003). Food can be one of the most diverse and memorable experiences that the consumer has when encountering different cultures and societies, either locally or as a tourist. This chapter begins by explaining how the infusion of a rich variety of foodstuffs and different cuisines and cultures is now an everyday aspect of international eating which has merged to create a very diverse food culture. The expanding global eating out market is associated not only with increased leisure travel, reduced seasonality of foods, improved food transportation, storage and shelf life but also with relaxed immigration laws. The potential for food tourism is examined in the context of the UK outbound and inbound markets and the evolving consumer attitudes to food choices in the global fast food industry. The recent developments in the fast food market, incorporating views on the impact of consumer choice on healthy eating and the re-emergence of regional, traditional food through the slow food movement and the impact of local, national and international food events and festivals on food tourism, are considered.

Food Culture

Over many years, tourism in Europe has continued to develop and expand, embracing many aspects of its different cultures. This concept of culture is "transferred and transmuted from generation to generation and forms the framework for social behaviour and systems" (Theocharous, Nuttall and Seddighi, 2000, p. 387). In Britain there are strong influences from many European and ethnic cultures that are ingrained in British society. Its rich cultural tapestry has not only seen the development of society's understanding of different cultures but also the diverse range of foods that have been an accepted part of British culture. As early as 1992, changing preferences in British food culture were evident. Mintel (1992) and a report by Market Assessment Publications (1992) indicated that the Great British chip shop was in decline and had been out-numbered by the Indian take-away. Subsequently, this cultural repositioning became increasingly evident, when a Key Note report (1994) gave a strong indication of the changing British palate towards relatively 'exotic' international foods that were becoming much more readily available. Olsen, Warde and Martens (2000) conducted a study of the eating out market in the UK as part of the Economic and Social Research Council (ESRC) Research Programme: "The Nation's Diet: The Social Science of Food Choice". Data were collected in 1995 from a stratified (by age, sex, social class and ethnic group) sample of 1001 respondents in three major cities (London, Bristol and Preston), in contrasting geographical areas of England. Questions were based broadly on eating out patterns in the 12 months prior to the study. The research concluded that 52% of the sample had eaten in an ethnic restaurant (Non-UK cuisine), which was a strong indication of the positioning of the ethnic restaurant in the British eating out market.

As the British food preferences have changed and developed, consumers' tastes for food from India, China, Spain and France have evolved with dishes like pizza and pasta, which originated in other cultures, merging to become an accepted part of a global food cuisine (James, 1996). Mintel (2003a) commissioned a consumer research report in the UK from the British Market Research Bureau (BMRB) that looked at the different aspects of ethnic food, tastes and ethnic ingredients (See Table 1) over a period of three years. For the purpose of the report, compiled in December 2002, a national representative sample of 1,019 adults aged 15+ years were asked: "Which of these types of food do you most enjoy?" Up to four responses were allowed and the mean number of individual responses was 2.16; therefore the sum of the percentages in each column in Table 1 exceeds 100.

Base: Adults Aged 15+ Type of Food	1999 N=982 %	2001 N=1,052 %	2002 N=1,019 %	Change 1999-2002 % point
British	78	82	83	+5
Chinese	57	59	59	+2
Italian	47	50	47	0
Indian/Pakistani/Bengali	38	39	42	+4
French	17	14	15	-2
Thai	10	12	11	+1
Mexican/Tex-Mex	9	9	9	0
American (USA)	12	11	7	-5
Greek	11	7	6	-5
Spanish	9	7	6	-3

Table 1: Type of Food Enjoyed the Most by UK Adults, 1999-2002
Source: adapted from BMRB/Mintel 2003a.

Statistics show British cuisine is the most popular food type (Table 1) but it is suspected that many consumers would find it difficult to define this cuisine in a culture that has such a variety of influences. This blending of cultural foods (creolisation) to form dishes that have origins from different cultures (James,1996) can be seen as a natural development and is also termed by Scarpato and Daniele (2003) as the 'new global cuisine'. Possibly due to this invasion of non-British cultural foods and the popularity of fast food in the UK, there has been a push for more traditional British cuisine with the 'British Food Fortnight' , designed to "nurture a renaissance in the pleasures of preparing and eating regional food and drink" (http://www:britishfoodfortnight.co.uk). The aims are to increase consumers' awareness of home produced food and drink in Britain by focusing on the health benefits of eating quality, fresh, seasonal and regional produce. In particular, educators are requested to target school children by holding special events whilst producers, retailers and hospitality companies are invited to take a proactive role in educating the public about the food and drink that their region produces. In this way, British Cuisine is trying to become more identifiable with local products and local distinctiveness. Table 1 also shows a wide selection of international cuisines that give a clear indication of the variety within British food tastes and culture. Examples of food culture in Britain can be seen throughout the UK, not just in the major cities, with many excellent speciality restaurants, ranging from Asian cuisine, which has been part of the food culture in Britain for more than 40 years, to Oriental cuisine and the emergence of Thai restaurants (Mintel, 2003a). Embroiled in these culinary developments are the many Italian, Spanish, French, Greek and other European food delights that are increasingly part of the food culture of Britain.

This increasing demand for foreign food is confirmed in Table 2, which analyses the ethnic food choices eaten in restaurants, pubs or as a takeaway in the UK, in the six months prior to November 2002 (Mintel, 2003a). Although the choices in the report are not a complete list of the available ethnic food products in the UK market, 74.4% of respondents in the report indicated purchasing from the selection of commonly offered ethnic foods, with 25.5% of respondents giving a negative response or selecting none of the choices available. Some of the recent popularity and diverse range of cuisines in the UK coincide with (i) the economic change and the increased disposable income, which has seen an 8% growth in the eating out market since 1996, worth over £22 billion (approximately €33 billion) in 2001 (Mintel, 2002) and (ii) changing eating patterns due to the busy work life schedules of modern society and the increase in convenient methods of eating that have given a 5% rise to the weekly number of consumers eating out (Mintel, 2004) with consumers spending less time on chores like cooking and more time pursuing social and leisure activities (Warde & Martens, 2000, p. 100).

> *Pizza*
>
> "Pizza, a simple Italian dish associated specially but not exclusively with Naples, has become almost ubiquitous. After it was taken to America by Italian emigrants it developed into an international food and pizzerias sprung up all over the world. The word 'pizza' itself was used as early as the year 997 AD at Gaeta, a port between Naples and Rome" (Davidson, 1999, p. 611).

Base: Adults Aged 15+	All Respondents* N=1,019 (100% of total sample) %	Ethnic Food Consumed in UK Restaurants/Pubs or from Takeaways** N=759 (74.5% of total sample) %
Chinese main course with meat	40	54
Medium Indian curry	29	39
Mild Indian curry	28	38
Indian bread	22	30
Any kebabs	19	26
Tandoori or Tikka	17	23
Thai curry	16	22
Hot Indian curry	13	18
Chinese crispy duck	14	18
Chilli con carne	11	15
Indian vegetarian curry	11	15
Chinese fish or seafood dish	10	14
Chinese soup	10	13
Other Mexican	8	11
Thai noodles	7	9
Any Greek or Turkish	6	8
Chinese Vegetarian	6	8
Other Thai main course	5	6
Any other ethnic food	4	5
Vegetarian Thai	3	5
Any Indonesian/Malaysian food	2	3
Japanese	2	3

Table 2: Types of Ethnic Food Eaten in a UK Restaurant or Pub or Bought as a Takeaway in the Last Six Months, November 2002

* Ethnic food purchases as a percentage; up to four responses were allowed; includes 25.5% indicating a negative response or selecting none of the choices available.
** Ethnic food purchases as a percentage; up to four responses were allowed; % based on respondents who had purchased form of ethnic food choices listed. *Source:* adapted from BMRB/Mintel 2003a

Although Table 2 does not take into account British cuisine, there are clear indications that available food preferences and eating habits in Britain are immersed in ethnic cuisines that have become part of British food culture. It appears that the British, like many European cultures, have embraced these changes enthusiastically through travel and exposure to the diversity of other cultures. Hence they have developed a much more open-minded, international approach to food through dining out and experiencing different cuisines and leisure pursuits abroad (Mintel, 2003b).

Food Tourism

Hall and Mitchell (2001, p. 308) defined food tourism as "a visitation to primary and secondary food producers, food festivals, restaurants and specific locations for which food tasting and/or experiencing the attributes of a specialist food production region are the primary motivation factor for travel". "For many people food tourism is an opportunity to find something real, traditional and meaningful, something which is produced by artisans and which says something about heritage and identity, whether our own or someone elses" (Hall, Sharples and Smith, 2003, p. 331). The popular UK holiday destinations listed in Table 3 offer more than sun and a relief from work; they allow tourists to see sights and experience different cultures first hand. In particular, Western European destinations such as Spain and France with their short journey times and relatively familiar food cultures are by far the most popular with UK tourists, having secured 41.5% of the outbound market in 2002. This increasing desire to experience different cultures is set to continue as UK residents visiting Western European countries rose by 2% for the first 3 months of 2004 on the same period in 2003 (Office of National Statistics, 2004a).

	2000		2001		2002	
	'000s	% share	'000s	% share	'000s	% share
Spain	11,154	19.6	11,790	20.2	12,525	21.1
France	11,903	20.9	11,959	20.5	12,112	20.4
Ireland	3,961	7.0	3,930	6.7	3,965	6.7
USA	4,331	7.6	3,990	6.8	3,602	6.1
Greece	2,709	4.8	3,215	5.5	2,958	5.0
Italy	2,327	4.1	2,471	4.2	2,650	4.5
Germany	2,411	4.2	2,242	3.8	2,275	3.8
Netherlands	2,044	3.6	2,095	3.6	2,149	3.6
Belgium	1,657	2.9	1,738	3.0	1,784	3.0
Portugal	1,612	2.8	1,598	2.7	1,779	3.0
Cyprus	1,310	2.3	1,476	2.5	1,302	2.2
Turkey	775	1.4	878	1.5	991	1.7
Caribbean	794	1.4	721	1.2	779	1.3

Table 3: UK Outbound Tourism by Destination Popularity, 2000-02
Source: adapted from Mintel (2003b).

From 2002-03, there was a corresponding 5% increase in the number of visitors to the UK from European destinations, jumping by over 15% in the first quarter of 2004 over the same period in 2003 (See Table 4). The impending enlargement of the European Union (EU) gave rise to a cumulative increase of 65% in travel to the UK from the potential EU member states in the first quarter of 2004 on the same period in 2002 following an increase of 38% on the same period in 2003 (See Table 4). Subsequent to the enlargement of the EU on 1ˢᵗ May 2004, the relaxation of travel restrictions has resulted in a major influx of both visitors and workers in the UK from Central and Eastern European countries. It is anticipated that the migration of EU citizens with 10 new cultural backgrounds to the UK will bring the foundations of another era of international cuisine.

	2002	2003	2002				2003				2004**
			Qtr 1	Qtr 2	Qtr 3	Qtr 4	Qtr 1	Qtr 2	Qtr 3	Qtr 4	Qtr 1
Austria	217	194	39	63	70	45	40	52	66	36	57
Belgium	863	855	181	235	241	205	152	240	194	270	162
Denmark	405	352	77	129	109	90	69	79	89	116	91
Finland	116	133	26	25	27	38	23	27	35	48	27
France	2,842	2,846	612	795	710	725	668	719	788	671	761
Germany	2,328	2,493	408	613	771	535	429	628	871	565	450
Greece	179	188	41	45	36	56	40	34	53	61	57
Irish Republic	1,962	2,206	464	443	591	464	574	511	587	535	567
Italy	997	1,060	190	223	323	260	218	229	321	292	274
Luxembourg	16	19	5	5	6	—	3	7	4	4	7
Netherlands	1,424	1,433	289	349	421	364	258	395	396	384	357
Portugal	205	226	45	43	63	54	42	54	57	72	58
Spain	789	857	156	173	241	218	197	161	274	224	227
Sweden	495	497	108	138	129	120	106	115	125	151	138
Czech Republic	135	185	25	33	58	19	36	56	61	32	41
Estonia	15	17	—	4	7	4	3	5	6	3	7
Hungary	77	87	10	24	24	19	17	22	26	23	40
Latvia	18	14	5	6	4	3	3	2	3	7	5
Lithuania	28	34	4	8	7	8	2	5	11	15	11
Poland	210	279	53	51	77	30	61	70	86	62	66
Slovakia	34	35	7	2	16	9	4	11	11	8	14
Slovenia	33	27	5	11	13	4	6	3	10	8	7
Cyprus	46	50	10	7	15	13	10	11	18	11	9
Malta	31	40	8	3	9	11	9	4	15	12	9
Total	13,463	14,128	2,771	3,428	3,968	3,294	2,970	3,443	4,108	3,608	3,442

Table 4: Number of Visits to the UK (000's) by Residents of the Enlarged EU, 2002-2004*

* The data represent visits for all purposes in 000 (thousands), country totals have been subject to rounding and as a result may not sum exactly to overall totals.

** Provisional estimates

Source: adapted from Office of National Statistics, International Passenger Survey (2004b).

Travel abroad includes not only experiencing the local (alcoholic) drinks and food of the area or country visited but also, increasingly, visitor activities focusing on traditional cooking and wine tasting tours as part of developing tourism strategy. This form of tourist activity is clearly evident in strong wine growing countries where organisations, governments and the wine industry are working together to promote wine tourism and develop strategies that will benefit the tourism industry (Hall, Sharples, Mitchell, Macionics and Cambourne, 2000; Van Westering and Neil, 2003; also see Chapter 2). It is also evidenced in many emerging wine countries around the world, where developing wine tourism strategies are seen as an important attraction to tourists (Williams and Dossa, 2003), with the concept of wine and culinary destinations being an important part of tourism marketing (Hashimoto and Telfer, 2003). Regarding the UK outbound market to Central and Eastern Europe, it is clear that Hungarian goulash, Czech dumplings and Polish sausages have already made an impact on the UK market. Considering new food tourism destinations, there appears to be potential for development in Georgia and Armenia, both of which possess many of the basic elements for a successful tourism industry including a friendly population, good food and attractive scenery. However, a more developed infrastructure and a more secure environment are necessary before these advantages can be exploited fully (http://www.researchandmarkets.com/reportinfo.asp?report_id=3932).

> **Fish and Chips**
>
> "Fish and chips may fairly be said to constitute one of the national dishes of England (and Scotland) but does not have a very long history. The combination in its familiar form is thought to date back to the 1860s, in Lancashire or London. However, the two component parts existed separately for more than half a century before then, when fried fish was a standard street food in the 1840s or earlier; chips are thought to have been on menus since the late 18th century"
> (Davidson 1999, p. 300).

As with wine, food is not only a strong expression of region but also of culture which can be used to differentiate a destination in a global tourism market (Hall, Sharples, Mitchell, Macionics, and Cambourne, 2003). This expression can be through a national, regional or local difference that stimulates the food as a tourism product or it can be through the product itself. Many countries and regions develop tourism strategies that involve a strong, identifiable product to help to reach their target market. A good example of this product development in the UK is Stilton cheese that was being sold from the Bell Inn, a coaching house on the Great North Road where travellers stopped to rest, in the village of Stilton during the first quarter of the eighteenth century. It was known locally as Quenby cheese although Quenby was 30 miles away. However, as travellers became accustomed to buying the cheese at the Bell Inn, it took on the name of Stilton. It was this early development as a local product that allowed Stilton to become an English cheese of international fame and blue Stilton is one of a handful of British cheeses granted the status of a 'protected designation origin' (PDO) by the European Commission. Only cheese produced in the three counties of Derbyshire, Leicestershire and Nottinghamshire and made according to a strict code may be called Stilton. There are just six dairies licensed to make Stilton. They are subject to regular audit by an independent inspection agency accredited to European Standard EN 45011 (Davidson, 1999, p. 754). There are many examples of products that become identifiable within a country or culture as a national product and develop in a similar way to Stilton, but this can be a slow process. Food products need to become recognised locally through promotion and marketing, thus creating links regionally that can go on to become internationally identifiable with a country and region. Myers and Alexander (1996) believed geographical location, culture and economic conditions are fundamental to understanding the expansion and trends in a commercial environment. Most food products already have a link to a region or culture articulated by Myers and Alexander, which is often expressed through a desire to keep a product or dish alive through low level production and distribution by food enthusiast similar to Hall, Sharples & Smiths' description (2003, p. 331). What is important is that the products are made available so that the food tourist can experience them and develop a desire and identity for those products.

> **Goulash**
>
> "In Hungary the word 'goulash' refers to the cattle driver or the 'cowboy'. The only place on a Hungarian menu where you will find the goulash (gulyás) is among the soups and it is called 'gulyás leves' meaning the soup of the cowboy. What is known all over the world as 'Hungarian goulash' is called in Hungary 'pörkölt' or 'pakrikás' if sour cream has been added to the pörkölt"
> (Davidson, 1999, p. 346).

Also, this expression of food tourism may be linked to an event that distinguishes the time of year that generates a strong tourism product. Food events and festivals are often the place where food products make their initial impact on the food tourist. This impact can act as a stepping stone for many products to become identifiable outside of their own geographical area with appearances at regional festivals. These types of event promote their region and local produce to suppliers and local/international tourists and consumers. Such examples can be seen in the UK with food festivals like Manchester, York, Nottingham and Nantwich and local events like the Ludlow Food Festival on the English/Welsh border (britishfoodfortnight.co.uk). The Ludlow food festival, which takes place every May, has become a gastronomic phenomenon with over 20,000 visitors attracted annually, with food and drink trials, food tasting and cookery demonstrations that are designed to create interest and bring fun and notoriety to a small market town. Ludlow hosts more Michelin-starred restaurants (http://www.viamichelin.com) than any other place in the UK outside London. This feature has helped Ludlow to build a reputation as a 'centre of excellence' for food, attributed partly to the annual food festival. Ludlow's gourmet chefs have a truly international reputation: Shaun Hill's, The Merchant House was recently voted 14th out of the top 50 restaurants in the world as well as 'Best Value Restaurant in the World' by Restaurant Magazine. Claude Bosi at Hibiscus has been awarded a second Michelin star, whilst Chris Bradley at Mr Underhill's also has one star (http://www.foodfestival.co.uk; http://www.ludlow.org.uk). Food events and festivals put products on show, often in settings that create some interest or authenticity to the origins of the product such as may be observed at English summer fêtes where traditional dress is often worn to symbolise some heritage or cultural connections. In many Central and Eastern European countries, there are examples of traditional costume being worn by food service staff working in restaurants set in historical buildings or 'authentic' environments such as Olde Hansa, Peppersack and Kuldse Notsu Korts in Tallin, Estonia. This close identification of a product with its heritage can increase the initial attention of international consumers and promote their interest and memory retention so building up brand loyalty, local repeat business and word-of-mouth marketing. Also, there is the opportunity for products to develop from the feedback provided by these consumers, which also allows producers to get to know consumers and understand their buying styles and needs. The need for marketing a food product at events and festivals not only develops the product but also develops the event's geographical location as a tourism destination. Such marketing is seen as an area that is lacking globally and receives very little attention when considering the role of food in destination tourism strategies, according to Du Rand, Heath and Alberts (2003). In the UK, destination marketing is seen as an important area, with regional tourism development initiatives utilising locally produced foodstuffs and beverages to strengthen an areas' tourism products, enhance visitor experiences and help to maintain and enhance the viability of the local food production and processing sector (Boyne, Hall, and Williams, 2003).

> *Paella*
>
> "Paella, to be precise the Valencian paella, is known universally as the traditional dish of Spanish cooking. It takes its name from the utensil in which it is cooked and from the Spanish region on the shores of the Mediterranean where it had its origins. This dish symbolises the union and heritage of two important cultures: the Romans who gave us the utensil; and the Arabs who brought us the basic food of humanity for centuries - rice"
> (Davidson, 1999, p. 566).

Mitchell and Hall (2003) identify the research needed in the area of the food tourist: to define, segment and analyse tourist motivations to experience food as part of the travel package. However, as with the food festivals, there are examples in many countries of tourists experimenting with local dishes in restaurants, hotels and cafés and creating the memorable moments of their trips. In 2000,

Enteleca Research and Consultancy conducted a home survey of 1600 English residents to examine the interest associated with regional food and drink whilst on holiday. The report focused on tourists' attitudes towards regional and local foods in the UK and sampled English resident holidaymakers and visitors to the South West, Cumbria, Yorkshire and the Heart of England. Overall, 72% of the respondents took an interest in local foods during their visit, with the majority being happy to try it and up to 69% of the respondents recognising that food made a positive contribution to their holiday. Respondents were divided further into five groups (Food Tourists, Interested Purchasers, Un-reached, Un-engaged, Laggards) according to the extent of their claims to be interested in food whilst on holiday. The interested purchasers' group, which accounts for nearly 33% of respondents, maintained that food in general can contribute to their enjoyment of their holiday and they purchase/eat local foods when the opportunity arises; this group is over and above the 11% (food tourists) who actively seek regional food and drink as part of their reason for choosing a destination. Another finding was that 26% of the total number of respondents expressed a strong interest in seeing restaurant menus that identify food that has been produced or sourced locally, suggesting that the development of the menu has a strong role to play in the marketing of a food-related business. Promoting local food can be utilised to sell products from emerging Central and Eastern European markets that have not always been accessible to tourists, especially with increasing travel activity across the EU; new cuisines are being introduced to Western European cultures whilst Central and Eastern Europeans are developing tastes for Western food cultures. Such food experiences can have a positive affect on consumers' food choices on returning home. Hall, Sharples and Smith (2003) found that when consumers return home having sampled the exotic, they treat similar food found at home as 'local' and give a simple meal a symbolic meaning and their intercultural experiences add to "the brand equity and cachet of the country and the cuisine" (Bestor, 2000 in Scarpato and Daniele, 2003, p. 301).

Fast Food Culture

The label 'fast food' came into being in the USA in the latter part of the twentieth century when drive-in eating places were flourishing. However, the notion of being able to go into a public eating place and to order something which would be available almost immediately, and could be consumed quickly, is obviously not a new one (Davidson, 1999, p. 289). Street food, which has been around throughout history, can be said to have been the first method used to produce food to be consumed quickly and has some similarities with the fast food culture. However, the fast food culture itself emerged through the McDonald brothers in the USA, who developed a mechanistic way of dispensing a limited choice of food very quickly to develop the 'McDonalds' brand and the fast food industry into the global phenomenon that we have today (Love, 1995). The continued rise of the 'fast food' market and the dominance of McDonalds in the global marketplace throughout the latter part of the twentieth century, threatened food culture; 'McDonaldisation' was and is still seen as the homogenisation of food (Page and Hall, 2003), opposing 'slow food' and destroying local and regional culinary delights (McCarthy and Kirby, 2004), giving rise to what Schlosser (2001) thought of as the negative aspects of food globalisation, that is homogenised and often unhealthy, fast and industrial cuisine.

There is little doubt that "food cultures are becoming more and more homogeneous as Western food conquers the world" (Finkelstine, 1989, p. 46). With globalisation, the fast food culture and the McDonalds brand have seen the humble hamburger and fries develop into one of the most identifiable food products in the world (Love, 1995). However, what some may regard as the destruction of local and national food culture, others may find comfort and take pleasure in, such as being able to eat a 'Big Mac' with its trade mark uniformity and lack of difference in a heterogeneous world culture. Although menu standardisation has led to the success of the McDonald brand and the fast food culture, originally this was not the formula McDonalds had planned for its international franchise. Developments of the McDonalds brand, with the expansion into Canada, Japan, and Europe aimed at developing McDonalds' international franchise by branding products that the consumers from those countries could identify with as part of their food culture and not as an American import. However, the 'branding approach' failed. It was found that it was easier to change local eating habits than to adapt menus to accommodate them (Love, 1995) and the "mechanistic success of the products and the development of McDonalds' unique supplier networks made it difficult and costly to transfer to less standardised products" (Vignali, 2001, p. 99). In consequence, the formula that had been successful in the United States was copied internationally to produce "a standardised strategy that became a homogenised approach which worked throughout the world" (Solomon, 1999, p. 416). Over time the global homogeneous identity and standardisation of fast food has become reassuringly 'local' in feel, encompassing in a foreign land or urban cityscape a wide diversity of individual consumers, with food from home at home and a place to locate or anchor oneself when abroad (James, 1996).

> ### Hamburger
>
> "Although the hamburger is one of the principal forms in which beef is consumed in the western world, its name has a relatively short history (first printed in 1890). However, it appears that the consumption of food in 'hamburger form', i.e. cooked round patties or rissoles of meat, dates back a very long way and not only in Europe. Ayto (1993) and Evan Jones (1981) provide good distinctions in the way in which the port of Hamburg, via seamen from there, came to have its name applied to particular version of this ubiquitous item. It seems that 'Hamburg steak' (in a Boston newspaper in 1884) preceded the snappier 'hamburger'. The St Louis World Fair of 1904 was a significant launching pad for the hamburger in a bun as we know it, although its growth to the status of a global food item required another four or five decades of the 20th century for completion" (Davidson, 1999, p. 369).

Survival in the market place has not all been easy for food suppliers and retailers; there has been some rejection of the fast food culture and McDonldisation over the years. McDonalds have attempted to address these issues by tailoring products increasingly to meet local cultural needs, for example by offering: vegetarian burgers for non-meat eaters; alcohol/champagne in France; and Halal meats in Muslim countries. These responses might be considered to be minimal in terms of what was seen as a fast food threat to other cultures (Ritzer, 2000) as they only reflect the needs and desires of minorities and local cultures. However, some international franchises suffered through years of militant action in France where campaigners saw McDonalds as an emblem of problems such as "environmental degradation, dietary dangers, the evils of capitalism, poor working conditions, faltering unionisation, neglected children and the threat of Americanisation" (Ritzer, 2000, p. 192), and even led to McDonalds abandoning plans to open some restaurants where tensions were high (Anastassion, 2000). In addition to the opposition from the national cultural aspect, the early part of 2004 has seen McDonalds doing some major repositioning in the market place with a focus on healthier eating options in reaction to increased global consumer awareness with respect to healthy eating. After promoting the 'supersize' (i.e. jumbo portions) in the UK in 1999, negative press pressured the company to announce its withdrawal of the supersize in December 2003 (BBC News, 2003). Other major changes have involved the new recipe for chicken nuggets with lower salt (McDonalds, 2004b), the offering of new healthier options, which has seen the most significant menu change in 30 years, and the introduction of nutritional information on packaging (McDonalds, 2004a).

Evolving Consumer Tastes: Healthy Eating and Slow Food

Healthy eating is possibly one of the most topical areas of food culture which it is thought might have the biggest influence on the food industry over the coming decades (Mackay, 2004). The World Health Organisation (WHO) reported the spread of fast food chains throughout Europe and Asia, on the rising tide of affluence, which it was believed subsequently contributed to the creation of fatter people in those countries, termed 'globesity' (BBC World Service, 2004). By 2004 the UK annual consumer expenditure on fast food was £10 billion, an increase of 80% over a 10 year period (Caterer, 2004) which caused the government health secretary to announce concerns over obesity and to raise it as one of the key issues in the public health white paper released late in 2004 (Reid, 2004). This problem is by no means isolated to the UK. The WHO reported obesity in adults in 1995 was estimated to be around 200 million worldwide (World Health Organisation, 2003); by 2000 this had reached epidemic proportions globally, with more than 1 billion adults overweight and at least 300 million of them clinically obese (World Health Organisation, 2004). Such are the current concerns for obesity and healthy eating the Food Standards Agency (FSA) recommended that the broadcasting regulator in the UK, OFCOM, should overhaul the way in which food was advertised to children, with special reference to eliminating the use of high-profile and often slim, attractive celebrities who endorsed high fat or high sugar products (Food Standards Agency, 2004).

> *Chow Mein*
>
> "Chow Mein is one of a pair of prominent Chinese-American dishes, the other being the somewhat similar 'Chop Suey'. Mariani (1994) notes that the term first appeared in print in 1903. Chow Mein is related to and takes its name from 'chao mian', a Chinese dish consisting of previously boiled noodles stir-fried with meat and vegetables. There is, however, an important difference. In Chow Mein the noodles are deep-fried in bundles, which are crisp and brittle when they emerge, whereas in the Chop Suey the noodles are soft" (Davidson, 1999, p. 183).

With the focus on healthier eating and the current concerns about obesity and fast food, the culture of food could be said to have come full circle. This process can be seen on a global level with the 'Slow Food' movement, which was founded in Bra, southern Piedmont, Italy in 1986 as an association but developed into an international movement in 1989 (http://www.slowfood.com; McCarthy and Kirby, 2004, p. 14). The Slow Food Movement advocates cuisine that is "predominantly regional, cooked traditionally and consumed in a leisurely manner" (Davidson, 1999, p. 289) and one of its manifesto pre-requisites invites consumers to rediscover the flavours and savours of regional cooking and banish the degrading effects of fast food. Although the movement has been around for 18 years there seems to be a new impetus as membership is on the increase. The movement boasts more than 60,000 members in more than 100 countries (McCarthy and Kirby, 2004, p. 14). Examples of slow food in the UK can be seen with Ludlow Marches 'convivium' (branch) set-up in 2002 and with the UK's fifth convivium founded at the Boath House Hotel Auldearn, Nairnshire, Scotland in 2003 (http://www.slowfoodludlow.org.uk/marches.html; Caterer, 2003b). The movement is continuing to raise awareness on issues dealing with local food and produce in an attempt to save dishes from being forgotten and fading away. In the UK consumers are becoming increasingly aware of issues pertaining to healthy eating and quality, possibly stemming from the highly publicised BSE scare in the 1990s, the foot and mouth epidemic in 2000 and the European poultry scandals in 2003 (Caterer, 2003a; Mintel, 2003c). These scares saw the fast food market slow down and, for the first time in its history, the dominant McDonalds slipped in to the red (Mintel, 2003c).

With this emphasis on quality produce and healthy-eating consumers became increasingly concerned with food quality, which allowed restaurateurs the opportunity to capitalise by promoting good quality food (Mintel, 2003c), especially in the expanding eating-out market. The quality of the food is now seen to be one of the important factors when choosing where to dine out; in some cases it is considered to be more important than cost (Mintel, 2003c). To this end it is often a good strategy for a restaurant or hotel to be associated with a quality mark or quality rating such as Egon Ronay, Automobile Association (AA) rosettes, Michelin, Harden's or Royal Automobile Club (RAC). Affiliation with one or more of these associations signals to the consumer that the outlet has been inspected to meet levels of quality and service which the consumer can trust and rely on. Along with the quality rating often comes substantial national or regional publicity, which can increase the profile of an establishment and, in some cases, an entry in a published guide promotes national and international coverage and often notoriety for the establishment (for further information see: http://www.viamichelin.com/viamichelin/gbr/tpl/hme/MaHomePage.htm; http://www.theaa.com/getaway/hotels/hotelshome.jsp; http://www.rac.co.uk/; http://www.egonronay.com/; http://www.johansens. com/404.aspx).

To develop a strong tourism product, there is a need for a great variety and choice of attractions, entertainment and an infrastructure to underpin the marketing of the location. To exemplify the role of food in the promotion and development of a tourism location, Manchester, one of most cosmopolitan cities in the UK, has been selected for a case study.

Case Study: Manchester – a City of Culinary Delight

Manchester is the UK's most popular tourist destination after London and Edinburgh, with 3.5 million tourists spending £463 million (€ 700 million) each year. Tourism in Manchester supports hundreds of thousands of businesses and individuals each year. The night time economy in the city centre alone is valued at £100 million (€150 million), due to the existence of over 450 licensed bars and restaurants in the centre (See http://www.manchester.gov.uk/business/econfacts/culture.htm; http://www.manchesteronline.co.uk for further details). Manchester is a vibrant city, which encouraged visitors to spend £10 million on short breaks in the city in 2002 (http://www.manchester.gov.uk/business/econfacts/culture.htm). Recent urban regeneration, including over £300 million (€450 million euros) invested to develop the city's cultural image and leisure attractions, has increased and enriched the choices for locals and visitors (http://www.manchester.gov.uk/business/econfacts/culture.htm). Developments include the Printworks entertainment and leisure complex, and the substantial Sportcity, constructed in the urban regeneration area of East Manchester for the 2002 Commonwealth Games. Also for the games, the Manchester Aquatics Centre comprising a swimming pool and leisure complex located close to the city centre was built. It is the only complex in the UK with two 50 metre pools as well as separate diving and leisure pools. Manchester City Centre has a large population of nearly 400,000 (Census, 2001) that comprises many diverse religions and cultures offering a rich and wide range of cultural cuisine to cater for the ethnic subgroups and which the locals and visitors alike have the opportunity to experience. In addition to Manchester's multi-cultural residents, the City has four Universities and houses a student population upwards of 78,000 (http://www.manchester.gov.uk/business/econfacts/intro.htm) which has further fuelled the massive fast food and takeaway market in and around the city centre.

One such example of this cultural experience can be found in Rusholme. Dating back to the 1960s, Rusholme's 'Curry Mile' is considered to be the largest single concentration of Asian restaurants in Europe with [at least] 52 restaurants and 65,000 customers passing through each week (Hyman, 2002, p. 38). This area of Manchester is a culinary delight not to be missed by either residents or visitors and it is a hive of activity the whole year round with its "lively bazaar-like stretch of neon-lit restaurants, halal butchers, kebab houses and Asian businesses" (Hyman, 2002, p. 38). Another such cultural delight can be found in 'China Town' in the centre of Manchester, with its large selection of speciality restaurants offering the best in Chinese cuisine. China Town has some of the most exclusive Chinese restaurants in Manchester including the famous 'Yang Sing', which has brought the taste of the orient to the city and claims to be the "most prestigious Cantonese restaurant in Europe, serving a wide range of authentic oriental dishes to suit all palates"

> *Curry*
>
> "Curry is a term adopted by the English language from India; it has changed its meaning in migrating and has become ubiquitous as a menu word. Taken from the Tamil word kari, it means spiced sauce with rice in southern India and soupy in consistency. It now denotes various kinds of dishes in numerous different part of the world but all are savoury and all spiced"
> (Davidson, 1999, p. 235).

(http://www.yang-sing.com). In addition to these gastronomic delights in cluster locations, there are numerous other speciality international restaurants scattered around the City, including a large selection of Italian pizzerias and restaurants, French bistros, Spanish tapas bars, Portuguese, Japanese and even some Mongolian cuisine in what has become a culinary melting pot with more than 1.5 million meals being eaten daily at more than 5,000 venues across the city (http://www.manchester.gov.uk/ business/econfacts/culture.htm).

To complement this culinary encyclopaedia, Manchester has its fair share of celebrity chefs, such as the youngest ever three Michelin star chef in the Lowry (http://www.roccofortehotels.com, 2004) and also an increasing number of restaurants developing gastronomic flair through to exclusive vegetarian cuisine which formed its roots in Manchester in 1847 (Battiwalla, 2002, p. 12). At the time of writing the only Michelin star in the City Centre is held by the Nico Central Bar and Brasserie which offers French cuisine in a franchised unit at the Midland Paramount hotel. Restaurants with AA rosette awards include Simply Heathcotes and Chandlers (in the Copthorne Hotel), both of which have predominantly British menus but also Chinese (Yang Sing and Tai Pan) and Mediterranean (Café Paradiso) food have been awarded this accolade. With a wide selection of

> *Sushi*
>
> "Perhaps the best known internationally of all Japanese specialities, Sushi consists essentially of 'fingers' of vinegared rice with pieces of very fresh fish or other seafood laid along them, served with thin slices of vinegared ginger (gari) and hot green tea. In this best known form, the one which belongs to Tokyo, sushi is an abbreviation for 'nigri-zushi', its full name"
> (Davidson, 1999, p. 771)

dishes from many cultures catering for the variety of consumer tastes and taking advantage of the vast array of ingredients and culinary skills in the area, some restaurants and hotels have been successful in adopting the Signature menus endorsed by local and national celebrity chefs. They have taken advantage of the 'creolisation' (James, 1996) of cultural foods and the 'new global cuisine' (Scarpato and Daniele, 2003) offering more than the standard international fare.

Access to information on food is important for visitors and tourists especially within a large city like Manchester. There are many sources a visitor or tourist can use, including: local papers, which may provide food recommendations; hotels and restaurants, that may provide access to coupons or word-of-mouth recommendations; flyers; tourism information points and Internet resources such as that set up by the Visitor Information Centre (http://www.manchester.gov.uk/visitorcentre/eat) to market food outlets. Examples of Manchester's dedicated local information web sources include:

Manchester Tart

"Appearing in Cassell's dictionary of cookery, published in the 1880s, Manchester tart is made from puff pastry made with greengage, apricot or strawberry jam. Breadcrumbs, milk and lemon peel, together with a little brandy and an egg yolk, are mixed to form the filling and beaten egg whites give the baked tart a meringue top. Modern incarnations of this confection, are rarely encountered. That recently championed by Marks & Spencer varies considerably from the Cassell's version and it is said different jams are used to reflect support for one or other of Manchester's football teams, City and United" (Mason, 2002, p. 36).

(i)   Manchester's monthly on-line dining magazine which may be found at (http://www.sugarvine.com/manchester/search/booking.asp). On-line bookings can be made with diners selecting their cuisine type from: Afro-Caribbean, American, Argentinian, British, Chinese, French, Greek, Indian, Irish, Italian, Japanese, Korean, Lebanese, Malaysian, Mexican, Middle Eastern Mongolian, Spanish, Thai et al. Religious and other food preferences such as kosher, Moslem, 'deli' and vegetarian are catered for. Advertisements for individual food outlets on this site include menus, prices, special offers and 360° panoramic video clips showing the interior of restaurants so that atmosphere can be assessed by the consumer, customer ratings and links to home websites.

(ii)   The Hi-life diners club (http://www.hi-life.co.uk), which is used to market food offerings to the local community to encourage them to eat out on a regular basis and to try new venues. There are over 80,000 local members who receive two meals for the price of one when dining out in over 1000 restaurants in the North West of England. The cost of the restaurant directory and card, which is marked each time it is used at a restaurant (and it can only be used once at each outlet), is £55 (€65 approx.) per annum currently with individual restrictions as determined by the restaurant manager – such as the offer is not available on Saturday nights after 7pm or on Valentines day. There is an additional optional charge for Platinum Membership with its select directory which allows dining within normally restricted periods and access to some of the top restaurants such as the River Room at the five star Lowry Hotel and the Moss Nook.

Visitors can research their cultural food options in advance of their visit and find the 'best of the city's dining experiences' at (http://www.manchesteronline.co.uk/food). It is also possible to register with 5pm.co.uk and to access and book the special offers of the day (available after 5pm) at http://www.manchesteronline.5pm.co.uk/index.cfm.

Access to dining facilities in Manchester for people with disabilities has been an issue under consideration since the early 1990s when research (Ineson, 1994) showed that out of 250 City Centre restaurants, only 10 had full access for such guests offering them a very limited cultural experience. For example, short of people with walking disabilities being carried (and this option was offered willingly to prospective guests), there was no access to Chinese restaurants due to all of them being located on more than one level in old buildings with steps at the entrances, no elevators and narrow steep stairs. By December 2001, it was gratifying to note that at least 61 central Manchester restaurants had full access

(http://www.manchester.gov.uk/visitorcentre/disabilit y) including one Chinese restaurant just two kilometres from the City Centre and intercultural dining experiences were possible in Italian, French, Mediterranean, Middle Eastern, vegetarian et al. establishments. The Disability Discrimination Act (DDA, 1995), which came into full force in October 2004, aims to end such discrimination by giving disabled people rights in the area of access to goods, facilities and services. In addition this Act allows the Government to set minimum standards so that disabled people can use public transport easily and as a result, UK nationals and overseas visitors have much improved access to the food experiences of their choice.

Black Pudding

"South Lancashire is essentially rich in formulae for these blood puddings, fried slices of which often feature as part of an English cooked breakfast. The puddings of Bury are best known. They are allegedly seasoned with marjoram, thyme, pennyroyal, mint and celery seeds but manufacturers keep their special mixtures secret. Food hygiene standards now prevent the use of pigs' blood as the primary ingredient and ox blood is used instead. White pieces of back fat dot the deep red-brown colour of the cut puddings. A popular street food, hot puddings with mustard are sold as snacks in some markets" (Mason, 2002, p. 36).

Eccles Cakes

"Small, round and formally associated with Eccles' Wakes Week, their guiding principles were stated in the late 19th century as 'currants, sweetness and lightness'. Sugar glazed puff pastry contributes the latter two qualities, as well as the pleasant crunch. [They are] not to be confused with the flatter, short crust based Chorley cakes" (Mason, 2002, p. 36).

Conclusion

Europe has many different cultures that create a variety of different foods and cuisines; in the UK these cultural influences have infused with British cuisine to help develop societies' understanding of different food cultures and accept them as their own. With this gastronomic evolution, the UK has also seen an increasing level of disposable income spent on dining out and travel which has allowed consumers to become increasingly knowledgeable regarding the variety of cuisine available and more discerning in terms of its cultural authenticity. Consumers are spending more time enjoying leisure pursuits, which is partly the reason for the increased spending on the hospitality and tourism sector and related products. During this growth stage the British consumer has become more experimental and willing to try products that may have been perceived previously as 'high risk' purchases. This trend is set to continue with increasing opportunities for consumers to visit new destinations as the EU expands and so to experience cultures not so easily accessible in the past. The growing variety of food available to purchase for home consumption has possibly helped to develop the tourists' taste for experimenting with different food whilst visiting other regions or on holiday abroad. Developments in food as a tourism product or as part of tourist experience and motivation for travel are an important part of a country's development as a tourist destination. This feature is recognised in many countries in Europe but the concept is possibly still under developed. In the light of recent European expansion, there is a good opportunity for EU countries to capitalise on the new travel markets created by this enlargement and to develop strong tourism strategies around food products and heritage issues relating to cultural authenticity. In Central and Eastern Europe opportunities are opening up not only to develop travel markets to western destinations but also to develop internal strategies around food and beverage products through national and regional food events and marketing opportunities within the hospitality sector. This access to local information fuels consumers' appetites for products that are new but may or may not be exotic and so continues to develop food tourism as a dynamic part of the tourism industry. Understanding the consumers is an important part of food tourism which brings the need for European hospitality personnel to appreciate the cultural differences of their customers and to develop a diverse range of knowledge and skills to meet their evolving knowledge and to offer an acceptable variety of meal experiences.

The fast food culture has evolved over 60 years into the global homogenisation of food, through brands like McDonalds but now it is changing to meet the changing consumer demands. These changes are in reaction to consumer awareness of health issues relating to food and diet and are seen as essential if fast food is to sustain its market share. With these added concerns and the development of food tourism, the re-emergence of traditional food products and cooking is apparent. The concept of cuisine that is predominantly regional, cooked traditionally is being re-introduced in opposition to the unhealthy aspect of fast food. It is clear that these developments and the wider health issues, in which Governments are becoming increasingly involved, are changing the ways in which people view and select their food. These changes are being encouraged through schools and the media, such as television programmes which promote healthy eating and time limitations on fast food advertising to avoid excessive exposure to child viewers. In such ways, consumers can be educated about food culture. In contrast, it is of interest and of some concern to note that, especially in the new EU countries, many fast food outlets are appearing and unhealthy 'international' food is replacing some of the traditional menu items in hotels and restaurants. During this period of raised awareness of healthy eating and matters of well being, perhaps managers and developers in such countries should tread carefully when considering 'opening their doors' to Western fast food; these 'innovations' should not be at the expense of their regional foods that may, in the long term, not only prove to offer healthier options but also to support lucrative tourism markets.

Student Activities

The activities focus on developing an understanding of food as part of a tourism product in the context of tourism related events and festivals and related hospitality sectors. The activities can be completed in any order as individual pieces of work or as part of a project.

1. Write a brief (500 words) outline on a local/national food item or dish of your choice that could be used to promote your regional/national identity to a food tourist. You may want to consider the origins and composition of the product/dish and how this may appeal and communicate a sense of origin to the consumer.

2. Choose a food outlet in your area and conduct a study on the menu content and style of food on offer. This work could include an overview of the business sector (i.e. hotel/restaurant/café/fast food), an analysis of the menu content (not a list of food items) and how the style of food appeals to the businesses' target market.

3. Conduct a comparative study of the food offerings from two local hospitality businesses with a view to evaluating their food culture and healthy eating perspectives. It is suggested that the businesses come from different sectors (i.e. hotel/restaurant/café/fast food) to enable you to distinguish between food cultures and healthy eating opportunities.

4. You have been asked to create a four day itinerary for a group of food tourists visiting your country for the first time. Your client wishes them to visit a different eating establishment each evening to sample the countries culinary delights and to attend at least one food event or festival during their stay. The client has also informed you that one member of the group is disabled and requires a walking stick and another is a vegetarian. Using the Internet as your primary research tool, identify the food outlets, event(s), accommodation and travel arrangement(s) to the venues for the four nights. Present the programme and itinerary in written format for your client to view and include references to the Internet sites you have chosen.

5. You have been asked to write an article to provide a profile of your region's food offerings for an international travel magazine. As part of the profile you are required to conduct a study on the local food events, festivals and products that could be marketed to help promote your region as a food tourism destination. The article (word count to be specified by your tutor) should be presented in a clear written format with appropriate references and a maximum of four illustrations.

6. The purpose of a business is to satisfy the needs of its customers; a business that fails to do this will not survive in a competitive environment. With this view in mind, conduct a study of the range of food outlets available in your area, possibly

including examples from the hotel, restaurant, café and fast food businesses; critically analyse and compare the different target markets for each business.

7. Conduct a study of tourist motivations to experience different cuisines whilst visiting your country/region as part of the travel package. For the study you will be required to produce a small questionnaire to gather data on tourists' food choices, attitude to different foods and reasons for travel. Write a report on your findings with recommendations for the development of food tourism in your country/region.

8. Draw conclusions from the information gathered from the studies in activities 6 & 7 to consider the availability and variety of food products in your area and whether the products meet the expectations of tourists. Develop recommendations on how businesses in your area could improve to meet the expectations of tourists.

References

Anastassion, L. (2000). McDonalds boué hors de la rue des Rosiers á Paris, *L'Hôtellerie*, June 22nd 2000, No 2671, p. 6.

Ayto, J. (1993). *The Diners Dictionary*, Oxford University Press, Oxford.

Battiwalla, D. (2002). Manchester. In C. Petrini, (ed.) *Slow, The Magazine of the Slow Food Movement*, Vol. V, January-March 2002, pp. 8-17.

BBC News, (2003). Going Large, *The 7 O'Clock News*, [on line] available from: http://www.bbc.co.uk/bbcthreenews/7oclocknews/features/supersize_040304.shtml, [accessed June 16th 2004].

BBC World Service, (2004). Fast Food Factory: Fries and Devine, *BBC WorldService*, [on line] available from: http://www.bbc.co.uk/worldservice/specials/1616_fastfood/page5.shtml, [accessed June 17th 2004].

Bessière, J. (1998). Local Development and Heritage: Traditional Food and Cuisine as Tourist Attractions in Rural Areas. *Sociologia Ruralis*, Vol. 38, No. 1, pp. 21-34.

Boyne, S. Hall, D. and Williams, F. (2003). Policy, Support and promotion for Food Related Iniciatives: A Market Approach to Regional Development, *Journal of Travel and Tourism Marketing*, Vol. 14, No. 3/4, pp. 131-154.

Caterer (2003a). In brief, FSA calls for chicken crackdown, *Caterer*, [on line] available from: http://caterer-online.com/archive/articledetail.asp?articleID=48945andnomenu, [accessed June 17th 2004].

Caterer (2003b). In brief, Take the slow road to gastronomic delight, *Caterer*, [on line] available from: http://caterer-online.com/archive/articledetail.asp?articleID=48945andnomenu, [accessed June 17th 2004].

Caterer (2004). UK spending £10b on fast food a year, *Caterer*, [on line] available from: http://caterer-online.com/archive/articledetail.asp?articleID=52474andnomenu, [accessed17[th] June 2004].

Census (2001). *National Statistics,* [on-line], available from: http://www.statistics.gov.uk/census2001/profiles/00bn.asp, [accessed June 7th 2004].

Cusack, I. (2000). African Cuisines: Recipes for National Building? *Journal for African Cultural Studies,* Vol. 13, No. 2, pp. 207-225.

Davidson, A. (1999). *The Oxford Companion to Food,* Oxford University Press, Oxford.

Disability Discrimination Act (1995). [on-line] available from: http://www.disability.gov.uk/dda/. [accessed March 8th 2005].

Du Rand, G. Heath, E. and Alberts, N. (2003). The role of local and regional; food in destination marketing: A South African Situation Analysis, *Journal of Travel and Tourism Marketing,* Vol. 14, No. 3/4, pp. 97-112.

Market Assessment Publications (1992). *Eating out and takeaways,* Market sector report, Business Publications Limited Group, pp. 18-19.

Enteleca Research and Consultancy (2000). Tourists Attitudes Towards Regional and Local Food. In C.M. Hall, L. Sharples, R. Mitchell, N. Macionics and B. Cambourne, (eds.) *Food Tourism Around the World,* Butterworth-Heinemann, Oxford, pp. 315-317.

Finkelstine, J. (1989). *Dining Out,* Polity Press, Cambridge.

Frochot, I. (2003). An Analysis or Regional Positioning and its Associated Food Images in French Regional Brochures, *Journal of Travel and Tourism Marketing,* Vol. 14, No., 3/4, pp. 77-96.

Food Standards Agency (2004). FSA wants to promote healthy eating, *Caterer,* [on line] available from: http://caterer-online.com/archive/articledetail.asp?articleID=52474andnomenu, [accessed June 17th 2004].

Hall, C. M. and Mitchell, R. (2001). Wine and Food Tourism. In N. Douglas, N., Douglas and R. Derrett, (eds.) *Special Interests Tourism: Context and Cases,* Wiley, Australia, pp. 307-329.

Hall, C. M. Sharples, L. Mitchell, R. Macionics, N. and Cambourne, B. (2000). *Wine Tourism Around the World,* Butterworth-Heinemann, Oxford.

Hall, C. M. Sharples, L. Mitchell, R. Macionics, N. and Cambourne, B. (2003). *Food Tourism Around the World,* Butterworth-Heinemann, Oxford.

Hall, C. M., Sharples, L. and Smith, A., (2003). The experience of consumption or the consumption of experiences? Challenges and issues in food tourism. In C.M. Hall, L. Sharples, R. Mitchell, N. Macionics and B. Cambourne, (eds.) *Food Tourism Around the World,* Butterworth-Heinemann, Oxford, pp. 314-335.

Hashimoto, A. and Telfer, D. (2003). Positioning an Emerging Wine Route in the Niagara Region: Understanding the Wine Tourism Market and its Implications for Marketing, *Journal of Travel and Tourism Marketing,* Vol., 14 No. 3/4, pp. 61-76.

Hyman, C. (2002). Sweet Street. In C. Petrini, (ed.) *Slow, The Magazine of the Slow Food Movement,* V, January-March 2002, pp. 38-43.

Ineson, E. M. (1994). Access to Quality Urban Food Service - perspectives of people with disabilities. In P. Murphy (ed.) *Quality Management in Urban Tourism: Balancing Business and the Environment,* Ministry of Small Business, Tourism and Culture, Province of British Columbia, Canada, pp. 444-454.

James, A. (1996). Global or local identities in contemporary British food cultures. In D. Howes, (ed.) *Cross Cultural Consumption*, Routledge, London, pp. 77-92.

Jones, E. (1981). *American Food: The Gastronomic Story*, 2nd edn., Random House, New York.

Key Notes Report. (1994). *Fast Food and Home Delivery Outlets*. Key Notes, Middlesex, pp. 10-12.

Love, J. F. (1995). *McDonald's: Behind the Arches*, Bantam Trade Paperback, New York.

Mackay, F. (2004). Healthy eating is the future, *Caterer*, [on line] available from: http://caterer-online.com/archive/articledetail.asp?articleID=51645andnomenu, [accessed June 17th 2004].

Manchester City Council, http://www.manchester.gov.uk/business/econfacts/culture.htm [accessed May 24th 2004].

Market Sector Report. (1992). Market Assessment: *Eating Out and Take Aways 1992*, BLA Business Publications Limited, pp. 18-19.

Mariani, J. (1994). *The Dictionary of American Food and Drink*, Hearst, New York.

Mason, L. (2002). Sweet Street. In C. Petrini, (ed.) *Slow, The Magazine of the Slow Food Movement*, V, January-March, p. 36.

McCarthy, M and Kirby, T. (2004). More Taste Less Speed, *The Independent*, April 1st, pp. 14-15.

McDonalds On-line, http://www.mcdonalds.co.uk, [accessed June 17th 2004].

McDonalds, (2004a). *McDonalds-New menu and information launched as part of ongoing commitment to informed choice*, McDonalds, [on line] available from: http://www.mcdonalds.co.uk/pages/global/newmenulaunched.html, [accessed June 17th 2004].

McDonalds, (2004b). *McDonalds-New menu and information launched as part of ongoing commitment to informed choice*, McDonalds, [on line] available from: http://www.mcdonalds.co.uk/pages/global/saltinchicken.html, [accessed June 17th 2004].

Mintel (1992). *Eating Out-1992*, Mintel International Group Limited, London, UK, [on-line] available from:. http://reports.mintel.com, [accessed June 7th 2004].

Mintel (2002). *British Lifestyle 2002: Expenditure on Eating Out,* Mintel International Group Limited, UK. [on-line] available from: http://reports.mintel.com/sinatra/mintel/searchexec/type=reports&variants=true&fulltext=British+Lifestyle+2002/report/repcode=S210&anchor=accessS210, [accessed June 7th 2004].

Mintel (2003a). *Thai and Other Emerging Ethnic Foods-UK,* Mintel International Group Limited, UK. [on-line] available from: http://reports.mintel.com/sinatra/mintel/searchexec/type=reports&variants=true&fulltext=Thai+and+Other+Emerging+Ethnic+Foods/report/repcode=C858&anchor=accessC858, [accessed June 7th 2004].

Mintel (2003b). *UK Outbound-2003*, Mintel International Group Limited, UK. [on-line] available from: http://reports.mintel.com/sinatra/mintel/searchexec/type=reports&variants=true&fulltext=UK+Outbound-2003/report/repcode=0101&anchor=access0101, [accessed June 7th 2004].

Mintel (2003c). *Eating Out Review-UK-June-2003*, Mintel International Group Limited, UK. [on-line] available from: http://reports.mintel.com/sinatra/mintel/searchexec/type=reports&variants=true&fulltext=Eating+Out+Review-UK-June-2003/report/repcode=L418&anchor=accessL418, [accessed June 7th 2004].

Mintel (2004). *Eating Out Habits-UK-April 2004*, Mintel International Group Limited, UK. [on-line] available from:
http://reports.mintel.com/sinatra/mintel/searchexec/type=reports&variants=true&fulltext=Eating+Out+Habits-UK-April+2004/report/repcode=0283&anchor=access0283, [accessed June 7th 2004].

Mitchell, R. and Hall, C. M. (2003). Consuming tourists: Food tourism consumer behaviour. In C.M. Hall, L. Sharples, R. Mitchell, N. Macionics and B. Cambourne, (eds.) *Food Tourism Around the World*, Butterworth-Heinemann, Oxford, pp. 60-80.

Myers, H. and Alexander, N. (1996). European food retailers' evaluation of global markets. International Journal of Retail & Distribution Management, Vol. 24 No. 6, 1996, pp. 34-43

Office of National Statistics (2004a). Overseas Travel and Tourism-April 2004, [on-line] available from: http://www.statistics.gov.uk, [accessed June 7th 2004].

Office of National Statistics (2004b). *Number of visits to the UK by the enlarged EU, 2002-2004*, [on-line] available from: http://www.statistics.gov.uk, [accessed June 12th 2004].

Olsen, W. K., Warde, A, and Martens, L. (2000). Social differentiation and the market for eating out in the UK, *International Journal of Hospitality Management*, Vol. 19, No. 2, pp. 173-190.

Page, S. and Hall, C. M. (2003). *Themes in Tourism: Managing Urban Tourism*, Prentice Hall: Pearson Education Limited, Essex, England.

Reid, J. (2004). *Obesity a priority for government*, Publications and Statistics, [on line] available from: http://www.dh.gov.uk/PublicationsAndStatistics/PressReleasesNotices, [accessed June 17th 2004].

Ritzer, G. (2000). *The McDonaldisation of Society*, Pine Forge Press, London.

Rocco Forte Hotels (2004). [on line] available from: http://www.roccofortehotels.com, [accessed June 17th 2004].

Scarpato, R. and Daniele, R. (2003). New global cuisine: Tourism, authenticity and a sense of place in post-modern gastronomy. In C.M. Hall, L. Sharples, R. Mitchell, N. Macionics and B. Cambourne, (eds.) *Food Tourism Around the World*, Butterworth-Heinemann, Oxford, pp. 296-313.

Schlosser, E. (2001). *Fast Food Nation, What the all American Meal is doing to the World*, Allen Lane, The Penguin Press.

Slow Food, http://www.slowfood.com/eng/sf_editore/sf_editore_rivista.lasso, [accessed June 7th 2004].

Solomon, M. R. (1999). *Consumer Behaviour*, 4th edn., Prentice Hall, New Jersey.

Theocharous, A. L., Nuttall, M, W. and Seddighi, H. R. (2000). *Political Instability and Tourism: A Cross-cultural Examination: Expressions of Culture, Identity and Meaning in Tourism*, Business Education Publishers Ltd., Sunderland, pp. 385-412.

Valentine, G. (1999). Consuming Pleasures: Food, Leisure and the Negotiations of Sexual Relations. In D. Crouch *Leisure/Tourism Geographies*, Routledge, London, pp. 164-180.

Van Westering, J. and Neil, E. (2003). The organisation of Wine Tourism in France: The involvement of the French public sector, *Journal of Travel and Tourism Marketing*, Vol. 14, No. 3/4 pp. 35-48.

Vignali, C. (2001). Mcdonalds: think global, act local-the marketing mix, *British Food Journal*, Vol. 103 No. 2, pp. 97-111.

Warde, A. and Martens, L. (2000). *Eating Out.* Cambridge University Press, Cambridge, England.

Williams, P. W. and Dossa, K. B. (2003). Non-Resident Wine Tourist Markets: Implications for British Columbia's Emerging Wine Tourism Industry. *Journal of Travel and Tourism Marketing*, Vol. 14, No. 3/4, pp. 1-34.

World Health Organisation (2003). *Controlling the Global Obesity Epidemic*, World Health Organisation, [on line] available from: http://www.bbc.co.uk/food/foodjunkies/chrono_fastfood.shtml, [accessed Jun 17th 2004].

World Health Organisation (2004). *Obesity and Overweight*, World Health Organisation, [on line] available from: http://www.who.int/dietphysicalactivity/publications /facts/obesity/en, [accessed June 17th 2004].

Suggested Further Reading

Bessière, J. (1998). Local Development and Heritage: Traditional Food and Cuisine as Tourist Attractions in Rural Areas, *Sociologia Ruralis*, Vol. 39, No.1, pp. 21-34.

Hall, C. M., Sharples, L., Mitchell, R., Macionics, N. and Cambourne, B. (2003) (eds.). *Food Tourism Around the World*, Butterworth-Heinemann, Oxford.

Love, J. F. (1995). *McDonald's: Behind the Arches*, Bantam Trade Paperback, New York.

Ritzer, G. (2000). *The McDonaldisation of Society*, Pine Forge Press, London.

Slow, The Magazine of the Slow Food Movement.

Chapter Two

The Development of Wine Tourism

Neil Symon

Overview

This chapter focuses on global wine production and wine consumption, highlighting the economic benefits of wine tourism and strategies for developing wine tourism. Tourists visiting vineyards have not only the opportunities to taste and to buy local wines but also can see for themselves how wines are made and in turn they can place them into the context of the wines that they purchase for home consumption. To savour such experiences, tourists need to leave the generally recognised centres of tourism and follow wine-routes or create their own. Therefore, there are economic effects on the surrounding areas, in particular hotels, restaurants, shops and fuel suppliers. To the small-scale wine producer such tourists can mean economic survival so it is beneficial to the locals to develop practical business strategies to accommodate the tourists. Each vineyard is unique in the style of wine produced due to variances in the soil, the varieties and blend of grapes, viticultural (grape growing) and vinification (wine making) methods, regional climate and micro-climates. However, each wine growing district has generic similarities. This chapter concludes with a planning exercise which employs a framework for a case study on the management of wine tourism. On this basis, for a chosen geographical region or a local area, strategies for increasing wine tourism can be devised and the practical implications of those strategies can be given specific consideration.

Introduction

Increasingly, tourists are looking for holiday experiences in which they can participate (Hall, Sharples, Cambourne and Macionis, 2000). A scholar of wine, when tasting, can read the label on the bottle and ascertain information about the country and region of origin, the grape or grapes used, whether it is dry or sweet and the alcohol by volume. Further reading can ascertain the viticultural and vinification methods, including the nature of the soil and the climate. However much the taster might read about the wine, nothing can bring the experience to life as does a visit to the vineyard. The Winemakers Federation of Australia (2005a, p. 1) defines wine tourism as: "a wide range of experiences built around tourist visitation to wineries and wine regions, including: wine tasting, wine and food, the enjoyment of regional environs, day trip or longer term recreation and many companion/complementary cultural, nature based and lifestyle activities available in wine regions", a definition agreed by Hall and Macionis (1998). The Australian Wine Industry Strategy 2025 (Winemakers' Federation of Australia, 2005b, p. 1) states: "The wine industry and the tourism industry share a common goal in capturing and presenting a unique sense of place to consumers, whether they be wine drinkers or tourists".

Country	2000	1999	1998	1998	1996	Average 1996-1999	%Change 2000VS.1996-99
World Total	275,892	277,171	256,399	256,399	270,531	266,390	3.57%
France	57,541	60,425	52,671	53,561	57,047	55,929	2.88%
Italy	51,620	56,454	54,188	50,894	58,772	55,077	(6.28%)
Spain	41,692	33,723	31,175	33,218	31,000	32,279	29.16%
United States	23,300	19,050	20,504	21,606	18,840	20,000	16.50%
Argentina	12,538	15,588	12,673	13,500	12,681	13,686	(8.38%)
Germany	9,852	12,123	10,834	8,495	8,642	10,024	(1.71%)
Austrailia	8,064	8,511	7,415	6,174	6,734	7,209	11.87%
South Africa	6,949	7,968	7,703	8,115	8,739	8,131	(14.54%)
Portugal	6,694	7,859	3,750	6,124	9,712	6,861	(2.44%)
Chile	6,419	4,807	5,475	4,459	3,824	4,664	37.64%
China	5,750	5,200	3,550	3,200	3,000	3,738	52.85%
Romania	5,456	6,054	5,002	6,688	7,663	6,352	(14.10%)
Brazil	3,704	3,190	2,782	2,743	3,128	2,961	25.10%
Greece	3,588	3,680	3,826	3,987	4,109	3,901	(8.78%)
Hungary	3,000	3,339	4,334	4,472	4,188	4,083	(26.53%)
Russia	2,903	2,903	2,180	2,230	2,550	2,466	17.73%
Moldova	2,402	1,332	1,700	3,123	3,598	2,438	(1.49%)
Austria	2,338	2,803	2,7803	1,802	2,110	2,355	(0.70%)
Bulgaria	2,099	2,026	2,129	3,371	3,534	2,765	(24.09%)
Croatia	2,094	2,094	2,277	2,260	1,958	2,147	(2.48%)
Yugoslavia	1,973	1,366	3,150	4,025	3,488	3,007	(34.39%)
Mexico	1,437	1,427	1,112	1,524	1,332	1,349	6.54%
Japan	1,328	1,328	1,301	1,301	675	1,151	15.35%
Switzerland	1,311	1,347	1,204	1,045	1,304	1,225	7.02%
Macedonia	1,220	1,220	1,227	1,136	1,010	1,148	6.25%
Uruguay	1,080	1,050	1,050	1,028	963	1,023	5.60%
Uzbekistan	1,080	1,080	1,140	1,470	1,020	1,178	(8.28%)
Georgia	750	830	830	830	700	798	(5.96%)
Slovenia	688	688	894	894	932	852	(19.25%)
New Zealand	602	602	606	458	573	560	7.55%
Ukraine	600	600	900	990	1,199	922	(34.94%)
Cyprus	545	555	710	534	559	590	(7.55%)
Slovakia	514	514	497	586	376	493	4.21%

continued

Country	2000	1999	1998	1998	1996	Average 1996-1999	%Change 2000VS.1996-99
World Total	275,892	277,171	256,399	256,399	270,531	266,390	3.57%
Canada	512	512	371	343	333	390	31.37%
Czech Republic	504	498	560	405	516	495	1.87%
Algeria	424	422	360	357	392	383	10.78%
Tunisia	412	468	352	372	221	353	16.63%
Azerbaijan	375	375	650	600	350	494	(24.05%)
Turkmenistan	354	354	360	180	168	266	33.33%
Turkey	320	320	278	336	363	324	(1.31%)
Morocco	300	493	298	376	284	363	(17.30%)
Kazakstan	227	227	191	111	114	161	41.21%
Lebanon	188	188	186	248	158	195	(3.59%)
Belarus	155	183	195	232	174	196	(20.92%)
Luxembourg	132	184	160	75	128	137	(3.47%)
Tajikstan	130	130	163	195	195	171	(23.87%)
Peru	127	127	120	120	111	120	6.28%
Albania	127	127	105	168	176	144	(11.81%)
Madagascar	89	91	90	89	88	90	(0.56%)
Paraguay	80	80	92	92	80	86	(6.98%)
Israel	80	80	90	90	90	88	(8.57%)
Bosnia-Herceg	48	58	54	54	54	55	(12.73%)
Lithuania	40	40	45	35	35	39	3.23%
Malta	35	35	32	32	32	33	6.87%
Armenia	35	35	24	65	78	51	(30.69%)
Egypt	27	27	27	26	26	27	1.89%
Bolivia	20	20	20	20	20	20	0.00%
Estonia	20	20	18	7	22	17	19.40%
United Kingdom	14	13	12	6	26	14	(1.75%)
Latvia	10	10	10	56	152	57	(82.46%)
Kyrgyzstan	4	6	8	20	23	14	(71.93%)
Belgium	2	2	1	1	1	1	60.00%
County Total	275,892	277,171	256,364	260,644	270,370	266,137	3.67%
Other Countries	0	0	35	815	161	262	(100.00%)
World Total	275,892	277,171	256,399	261,459	270,361	266,390	3.57%

**Table 1: World Wine Production By Country (1); Hectolitres (000) (2)
Actual 1996-2000; Average for years 1996–1999 and percent change 2000 v. 1996-1999**
(1) Ranked by production in 2000. (2) Conversion: After adding three zeros to the figures to get hectolitres, multiply hectolitres times 26.418 to convert to gallons.
Source: Wine Institute (2004).

Quality wine is produced between the latitudes of 30° and 50° north and 30° and 50° south due to the hours of sunshine and temperatures achieved. Table 1 identifies the world wine production by country ranked by quantity in the year 2000. France produced 57541 hectolitres (hl) of wine (20.8% of the global total), Italy 51620 hl, 18.7%; Spain 416921 hl, 15.1%; United States of America 23300 hl, 8.4%. These countries accounted for 63% of the world's wine production. Examples from Central and Eastern Europe include Romania (12th in the world rankings), followed by Hungary, Russia and Moldova (15th to 17th respectively), Bulgaria (19th), Croatia and Yugoslavia (20th and 21st). Further down the table are Slovakia and the Czech Republic (33rd and 35th in the world) with 514 hl, 0.186% and 504 hl, 0.182% respectively. The United Kingdom (UK), being a marginal producer of wine due to its northerly position, produces only 14 hectolitres which represents 0.005% of the world wine production. Of the 44, UK vineyards listed at the time of writing (See http://www.english-wine.com/content.html#index) 28 (64%) accept visitors. Australia, which produced 8064 hl, 2.92% of the world wine production has an organised and highly effective wine tourism system. According to the WFA (Winemakers' Federation of Australia, 2005c), the economic and social benefits of wine tourism to wine regions and the wine industry include: increased number of visitors (domestic and international) and repeat visits; extended length of stay and money spent by visitors; enhanced visitor satisfaction by increasing activities for tourists; and expanded market for cellar door sales. Szivas (1999) extends this theme by saying that the tourist flow can be dispersed from established tourist centres, thus relieving the pressure on them; a peripheral region can use wine tourism as the basis to develop their tourism industry.

Benefits of Wine Tourism

The importance to a winery of tourism depends upon its size. For many small wineries tourism can be the core business (Hall. et al., 2000), and in 1999 it was estimated that about 68% of wineries relied on cellar door sales for their income (Jolley, 2002). Over the period 1986-1998 world wine production decreased by an average rate of 1.7% per annum, whilst world wine consumption declined over the same period by 0.8% per annum (Stanford, 2001). Every winery is at risk from a shrinking market; however it is the smaller wineries that are more at risk due to their limited resources.

Much research has been carried out on Australian Wine Tourism. In Queensland during the five-year period up to 2002 Australian (A)$60 (approx. €35) million was invested into the wine industry, increasing the number of cellar door outlets from 30 to 90 (Research Department, Tourism Queensland, 2003), and within Australia, 5.3% of short trip tourists (three nights or fewer) and 8.1% of long trip tourists (greater than three nights) visited a winery during their stay. The result was, in 1999, 425,000 international tourists visited a winery that supplemented the 490,000 domestic short trip tourists and 766,000 long trip domestic tourists, giving a total of 1,681,000 tourists visiting wineries. (Roy Morgan Research, 2002). Subsequent research (South Australian Tourism Commission, 2002) showed that in 2001, 3,979,000 people visited Australian wineries, with South Australia claiming 20% (815,000) of these visitors. Apart from buying wines, tourists also buy souvenirs and other merchandise (Foo, 1999). In addition to tourists, wineries also have numerous visits from locals who buy wine from the cellar door. It has been estimated that during 2001, the 210 wineries of New South Wales (NSW) received 4.1 million visits (Tarr, 2003), generating A$ 353 (approx. €205) million.

Having looked at the benefits to the wine industry, it is important to review the benefits to the local economy of the wine region. Whilst at a winery, visitors can (a) have a good time; (b) extend their knowledge of wines, the winery and wine region; and (c) taste and perhaps buy the wines. However, many tourists include winery visits as part of an overall package whereby they can experience restaurants, international foods and wine, socialising, cultural activities such as visiting art galleries, visiting historical places and visiting parks and gardens (Roy Morgan Research, 2002); international visitors have a higher interest than other visitors in cultural activities such as visiting museums, art galleries and wine festivals (Winemakers' Federation of Australia, 2005c). Within New South Wales, approximately 2,800 people are employed in various roles in wineries, not just in viticulture and viniculture, but also cellar door services, restaurant and food services and accommodation. Moreover, 35% of these staff are employed in visitor services and retail operations. The estimated total turnover of wineries with cellar doors in NSW was A$92.9 (approx. €54) million in 2001 (Tarr, 2003). From these examples, the potential for wine tourism to provide work for the locals and to generate income is apparent.

Wine Tourism Strategy

In the previous section the reasons why tourists wish to visit wineries have been discussed, showing the benefits in both fiscal and numerical terms. "Strategy 2025: The Australian Wine Industry" (Winemakers' Federation of Australia, (2005b, p. 2) states: "The wine industry and the tourism industry share a common goal in capturing and presenting a unique sense of place to consumers, whether they be wine drinkers or tourists". The question that must be addressed is how these industries can develop their products and services to maximise returns.

Winemakers' Federation of Australia (2005b, p. 2) identifies four key areas:

> ➢ "Ensuring that the wine industry is aware of the opportunities to increase visitation and yield for their business related to participation in wine tourism"

> ➢ "Improving the opportunities for interaction and collaboration between the wine and tourism industries resulting in a higher level of understanding and a strategic business commitment to wine tourism"

> ➢ "Providing tools to assist winemakers and tourism operators to present higher quality wine tourism products and services that will result in innovation in wine tourism, a higher level of consumer appeal for the experiences that are available and ultimately higher visitation and yields"

> ➢ "Heightened definition, promotion and awareness of the Australian wine tourism experience in both domestic and international markets that will deliver higher visitation and yields'

The strategies devised for the key areas are outlined below. Research in Australia identified some important requirements for consideration in the implementation of a strategy (WFA, 2002).

1.   Infrastructure Requirements

Special attention needs to be paid to the infrastructure requirements as detailed in Table 2.

Infrastructure Requirements	Details
Signage	Signs at the front gate set the tone – the style of the sign, the information on it (such as opening hours), all create a first impression
Car park	Availability of parking is important. It is also important that visitors do not experience confusion about where to park.
Landscaping	The style, maintenance and look of the landscaping help to create a good first impression.
Attention to outdoor areas	Outside facilities, such as places for people to linger on a terrace, a place for picnics, and especially children's play areas are facilities to be considered. Many wine tourists have children who get bored easily – if they have somewhere safe to play outside, the parents will have more time to taste the wines, relax and buy.
Indoor-outdoor connections and relationships	Both visual and physical, such as are achieved through astute structural and design linkages (doorways, windows with a scenic outlook, etc.) should be explored to further enhance the overall feel and visual/physical flow of the place
Indoor ambience	Aim to create an inviting atmosphere upon entry to the cellar door; include design elements and features that feed a variety of the visitors' senses.
Walls	Wall space can be used to educate the visitor on the wines in a subtle and interesting way, such as history of the vineyard – old photos if it is a winery with a significant history and heritage
Wine information	Information on grape varieties, picking time, how the wine is made, how the climate influences the flavour
Promoting the best of the wider region	Information on display of the local region is another idea for making the cellar door a total experience

Table 2: Infrastructure Requirements
Source: Winemakers' Federation of Australia (2005d, p2).

2.   Accommodation Preferences

Australian winery visitors have a preference for staying in bed and breakfast accommodation (Roy Morgan Research, 2002).

3.   Typical Nature of Travel Party

Most Australian wine tourists are couples, with the majority being older travellers (retirees) (Parfitt, 1998). Throughout the winter of 1998, wine travellers fell into the travel party categories indicated in Table 3.

Travel Party	Total Visitors % (N=408)	Passing Visitors % (N=196)	Weekend Visitors % (N=100)	Weekday Visitors % (N=112)
Alone	5.4	9.5	0.0	3.1
Couple	70.3	82.8	50.8	65.6
Family with children	4.2	2.6	5.1	6.3
Groups of friends	13.4	2.6	35.6	12.5
Relatives	5.9	2.6	6.8	10.9
Other	0.8	0.1	1.7	1.6
Totals	**100**	**100**	**100**	**100**

Table 3: Profile of Wine Tourists by Composition and Nature of Travel Party (N=408)
Source: Parfitt, N. (1998), p.7.

4.   Mode of Transport

Roy Morgan Research (2002) identified that, in Australia, visitors to wineries on long or short trips tend to use their own car/4WD or hire a car/4WD for transport. It is questionable whether the promotion of self-drive tours is advisable. Whilst a trained wine taster will spit tasting samples, it may be assumed that members of the public will swallow the wine, thus increasing the possibility of driving under the influence of alcohol hence attaching an element of risk to the visit.

5.   Demographic Profile of Overnight Visitors to Wineries

Roy Morgan Research (2002) found that 84% of short trip and 77.4% of long trip travellers who visited wineries had drunk wine in the last 4 weeks and 54% of the latter group agreed that they now drunk more wine than they used to. A diploma or degree was held by 40.7% of the former group and 36.9% of the latter. It could be argued on the basis of such data that the most common profile of visitors to wineries not surprisingly drink wine but also belong to the 50 plus age group and are 'fairly well educated'.

6.   Barriers to Wine Tourism

  ➢ Historically, the benefits of tourism have gone to the tour operators and other non-wine businesses whilst the wineries bear the costs (Parfitt, 1998);

  ➢ Environmental issues will need to be addressed. Wine production is a rural occupation and any increase in tourist numbers will necessarily increase the environmental impact on an area. In 1998, the Napa Valley in California had about 100,000 residents, but visitor number approximated 4 million (Conaway, 1990), reaching 5 million by 1998 (Skinner, 2000);

  ➢ Napa Valley roads are congested on summer weekends (Skinner, 2000) thus disrupting the harvest; and

➤   The alternative railway must sound its whistle at crossings creating noise pollution and further disrupting the harvest (Skinner, 2000).

Conclusion

Because of their nature, wine growing regions are located in rural areas which hitherto had not attracted tourism. It has been demonstrated that wine tourism can bring significant economic benefits to wine growing regions. For individual wineries, opening their cellar doors and selling to tourists can mean economic survival. However, as can be seen from the Napa Valley experience in California, large-scale commercialised tourism can disrupt normal daily life in these rural areas and, equally importantly, make it very difficult to produce the wines that the tourists wish to see and sample. Therefore, it is imperative to devise wine tourism strategies that balance the needs of the tourists with not only the local economy and infrastructure but also the wine production of the winery.

Student Activities

In devising a wine tourism strategy for an area or region, it is necessary to understand what motivates and influences visitor to wineries. As an initial step in devising a strategy, planners are advised to brainstorm some ideas to improve on the model below.

1.   Repeat visitors

Different wineries offer different experiences to visitors. Rene Henry, who has been involved in the wine industry, said in Wines and Vines (Howie, 1999, pp. 39-40): "I could not believe the crowds, the ranks of tour buses unloading 40 visitors at a time. The tasting room was packed, and a board announced which wines were available for tasting – for a fee". Also, he found that staff lacked knowledge and service was poor (Dodd, 1999). In accordance with Henry's viewpoint, Dodd (1999) believes that winery managers do not always appreciate the benefits of returning visitors and developing consumer relationships. Figure 1 identifies the circle of influence on the winery visitor. Dodd (1999) discusses whether the model in Figure 1 encompasses fully the influences upon a winery visitor. Do you think that you could improve on the model?

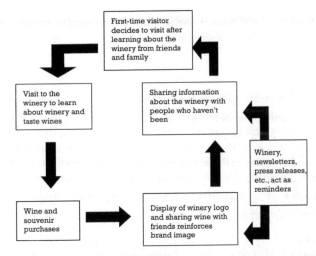

Figure 1: Circle of Influence of Decision-making Processes of the Winery Visitor
Source: Dodd (1999, p.25)

Discuss with your tutor or classmates ways in which boxes and/or arrows might be added or removed or rearranged where you think appropriate and justify your reason(s).

2. Implementing your strategy

The Winemakers' Federation of Australia created a Strategic Business Plan 2002 – 2005 (WFA, 2002) that identified four key areas to ensure increased returns for wineries and wine tourism operators through improved products and services and heightened awareness.

➤ "Ensuring that the wine industry is aware of the opportunities to increase visitation and yield for their business related to participation in wine tourism";

➤ "Improving the opportunities for interaction and collaboration between the wine and tourism industries resulting in a higher level of understanding and a strategic business commitment to wine tourism";

➤ "Providing tools to assist winemakers and tourism operators to present higher quality wine tourism products and services that will result in innovation in wine tourism, a higher level of consumer appeal for the experiences that are available and ultimately higher visitation and yields"; and

➤ "Heightened definition, promotion and awareness of the Australian wine tourism experience in both domestic and international markets that will deliver higher visitation and yields".

Using a wine region or country of your choice, use the following table to write a report on the development of a strategy for wine tourism. The strategies identified in the boxes below are those of the WFA, but the content of the 'major projects that must undertaken' should be your own ideas. To help you on your way, the original WFA major projects and anticipated key benefits/outcomes are included in *italics*. These may or may not be appropriate to your wine region or country. If you cannot think of a suitable wine growing district, consider the strategies for breweries, cider and perry, and distilleries.

References

Conaway, J. (1990). *Napa*, Avon Books, New York.

Dodd, T. (1999). Attracting Repeat Customers to Wineries, *International Journal of Wine Marketing*, Vol. 11, No. 2, pp. 18-28.

Foo, L.M. (1999). A profile of International Visitors to Australian Wineries, Tourism Research Report, *Journal of the Bureau of Tourism Research*, Vol. 1, No. 1, pp. 41-44.

Hall, C. M., Sharples, L., Cambourne, B. and Macionis, N. (2000). *Wine Tourism around the world; developing, management and markets*, Butterworth-Heinemann, Oxford.

Hall, C. M. and Macionis, N. (1998). Wine tourism in Australia and New Zealand. In R.W. Butler, C.M. Hall and L.M. Jenkins (eds.) *Tourism and recreation in rural areas*, John Wiley and Sons, Chichester, pp. 267-98.

Howie, M. (1999). Napa Valley disappoints Rene A. Henry, *Wines and Vines*, May, pp. 39-40.

http://www.english-wine.com/content.html#index.

Jolley, A. (2002). *The Wine Industry, Wine Tourism and Tourism in General*, Supporting paper No 5, Centre for Strategic Economic Studies, Victoria University, Melbourne.

Parfitt, N. (1998). The Southern Downs Visitor Survey: Research Findings. In *Wine Tourism*, Research Department, Tourism Queensland (2003). [on-line] available from: http://www.tq.com.au/index.cfm?16C409C3-D3E5-21DE-AD0E-03FF0FF9FA06#w [accessed November 17th 2003].

Roy Morgan Research Pty Ltd. (2002). Wine and Tourism, *Tourism & Travel Market Insight*, No. 5, March 8th, pp. 1-6.

Skinner, A. (2000). Napa valley, California: a model of wine region development. In C.M. Hall, L. Sharples, B. Cambourne and N. Macionis. *Wine Tourism around the world; developing management and markets*, Butterworth-Heinemann, Oxford, pp. 293-296.

Stanford, L. (2001). Vintage 2001 – the new order emerging? Wine of Australia, PowerPoint presentation [on-line] available from: http://www.agribusiness.asn.au/members/proceedings/Wine_2001.pdf [accessed November 17th 2003].

Szivas, E. (1999). The Development of Wine Tourism in Hungary, *International Journal of Wine Marketing*, Vol. 11, No. 2, pp. 7-17.

Tarr, D. (2003). *Wine Tourism*, Powerpoint Presentation, Tourism New South Wales [on-line] available from: http://corporate.tourism.nsw.gov.au/scripts/runisa.dll?CORPORATELIVE.65630:HOMEPAGE: 1513702486:pp=UPPER,pc=HOME [accessed November 17th 2003]

Winemakers' Federation of Australia (WFA) (2002). *Wine Tourism Strategic Business Plan 2002-2005: Embrace the Challenge*, [on-line] available from: http://www.wfa.org.au/PDF/NWTS%20Strategic%20Plan.pdf [accessed March 22nd 2005].

Winemakers' Federation of Australia (WFA) (2005a). *Your guide to wine tourism; understanding wine tourism markets* [on-line] available from: http://www.wfa.org.au/PDF/Fact%20Sheet%201.pdf [accessed February 14th 2003].

Winemakers' Federation of Australia (WFA) (2005b). *The Strategy 2025: The Australian Wine Industry Looks Ahead* [on-line] available from: http://www.winetitles.com.au/awol/overview/strategy2025/[accessed March 22nd 2005].

Winemakers' Federation of Australia (WFA) (2005c). *Your Guide to Wine Tourism: Understanding Wine Tourism Markets,* [on-line] available from: http://www.wfa.org.au/PDF/Fact%20Sheet%202.pdf [accessed March 22nd 2005].

Winemakers' Federation of Australia (WFA) (2005d). *Your Guide to Wine Tourism: The Cellar Door Experience,* [on-line] available from: http://www.wfa.org.au/PDF/Fact%20Sheet%204.pdf [accessed March 22nd 2005].

Wine Institute (2004). *World wine production by country (1); hectolitres (000) (2) actual 1996-2000; average for years 1996– 1999 and percent change 2000 v. 1996 – 1999,* [on-line] available from: http://www.wineinstitute.org/communications/statistics/keyfacts_worldwineproduction02.htm [accessed March 22nd 2005].

Suggested Further Reading

Beverland, M. (1998). Wine Tourism in New Zealand: maybe the industry has got it right, *International Journal of Wine Marketing* Vol. 10, No. 2, pp. 24-33.

Beverland, M. (2000). Wine Tourism: a tale of two conferences, *International Journal of Wine Marketing*, Vol. 12, No. 2, pp. 73-74.

Beverland, M. (1999). Wine Tourists: a missed opportunity or a misplaced priority? *Pacific Tourism Review*, Vol. 3, No. 2, pp. 119-131.

Broom, D. (1996). Take the high road, *Decanter*, Vol. 22, No.3, pp. 108-113.

Brown, G. (1995). Whiskied away, *Decanter*, Vol. 20, No. 5, pp. 48-50.

Carlsen, J. and Dowling, R. (1998). Wine tourism marketing issues in Australia, *International Journal of Wine Marketing*, Vol. 10, No. 3, pp. 23-32.

Carlsen, J. and Dowling, R. (2001). Regional Wine Tourism: a development plan for Western Australia, *Tourism Recreation Research*, Vol. 26, No. 2, pp. 45-52.

Dodd, T. and Beverland, M. (2001). Winery Tourism life-cycle development: a proposed model, *Tourism Recreation Research*, Vol. 26, No.2, pp. 11-21.

Frochot, I. (2001). French wine brotherhoods and wine tourism: a complex relationship, *Tourism Recreation Research*, Vol. 26, No. 2, pp .53-62.

Getz, D., Dowling, R., Carlsen, J. and Anderson, D. (1999). Critical Success Factors for Wine Tourism, *International Journal of Wine Marketing*, Vol. 11, No.3, pp. 20-43.

Hall. C. M. (2003). (ed.) *Wine, food and tourism marketing*, Haworth Hospitality Press, Binghampton, USA.

Knight, J. and Charters, S. (1999). Education in a West Australian wine tourism context, *International Journal of Wine Marketing*, Vol. 11, No. 1, pp. 7-18.

Kovačić, D. and Radman, M. (2003). Farmers' wine fair: a case study, *British Food Journal,* Vol. 105, No. 3, pp. 204-210.

Lockshin, L. and Spawton, T. (2001). Using involvement and brand equity to develop a wine tourism strategy, *International Journal of Wine Marketing,* Vol.13, No.1, pp. 72-81.

Martin, A. and Haugh, H. (1999). The Malt Whisky Trail: the tourism and marketing potential of the whisky distillery visitor centre, *International Journal of Wine Marketing,* Vol. 11, No. 2, pp. 42-52.

McBoyle, G. (1996). Green Tourism and Scottish distilleries, *Tourism Management,* Vol. 17, No. 4, pp. 255-263.

Nuernberger, K. (2003). *The Okanagan Cultural Corridor Project 2002, A review of the literature,* Research Services, Tourism British Columbia [on-line] available from: http://www.google.co.uk/search?hl=en&q=Nuernberger%2C+K.+%282003%29.+The+Okanagan +Cultural+Corridor+Project+2002%2C+A+review+of+the+literature%2C+&btnG=Search&meta= [accessed February 14th 2005].

Roberts, L. and Simpson, F. (1999). Developing Partnership Approaches to Tourism in Central and Eastern Europe, *Journal of Sustainable Tourism,* Vol. 7, Nos. 3 & 4, pp. 314-330.

Telfer, D (2001). From a wine tourism village to a regional wine route: an investigation of the competitive advantage of embedded clusters in Niagara, Canada, *Tourism Recreation Research,* Vol. 26, No. 2, pp. 23-33.

Telfer, D. (2001). Strategic alliances along the Niagara Wine Route, *Tourism Management,* Vol. 22, No. 1, pp. 21-30.

Telfer, D. and Hashimoto, A. (2000). Niagara Icewine tourism: Japanese souvenir purchases at Inniskillin Winery, *Tourism and Hospitality Research,* Vol. 2, No. 4, pp. 343-356.

Williams, P. (2001). The evolving images of wine tourism destinations, *Tourism Recreation Research*, Vol. 26, No.2, pp. 3-10

Note:

Winemakers' Federation of Australia (2005) have collated a database of wine tourism publications and research containing information on research papers, articles, journals, conference proceedings and books related to wine tourism. The intention is to facilitate easier access to existing information and encourage greater coordination and collaboration related to wine tourism research activities. [on-line] available from: http://www.wfa.org.au/projects/winetourism.html [accessed February 14th 2005].

	Glossary	
	AWTA	Australian Wine Tourism Alliance
	WFA	Winemakers' Federation of Australia
	STOs	State Tourism Organisations
	AWBC	Australian Wine and Brandy Corporation
	AWEC	Australian Wine Export Council
	ATC	Australian Tourism Commission
	Framework for report, adapted from WFA (2002)	

	Strategy	**Major Projects**	**Key Outcomes**
1.	Facilitate better coordination and communication of activities	*Review AWTA* *Establish Advisory Committee* *Establish Wine Tourism section within WFA web site and newsletters* *Review National Wine Tourism Conference* *Clarify wine and tourism organisational structure and disseminate information* *Identify, establish and/or strengthen other key relationships (for example, food, STOs, AWBC, AWEC, ATC)*	*Raised understanding and awareness of benefits of assessment process and relevant State[1] contacts.* *Preparation of case studies related to successful cellar door and signage programmes and relevant local/regional/national contacts as appropriate*
2.	*Improve wine industry knowledge (Training and Accreditation)*	(Write here what you consider to be the major projects that should be undertaken to facilitate the strategy opposite)	(Write here what you intend to achieve by your strategy and major projects)
3.	*Improve wine tourism research*		
4.	*Improve supporting services and infrastructure*		
5.	*Improve consumer and travel trade information quality and access*		
6.	*Domestic marketing and promotion*		
7.	*International marketing and promotion*		

---

[1] State in this context means one of the States of Australia, such as New South Wales, Victoria, Western Australia or Queensland.

Chapter Three

Accommodation Development:
focusing on a case study of Eastern Europe

Neil Robinson

Overview

The role of accommodation is a key component within any destination's service infrastructure; not only does the accommodation provision facilitate stay and therefore increase customer spend, it also acts as a benchmark in relation to the wider service provision within the destination (Youell, 1998). Accommodation demand has increased greatly over recent years, with provision being improved continually and customer expectations rising all the time. Against this backdrop Western Europe's politically stable and financially secure arena has further supported and facilitated accommodation growth. This phenomenon could offer much social and financial security for Central and Eastern Europe if it can be controlled and monitored accordingly. This chapter aims to examine in detail the provision for accommodation within a European context and identify growth and development patterns. The chapter provides a general overview of accommodation, including definitions and a chronological review of its development, with attention being given to the role which accommodation plays in the tourism supply chain. The utilisation of a case study of European origin further reinforces understanding and contextualises future development opportunities within Central and Eastern Europe.

Introduction

The accommodation concept has developed considerably in the last two decades and nowhere is this more the case than in Europe, where provision and service have accelerated the pace of change for both tourist and host alike (Davidson, 1992). Indeed the development of accommodation has impacted greatly on tourism provision, offering an opportunity for increased social well-being and improved urban environments and at the same time creating new opportunities for business. Matley (1976) encapsulated this notion perfectly and goes on to argue that the popularity of any urban environment is very much dependent upon its superstructure and infrastructure support. More recently (Page 1995; Cooper, Fletcher, Gilbert and Wanhill, 1998) have highlighted the relationships among accommodation, attractions and infrastructure, as being fundamental to any destination's development. Sometimes simply referred to as hospitality, the accommodation sector provides leisure and business tourists with somewhere to stay and may offer sustenance to locals, travellers or visitors (adapted from Youell, 1998, p. 28). As a key component of the tourism industry, accommodation acts as a support mechanism for the tourist at those times when traditional comforts normally associated with the home, are geographically inaccessible. Over the last 30 years, the provision of accommodation has seen a huge growth in terms of development and demand. In many cases this growth has been due to increased consumer awareness, higher disposable incomes and greater integration across Europe, resulting in higher demand for accommodation and travel related services (Pearce 1995). This demand, if managed correctly, has the potential to increase economic stability in countries where traditional industries have been in demise for a number of years. Recent developments in the accommodation sector owe much to the continued growth of tourism, both at national and international levels. Indeed it would be hard to imagine tourism growth without development in local accommodation, as many tourists rely heavily on such services whilst visiting destinations.

In Europe generally, the standard of accommodation has improved greatly over recent years. In many cases, improvements have been a consequence of increased consumer affluence, international globalisation and the development of an expectant service culture, resulting in a more highly sophisticated customer. The increase in hospitality demand has expanded greatly over the last 100 years, with global hospitality brands and product standardisation being at the forefront of this evolution (Cooper et al., 1998). Indeed this global growth in hospitality infrastructure was facilitated further by the post war economic boom of the 1950s and 1960s, resulting in the creation of a service industry that encapsulates tourism, leisure and hospitality ventures.

Historical Development of Accommodation

Although traditionally associated with the hospitality and tourism industries, the utilisation of accommodation was in existence long before the advent of the service sector in the eighteenth and nineteenth centuries (Holloway 2002). In general, the rising living standards associated with the twentieth century have impacted positively upon peoples' lives and facilitated individuals' propensities to travel. Hospitality provision, although more commonly associated with the present, can be traced back to biblical origin, often being associated with religious events and trade.

History informs us that the Egyptians (circa 3200 BC) participated in religious events, requiring participants to move from one geographical location to another so creating a demand for accommodation which would have been basic and a far cry from today's hospitality provision, with payment probably being in the form of barter or exchange. From this early period the development of a hospitality industry can be identified.

Although the early Egyptian period might be recognised as possibly the first in which an 'accommodation industry' was apparent, during the later Greek period, accommodation development began to realise its full potential. The first Olympic Games in 776 BC acted as a real catalyst for the accommodation industry with participant athletes and visitors requiring the provision of food, beverage and accommodation, a requirement which Greece was quick to embrace as key component of Greek culture and civilisation (Torkildsen, 1999). The utilisation of leisure time as a facilitator of social interaction and well-being has been documented extensively in history; for example Roman civilisation typified this, with leisure provision being central to the Roman culture both in terms of population fitness and entertainment (Haywood, Kew and Bramham, 1995). In parallel, infrastructure provision in the form of road networks developed under the expanded Roman Empire, opened up many trade routes incorporating mechanisms for hospitality provision. The impact of the Roman Empire should be in no way understated and it can be argued with the increasing power that the Roman Empire held over its colonies, the birth of international travel emerged. In many cases, this manifested itself in travel for both business and leisure, with the medical benefits of Spa waters being advocated by the Romans as instruments to aid life and with this came yet another source of accommodation provision. From the evidence, hospitality provision during the Roman period was linked mainly to business, worship and in some cases social interaction, with accommodation being set up across main trade links and areas of significant economic interest. Indeed the Bible informs us that Bethlehem was a key trade location used by the Romans for the purpose of collecting taxes, with accommodation provision in the form of Inns, at which paying visitors could reside (Livingstone, 2000).

Post 400 AD, with the demise of the Roman Empire, the provision for travel became limited and this decline impacted upon hospitality provision. The rise of Christianity developed an ethos centring on prayer and worship, with recreation and travel being religious in origin rather than for enjoyment and physical well-being. It is from Christianity that the term 'holiday', which was developed from holy day, designed to encourage the populace to break from work and to participate in prayer, originated (Hoad, 1996; Torkildsen, 1999).

For centuries, hospitality provision remained underdeveloped, offering little in the way of personalised service and only really being experienced by those people in power or those who belonged to religious order. Further impacts on hospitality provision followed during the sixteenth century when the Reformation hindered hospitality development and travel in Europe due mainly to the growing role of the Protestant Church in preaching non-tolerance in the pursuit of pleasure, absolute commitment to the Protestant work ethic and a revulsion of the Catholic Church (Cannon, 2001).

The next date in the chronological review that is worthy of mention is the late 1600s, characterised by the emergence of the Grand Tour within Europe which acted as a kind of educational development system, designed to inform and familiarise wealthy nobility of the cultural richness and characteristics of Europe (Burkart and Medlick, 1989; Cannon, 2001). The Grand Tour, although exclusive in design, enabled the ruling elite of the day to experience first hand European living on a spatial scale. Destinations included Rome, Paris, Florence and Venice. The requirement for accommodation and additional support service created an unprecedented demand in Europe and, even today, many of these European cities promote accommodation stock developed originally for participants in the Grand Tour. The Grand Tour maintained its popularity right through to the early 1800s.

Although the health benefits associated with travel were recognised in the Roman and Greek periods, it is also worth noting that from the mid-sixteenth to the early eighteenth centuries, Europe's popularity as a destination for individuals seeking the benefits of spa waters increased (See also Chapter 7 p. 119 et seq). Seen as an elixir for life and health an increasing number of the middle class became indoctrinated by the benefits of bathing in and drinking spa water (Urry, 2002). As the popularity of such pastimes grew, the provision of accommodation also changed, with boarding provision and guesthouses providing services at key locations, both in Britain and mainland Europe. In Britain, for example, Royal patronage facilitated further the fashion of such activities with locations such as Leamington Spa, Buxton, Scarborough and Harrogate all proving popular as spa resorts and in turn further developing the accommodation sector in the United Kingdom (UK).

Industrial Impacts

The seventeenth and eighteenth centuries saw major changes in production and distribution techniques bringing with them fundamental changes to the manufacturing base and lifestyles of people within the UK and Europe (Burton, 2001). Alongside these changes, developments from traditional methods to more mechanistic methods of production saw urbanisation increase, on a scale never before witnessed, not only in the UK but also in mainland Europe. Gone were the old labour-intensive production techniques and in their place, mechanistic approaches which utilised heavy machinery for mass production and increased outputs. With these changes came huge pressures on the infrastructure. Migrating labour forces left their rural bases in exchange for employment in the cities and such movement impacted on both the rural and the city populations. The migration to the cities resulted in overcrowding which led to a multitude of problems including poor housing, sanitation and working conditions. In an attempt to alleviate these social conditions, and with the introduction of public Bank Holidays, created in 1871 (Youell, 1998), visits to the seaside and local countryside became commonplace and, as the days were extended to short breaks, so additional accommodation was developed to cater for the visitors' needs.

Technological Impacts

The role of technology in the form of transportation has been instrumental in developing hospitality provision over the ages. Indeed it can be argued that the pace of hospitality development would have been reduced greatly had it not been for the creation and maintenance of transport networks. The stagecoach networks of the seventeenth and eighteenth century established routes over which paying travellers would traverse linking the major cities of Europe, facilitating both business and commerce. "The development of the sprung coach was a huge advance for those who were obliged to travel. The invention in its most primitive form is traced to the Hungarian town of Kocs in the fifteenth century" (Holloway, 2002, p. 16). In England a number of transport corridors emerged including York to London and Manchester to Carlisle, and along these routes Inns and accommodation provision were established (Burkart and Medlick, 1989). Such facilities became invaluable and allowed the travellers to rest and obtain food and beverage; at the same time the stagecoach horses could be stabled and fed. Although underdeveloped by today's standards, the stagecoach accommodation ensured that guests, who were often journeying over several days, could be offered food and accommodation on route.

The advent of the steam engine proved effective in aiding transportation, leading inevitably to the creation of railway networks. The steam engine became an integral part of the industrial revolution assisting production in factories and mills and changed transportation fundamentally (For example, George Stephenson's Rocket, 1829, at http://www.bbc.co.uk/history/society_culture/industrialisation/launch_ani_rocket.shtml). Not only did the railway help to transport the over worked populace to such recreational environments but it was also key to the creation of inner-city hospitality provision in the form of the railway hotel. The railway hotel was established primarily to cater for the growing number of travellers to UK cities. Such hotels were often in very close proximity to the railway and offered the guest unprecedented luxury in terms of dining and accommodation. For example, The Midland Hotel, Manchester, UK was originally a British Railway hotel and was operated by the Holiday Inn group but it has been acquired recently by Quintessential Hotels (See http://www.manchesteronline.co.uk/business/dealsreview/s/124/124397_midland_in_line_for_12 m_makeover_.html). It was located close to the main central station, which has now been converted into Greater Manchester Conference and Exhibition (GMEX) centre (http://www.manchester2002-uk.com/buildings/fire&railways.html).

This chronological journey has taken the reader from the early origins of accommodation provision, right through to the growth in surface transportation of the late 1800s. From this historical perspective, lessons can be learned regarding the emergence and development of the accommodation sector today. People now travel more widely than ever for leisure, business and health reasons; transport infrastructure and attractions, events and entertainment remain inextricably linked with accommodation development. Moreover, visitors are beginning to expect technological developments that permit them to communicate world-wide from their current locations, in particular from their guest rooms.

Therefore, within the last 30 years, international visitors' expectations regarding accommodation provision have changed dramatically with the global development of tourism and increased consumer wealth of the latter part of the twentieth century having impacted positively on accommodation growth. Alongside these contributory factors, better health provision, higher educational standards and socially aware consumers, who are living longer, highly sophisticated and secure financially, have all benefited accommodation development. Indeed Western Europe has benefited greatly post World War II (WWII) from huge amounts being invested to create an environment for development and growth. However, this was not the case throughout all of Europe. The second part of this chapter identifies future accommodation development opportunities in Central and Eastern Europe where both local and foreign investments have provided opportunities for both national and international growth in the accommodation sector over the last decade. The following section is focused on the Czech Republic in which, in 2002, one in eight people was employed in tourism or a related sector (Čermáková, 2003) but other countries could be reviewed in a similar way.

The Central and Eastern European Perspective

Although much of Europe can boast a rich cultural environment that offers the visiting traveller a unique experience in terms of language, traditions and architecture, this has not always been the case as Europe suffered greatly during WWII, with much of its infrastructure and superstructure being decimated. Post WWII, Europe began its long road to stability and it was during this period that Europe itself began to be divided between the traditional Western democratic lines and the regimes of the East.

Eastern Europe is traditionally the name given to those countries which have in the past followed a non-democratic political system, and which ruled based upon a communist doctrine (Palmowski, 2003). This political system, although highly developed in Russia, stretched across much of Europe after WWII with countries such as Poland, Czechoslovakia, Romania and Bulgaria all being considered part of Eastern Europe. Such a political system, although Socialist in origin, saw much oppression against its own people with the limiting of free speech and the development of a two level hierarchy, namely the ruling elite in the form of the Communist Party and the proletariat/workers (Marx and Engels, 1930).

After WWII, a "truncated Czechoslovakia fell within the Soviet sphere of influence. In 1968, the invasion by Warsaw Pact troops ended the efforts of the country's leaders to liberalise Communist party rule and create 'socialism with a human face'. Anti-Soviet demonstrations the following year ushered in a period of harsh repression" (http://www.travelblog.org/World/ez-info.html, p.1; derived from the Central Intelligence Agency, 2004). In 1970, Europe was split into two clear geographical sections and Eastern Europe comprised Albania, Bulgaria, Czechoslovakia, East Germany, Hungary, Poland, Romania, The Soviet Union and Yugoslavia. (For map see http://users.erols.com/mwhite28/euro1970.htm). The mass destruction caused by the war, the marked contrasts between the capitalist regimes of the Western countries and the communist regimes of the East impacted greatly on tourism and accommodation development. A bipolar division was created, the two major impacts of which were still apparent to some extent at the end of the last century (Daskalovski, 1999):

1.   Polarisation of Eastern Europe

> ➤   Restrictions on travel/individual movement of Eastern European nationals

> ➤   Low levels of income for Eastern Europeans

> ➤   Limited access to media and often controlled by the state

2.   Western Europe distanced itself from the East

> ➤   Benefits from the trade associated with a free market economy

> ➤   Development of infrastructure (facilitated by loans)

> ➤   Development of a tourism economy

The consequence of this divisive situation, with pro-communist leaders running the countries and limiting external trade and refusing to open up the countries borders (Beck, Mast and Tapper, 1997), was that for about 20 years Central and Eastern Europe saw relatively few international tourists in comparison with the relatively free and affluent West. Transport links were often poor and infrequent due to lack of demand. To compound the situation, because access to the East was restricted, the international visitors' demand for accommodation was comparatively low. In consequence, there were very few hotels that met Western international standards and the service tended to be slow and inefficient, exacerbated by the very low wages and a lack of knowledge or training. During this period, the European Community (EC) was established on April 8th 1965 and it became effective on July 1st 1967. Its aim was to integrate the European Atomic Energy Community (Euratom), the European Coal and Steel Community (ESC), and the European Economic Community (EEC or Common Market); the EC plans were to establish a completely integrated common market and an eventual federation of Europe and the 12 inaugural members were Belgium, Denmark, France, Germany, Greece, Ireland, Italy, Luxembourg, Netherlands, Portugal, Spain and the United Kingdom (See Table 1). It might be argued that this development compounded the East-West divide.

Phase 1:   Members on November 1st 1993 (N=12)

Belgium (€); Denmark; France (€); Germany (€); Greece (€); Ireland (€); Italy (€); Luxembourg (€); Netherlands (€); Portugal (€); Spain (€); United Kingdom of Great Britain and Northern Ireland.

Phase 2:   Members on January 1st 1995 (N=15)

Austria (€); Finland (€); Sweden.

Phase 3:   Members on May 1st 2004 (N=25)

Cyprus (Greek part); Czech Republic; Estonia; Hungary; Latvia; Lithuania; Malta; Poland; Slovakia; Slovenia.

Table 1: Membership of the European Union and Euro Currency (€) Utilisation
Sources: Adapted from: http://userpage.chemie.fu-berlin.de/adressen/eu.html and http://www.oanda.com/site/euro.shtml

Following the example case of the Czech Republic, in 1989, the Soviet system collapsed in Moscow, bringing with it a new period of change, often referred to as "the fall of the iron curtain" (Hall, 1991). This collapse enabled many of the former Eastern Block countries to become self governing and independent once again. "With the collapse of Soviet authority in 1989, Czechoslovakia regained its freedom through a peaceful 'Velvet Revolution' and the country's economic focus moved from heavy to the service industries. Foreign investment in the accommodation sector resulted in jobs for the local people and an influx of 'hard' foreign currency. On January 1st 1993, the country underwent a 'velvet divorce' into its two national components, the Czech Republic and Slovakia" (at http://www.travelblog.org/World/ez-info.html, p.1; derived from the Central Intelligence Agency, 2004). Also in 1993, the EC (which had more recently been referred to as the EEC (European Economic Community) became known as the European Union (EU), a union of 15 independent states based on the European Communities and founded to enhance political, economic and social cooperation. In 1995, three further countries joined the EU then in 2004 there was a much-awaited and welcome influx from Central and Eastern Europe (See Table 1), including the Czech Republic. Following this liberation, many new opportunities and challenges faced this former Eastern European member state including:

> Increased integration with the world markets

> European Union membership (In December 2002, the Czech Republic was invited to join the EU)

> Further EU integration (the Czech Republic joined the EU in 2004)

> Infrastructure and superstructure development to aid the emergence of a tourism economy

> Training and education of personnel to work in a Westernised service economy

> Social issues (crime etc)

Source: Adapted from Youell (1998) pp. 59-61, 72, 90-91.

The Euro (symbol: €), the 'single currency' of the European Monetary Union, was adopted on January 1st 1999 by 11 EU Member States, and two years later by Greece. On January 1st 2002, these 12 countries introduced the Euro banknotes and coins as official legal tender (See Table 1 and http://www.oanda.com/site/euro.shtml for further details). The impact of the Eurpeoan Union and the common currency was remarkable in terms of tourist arrivals and, in turn, accommodation development.

Accommodation Provision

A key component of the tourism industry is its provision of accommodation and therefore any tourism development needs to begin by considering present provision in relation to expected provision. Central and Eastern European countries lost time relative to Western European countries regarding accommodation development. In their favour, there remained as part of their infrastructure many very opulent historical buildings awaiting investment. However, they have experienced years of under investment in terms of infrastructure and superstructure expenditure.

These two components were keys to aiding the transition from former Eastern Block origins to newly created democratic states; a number of problems continue to hinder Eastern European entrants to the EU as identified in Table 2.

Accommodation in Eastern Europe (problems and challenges)	
Inadequate infrastructure.	Transport etc, poorly developed, possibly non existent in areas, impact on tourists etc.
Poor image.	Heavy engineering origin, traditional industries, pollution/landscape impacts.
Poorly developed policies.	Uncoordinated development, poor provision etc.
Poor accommodation stock.	Below Western European standards.
Lack of attractions/ entertainment.	Facilities in short supply, good scenery under developed.
Low service standards.	Lack of consistency in some hotels and restaurants (emerging from Stalinist grip).
Depressed economic situation	Historic debts, moving to free market economy, limited investment.
Little product development.	Limited innovation.
Insufficient market research.	Limited tourist research carried out, therefore lack of reliable data on which to base market planning.

Table 2: Accommodation in Eastern Europe (problems and challenges)
Source: Adapted from Youell (1998) pp. 61-62.

Since the late 1980s, visitor flows from Western Europe to Central and Eatern Europe have increased dramatically as a consequence of improved transport links and relaxed border access. In turn, there is substantial evidence of industrial integration across Europe through take-overs and mergers as organisations seek to achieve an increased share of the existing market, or to enter new markets perhaps initially through franchises which have posed limited risks (Ineson and Stone, 2005). Nevertheless, it is clear that in order to promote accommodation development in the former Eastern European countries, further consideration needs to be given to transport, in particular air, road and rail access. Although most of the countries have their own airlines, some travellers may need to be convinced as to their efficiency and safety. By pricing themselves competitively, and by increasing their geographical destination boundaries, Central and Eastern European airlines, such as CSA Czech Airlines for example, have strengthened their position in the international market. In June 2004, the year-on-year increase in the number of passengers using Prague-Ruzyne International Airport reached 28.9% ..... Ing. Martin Kačur, CEO of the Czech Airports Authority (CAA) and Prague Airport states that this success is due to the CAA' s "high-quality services, active business policies and persistent efforts aimed at creating a competitive environment". Furthermore, on July 1st 2004, ownership of the regional airports of Ostrava and Karlovy Vary (and Brno, which used to be rented out to a private operator) was transferred from the CAA to the individual regions because of their very good commercial results in 2003 (Kovarikova for the CAA, 2004).

In terms of assessing a country's potential for business development, a system based on quantitative data, business surveys and expert assessments, reflecting the main criteria used by companies in formulating their global business strategies and investment-location decisions, has been developed by the Economist Intelligence Unit. Their "global business rankings model is applied to the world's 60 largest countries, which account for more than 95% of global output, trade, and FDI (Foreign Direct Investment). It measures the quality or attractiveness of the business environment and its key components. The model considers 70 factors, across 10 categories, which affect the opportunities for, and hindrances to, the conduct of business. The resulting scores allow the countries to be ranked in order of attractiveness to business. The model is used to generate scores and rankings for the past fivr years, and also for the next fivr years (using the Economist Intelligence Unit's economic forecasts and assessments of likely business and political developments)" (Allen, 2003, p. 1). Six of these countries are in Central and Eastern Europe and their ranks (scores) are as follows (mean score for all 60 countries is 6.89 and range is 8.64 to 4.51): Czech Republic 26 (7.3); Hungary 28 (7.12); Poland 29 (7.07); Slovakia 34 (6.47); Bulgaria 40 (6.19) and Romania 49 (5.64) for the projected 2003-2007 period (Allen, 2003, p. 1). It seems apparent that these relative scores have some association with membership of the European Union as the higher ranked entrants are already members. It is of interest to note that the Czech Republic was ranked 26 for the projected 2003-2007 period, the highest of the Central and Eastern European countries.

Hence, Central and Eastern Europe have succeeded in attracting increasing numbers of global visitors in the last few years, assisted by the growing numbers of business visitors to and from Western Europe who have increased consumer confidence in general. Recent competition for air passengers is evident as European budget airlines such as Easyjet (http://www.easyjet.com/), Germanwings (http://www2.germanwings.com/), Jet2.com (http://www.jet2.com/), Ryanair (http://www.ryanair.com/) and SkyEurope (http://www.skyeurope.com/) hope to succeed by marketing to existing local consumers. Such efforts can provide a valuable source of income for Central and Eastern European accommodation providers as some overseas airlines also offer packages or accommodation 'add-ons'. However, the downside is that the national airlines may struggle to compete as their foreign counterparts offer lower and lower prices and try to beat the locals down in terms of accommodation costs by 'bulk purchasing'.

Cities tend to be the major attractors for tourists in new destinations, particularly when the country has no coastline, and they do attract most of the funding initially so they have the greatest supply and best quality of accommodation. Furthermore, there is a local labour market so, in turn, private accommodation investors are attracted at the outset to the cities, in particular to the suburbs where they can often acquire much cheaper land but with good public transport links. Very often, city transport is excellent in Central and Eastern Europe, with metros built by the Russians along with good tram links. However, many of the country roads have poor or unmade surfaces, signposts may be unintelligible to foreigners due to their linguistic inadequacy or even 'non-existent'. The latter can cause orientation and access problems also for non-local national visitors. Therefore accommodation development appears to be very worthwhile in the cities and on the major trunk roads but poses a major challenge in rural areas and might incur considerable expense. Generally in Central and Eastern Europe travel by rail is relatively inexpensive and traditionally has been cheaper than coach travel. However, most of the trains do not match up to Western European quality standards. In consequence, visitors tend to travel first class or may avoid them completely. Furthermore, tourism is composed of a wide network of micro, small and medium sized enterprises (SMEs) and it can create opportunities for small entrepreneurs as start-up costs and barriers to entry are generally low. In the hotel sector, it is estimated that 80% of the bed capacity worldwide corresponds to small and independent, non-chain establishments, including many family-owned enterprises. Similarly, small entrepreneurs provide many other tourism services, especially in developing countries (Yunis, 2004). SMEs are a vital part of all EU economies, accounting for 65% of EU turnover and they dominate the hotel and catering sectors ranging from sole traders to independent medium-sized businesses (Beckett, 1997). Therefore, although there may be the potential for locals to develop SME accommodation, they may be reluctant to do so unless they are adjacent, or close, to major transport access points.

Without doubt, the accommodation stock is increasing in Central and Eastern Europe. The average annual growth in the number of rooms in hotels and similar establishments from 1999-2000 was 1.9% in Central and Eastern Europe (defined as Armenia, Azerbaijan, Belarus, Bulgaria, Czech Republic, Estonia, Former U.S.S.R., Georgia, Hungary, Kazakhstan, Kyrgyzstan, Latvia, Lithuania, Poland, Rep Moldova, Romania, Russian Federation, Slovakia, Tajikistan, Turkmenistan, Ukraine, Uzbekistan) and also in Western Europe (defined as Austria, Belgium, France, Germany, Liechtenstein, Luxembourg, Monaco, Netherlands, Switzerland). However, in the following year, the growth rate was 1.1% in Central and Eastern Europe, exceeding Western Europe's 0.8% (World Tourism Organisation, 2003). Furthermore, the former's overall percentage increase in international tourist arrivals from 2001-02 was 2.9% in contrast with 1.4% in the latter. In fact, Central and Eastern Europe's 16.3% total share of the European international tourist arrivals market in 2002 is remarkable when contrasted with Northern Europe's (defined as Denmark, Finland, Iceland, Ireland, Norway, Sweden and the United Kingdom) 11.6% share (World Tourism Organisation, 2003). The next step is to bring the facilities and services in line with Western European standards through staff training and the development of a compatible and uniform accommodation grading system (See Chapter 4 for further detail).

Although facilities for mega and hallmark events (See Chapter 5, p. 76) may be in short supply, the history, art and musical talents evident in Central and Eastern European countries are becoming strong international tourist attractors. They are being supplemented by a growing number of heritage, rural and man made attractions (See Chapter 6, p.108-111) with some financial support from the EU, particularly for SME developments. Furthermore, natural attractions such as Borovets in the Rila mountains in Bulgaria, which has been marketed as a budget ski resort, and coastal areas such as the Black Sea in Bulgaria are taking over from Switzerland, France and Spain as 'cheap' and popular destinations for Western holidaymakers so their accommodation stock has seen phenomenal growth in the last few years.

According to De Vet, Boot and Hollanders (1998), Central and Eastern European countries face major challenges in funding and finance, in particular lack of resources. "For areas qualifying for Objective 1-status, which will be most of Central and Eastern Europe, the European Commission is prepared to contribute up to 75% of all public investment costs. This implies that an amount of 25% will need to be found elsewhere, which is an enormous challenge for governments with relatively small budgets. In the case of Estonia, for example, a total Structural Funds support equalling 4% of GDP could theoretically result in an annual Structural Funds support of ECU (European Currency Unit) 400 million, assuming a continuing economic growth over the years. This would require the Estonian public authorities to come up with a co-finance amount of ECU 133 million, an amount that is higher than the current budget for all public investments, including many expenses that would not qualify for Structural Funds support" (De Vet et al., 1998). They suggest that 85% would be a more realistic figure.

Until the 1990s, in most of the Central and Eastern European countries there was a dearth of statistical data. Existing data were often inaccessible or unreliable or lost; the case of the Czech Republic worsened following the floods in Prague in 2002. Czech Tourism recognises its key role in promoting rural tourism and, in addition, has stressed the importance of market research and major survey work (Čermáková, 2003). Following a series of seminars attended by 172 delegates in

Hungary, Slovakia, Bulgaria, Romania, Poland and Estonia between 1999-2004, ways in which educators and industrialists could work together for their mutual benefit and for the benefit of the European tourism industry, the role of students was acknowledged in the context of market research and data collection (See Ineson and Stone, 2005, for further details).

Service provision and accommodation standards have improved rapidly in the last decade with the influx of Western hotel groups looking to develop their profiles in the locality and ultimately reap financial rewards. The key to any future success appears to be the use of public/private partnerships with joint programmes run in conjunction with Westernised service providers, acting as mentors along this complex and uncertain road. This approach has worked effectively in some African states where service provision has been somewhat underdeveloped and it has been alleviated with the intervention and assistance of private sector consortiums, offering training and development related services (Jenkins, 1997). The issues raised in Table 2 need to be addressed, otherwise there may be fundamental limits to such development which, in turn, could impact negatively upon destination image.

It is important that any assistance is sustainable. Rather than developing hospitality ventures which are solely staffed and operated by foreign nationals, consideration should be given to the employment and training of Central and Eastern European nationals, in particular the local community. To ensure that any financial leakages are limited and that any profits can be reinvested in the country of origin, it is important that Central and Eastern European countries can be self-sufficient in service personnel, both at operational and executive level.

Conclusion

The service economy may be perceived as a cure for a country's former ills and a creator of jobs and prosperity for all. In addition, the hospitality industry offers the potential for the creation of cleaner economies with less reliance upon traditional and less environmentally sound manufacturing based industries. Central and Eastern Europe may seem to be in a phase of great opportunity in terms of their hospitality provision, in as much that it needs to consider seriously long-term strategic development of a hospitality industry which has financial implications and potential opportunity costs. Page (1995) is quick to point out that this 'boosterists tendency', a term used to describe the investment by governments in local infrastructure with the hope that additional inward investment will follow from the private companies, is often riddled with uncertainty and does not guarantee additional spin-offs. Once a decision has been taken to join the hospitality elite and to develop accommodation accordingly, it is very hard to change direction. The key to any circumnavigation is the involvement of the community, an approach that Murphy (1993) has been quick to advocate. This method would ensure that those individuals whose lives are to be impacted upon by such developments are consulted and involved in any planning or development. Consequently the expansion of Central and Eastern Europe's hospitality provision may lie with those government agencies that are responsible for approving any building programmes.

Presently many areas of the former Eastern Europe states have a series of almost blank canvasses in terms of hospitality provision; this lack of infrastructure has many advantages as development can be moulded around the needs of the community rather than utilising traditional approaches which may show little concern for location and community needs. The success of Central and Eastern Europe's hospitality expansion lies in its planning programme, both in terms of physical and human resource planning.

Student Activities

The Robinson Consultancy Group (RCG) PEST analysis

Head Office:	London (UK)
Business Type:	Consultancy
Established:	1971
Customer Profile:	Hospitality/service based enterprises.

The Robinson Consultancy Group (RCG) is a UK based company specialising in management services for the hospitality industry, with clients in the UK and mainland Europe. The group has been in existence since 1971 and has been the creation of Mr Daniel Robinson, who after working for many years in the service sector decided to set up and run his own consultancy group. The group has been involved traditionally in preparing business plans, marketing strategies and feasibility studies for clients looking to set up and operate business ventures overseas. The recent growth and development of tourism in Central and Eastern Europe has resulted in an influx of international hotel groups investing there. One such hotel group (Moorland Hotels) has asked the RCG to prepare a PEST analysis in relation to the business environment in a country newly admitted to the European Union. The Moorland Hotels Group is particularly interested in setting up a hotel venture, ideally in one of the locations listed below:

Czech Republic; Estonia; Hungary; Latvia; Lithuania; Poland; Slovakia; Slovenia

Please note: Students should not feel restricted to carrying out a PEST analysis only on the countries which are listed above. Students are encouraged to research a country or city location of their own choosing and present a PEST analysis accordingly.

Student Activity

As an employee of the RCG you have been asked to carry out a PEST analysis (on behalf of the Moorland Hotels group) (Ref. **Supporting Information PEST Analysis**) with a view to identifying the best location for a proposed hotel development.

In this scenario the PEST analysis is used to assess the Political, Economic, Socio-cultural and Technological factors which may hinder or facilitate business expansion in that city or country.

Socio-cultural Factors

The social and cultural influences on business vary from country to country. It is very important that such factors are considered, including:

What is PEST Analysis?

It is very important that an organisation considers its environment before beginning the marketing process. In fact, environmental analysis should be continuous and feed all aspects of planning. The organisation's marketing environment is made up from:

1. The internal environment, for example, staff (or internal customers), office technology, wages and finance, etc.

2. The micro-environment, for example, our external customers, agents and distributors, suppliers, our competitors, etc.

3. The macro-environment, for example, Political (and legal) forces, Economic forces, Socio-cultural forces, and Technological forces. These are known as **PEST** factors.

Political Factors

The political arena has a huge influence upon the regulation of businesses, and the spending power of consumers and other businesses. You must consider issues such as:

1. How stable is the political environment?

2. Will government policy influence laws that regulate or tax your business?

3. What is the government's position on marketing ethics?

4. What is the government's policy on the economy?

5. Does the government have a view on culture and religion?

6. Is the government involved in trading agreements such as EU, North American Free Trade Agreement (NAFTA), Association of South East Asian Nations (ASEAN), or others?

Economic Factors

Marketers need to consider the state of a trading economy in the short and long-terms. This is especially true when planning for international marketing. You need to look at:

1. Interest rates.

2. The level of inflation; Employment level per capita.

3. Long-term prospects for the economy; Gross Domestic Product (GDP) per capita, etc.

Socio-cultural Factors

The social and cultural influences on business vary from country to country. It is very important that such factors are considered. Factors include:

1. What is the dominant religion?

2. What are attitudes to foreign products and services?

3. Does language impact upon the diffusion of products onto markets?

4. How much time do consumers have for leisure?

5. What are the roles of men and women within society?

6. How long are the population living? Are the older generations wealthy?

7. Do the population have a strong/weak opinion on green issues?

Technological Factors

Technology is vital for competitive advantage, and is a major driver of globalisation. Consider the following points:

1. Does technology allow for products and services to be made more cheaply and to a better standard of quality?

2. Do the technologies offer consumers and businesses more innovative products and services such as Internet banking, new generation mobile telephones, etc?

3. How is distribution changed by new technologies, for example, books via the Internet, flight tickets, auctions, etc?

4. Does technology offer companies a new way to communicate with consumers, for example, banners, Customer Relationship Management (CRM), etc?

Source: www.marketingteacher.com/Lessons/lesson_PEST.htm (adapted).

References

Allen, S., for the Economic Intelligence Unit (2003). *Economist Intelligence Unit ranks Canada as best place to do business,* Press release, July 17th. [on-line] available from: http://store.eiu.com/ [accessed March 10th 2005].

Beck, P., Mast M. and Tapper, P. (1997). *The History of Eastern Europe for Beginners (Writers and Readers),* Writers & Readers Publishing Inc., New York.

Beckett, M. (1997). *The contribution of smaller firms,* for the Department of Trade and Industry, [on-line] available from: http://www.dti.gov.uk/comp/benchmark/sects/3contri.htm [accessed on March 2nd 2005].

Burkart, A.J. and Medlik, S. (1989). *Tourism: Past, Present and Future,* 2nd edn. Heinemann, Oxford.

Burton, A. (2001). *Remains of a Revolution,* Penguin, London.

Cannon, J. (ed.) (2001). *A Dictionary of British History,* Oxford University Press, Oxford.

Central Intelligence Agency (2004). *The World Fact Book* [on-line], available from: http://www.cia.gov/cia/publications/ [accessed March 24th 2004].

Čermáková, H. (2003). *CzechTourism.* [on-line] available from: http://www.czechtourism.com/index.php?search=%C4%8Cerm%C3%A1kov%C3%A1&x=10&y =6 [accessed March 9th 2005].

Cooper, C. Fletcher, J. Gilbert and D. Wanhill, S. (1998). *Tourism Principles and Practice,* Longman, London.

Daskalovski, Z. (1999). *Ten Years After: Schengen's Iron Curtain,* [on-line] available from: http://www.ce-review.org/99/25/daskalovski25.html [accessed February 28th 2005].

Davidson, R. (1992). *Tourism in Europe,* Pitman, London.

De Vet, J.M., Boot, L. and Hollanders, M. (1998), Laat de Structuurfondsen niet crashen (Don't Allow the Structural Funds to Crash), *Economisch Statistische Berichten,* July 31st, Rotterdam.

Hall, D. (1991). *Tourism and economic development in Eastern Europe and the Soviet Union,* Belhaven Press, London.

Haywood, L., Kew, F. and Bramham, P. (1995). *Understanding Leisure,* 2nd edn. Stanley Thornes, Cheltenham.

Hoad, T.F. (ed.) (1996). *The Concise Oxford Dictionary of English Etymology,* Oxford University Press, Oxford.

Holloway, J.C. (2002). *The Business of Tourism,* 6th edn, Longman, Harlow.

http://www2.germanwings.com/.

http://www.easyjet.com/.

http://www.jet2.com.

http://www.manchesteronline.co.uk/business/dealsreview/s/124/124397_midland_in_line_for_12 m_makeover_.html.

http://www.ryanair.com/.

http://www.skyeurope.com/.

http://users.erols.com/mwhite28/euro1970.htm [accessed February 28th 2005].

Ineson, E.M. and Stone, G.J. (2005). The development of industry–education links in Central and Eastern Europe. In D. Hind, (ed.) with P. Constanti and J. Theodore, *Tourism in Europe: research reflections on the implications of EU enlargement*, Business Education Publishers, Sunderland, Chap. 21.

Kovarikova, A. (2004) *Press release on behalf of the Czech Airports Authority*, [on-line] available from: http://www.csl.cz/en/spolecnost/tisk_media/tiskovezpravy/tiskovezpravy_69.htm, [accessed March 8th 2005].

Jenkins, C. L. (1997). *Third World Issues – Tourism Policies in Developing Countries*. In S. Medlik, *Managing Tourism*, Butterworth-Heinemann, Oxford, pp. 269-277.

Livingstone, E. A. (2000). *The Concise Oxford Dictionary of the Christian Church*, 2nd edn. Oxford University Press, Oxford.

Marx, K. and Engels, F. (1930). *Das Kapital*, Dent, London.

Matley, I.M. (1976). *The Geography of International Tourism*, Association of American Geographers, Washington.

Murphy, P.E. (1993). *Tourism. A Community Approach*, 3rd edn, Metheun, London.

Page, S. (1995). *Urban Tourism*, Routledge, London.

Palmowski, J. (2003). *A Dictionary of Contemporary World History*, 2nd edn., Oxford University Press, Oxford.

Pearce, D.G. (1995). *Tourism Today: a Geographical Analysis*, 2nd edn., Longman, Harlow.

Torkildsen, G. (1999). *Leisure and Recreation Management*, 4th edn., Spon, London.

Urry, J. (2002). *The tourist gaze*, 2nd edn., Sage Publications, London.

World Tourism Organisation (2003). [on-line] available from: http://www.world-tourism.org/facts/tmt.html, [accessed February 28th 2005].

Yunis, E. (2004). *Tourism: poverty, alleviation and microcredit: a first glance*, [on-line] available from: http://www.uncdf.org/english/microfinance/newsletter/pages/july_2004/news_tourism.php, [accessed March 2nd 2005].

Youell, R. (1998). *Tourism, an Introduction*, Longman, Harlow.

Suggested Further Reading

Ashworth, S. (2003). Central Europe, 5th edn., Lonely Planet Publications, London.

Greenaway, P. (ed.) (2003). Eastern Europe, 7th edn., Lonely Planet Publications, London.

http://www.travelcook.com/English/

http://www.timeout.com/prague/accom/

http://www.odci.gov/cia/publications/factbook/print/ez.html

Jones, P. (ed.) (2002). *Introduction to Hospitality Operations,* 2nd edn, Continuum, London.

Witt. S., Brooke, M. and Buckley, P. (1995). *The Management of International Tourism,* 2nd edn., Routledge, London.

Chapter Four

Hotel Classification and Grading: towards the development of a unified system

John Fenby

Overview

There is no European, or wider international, unified, consistently applied and sufficiently thorough hotel star rating system (cf. World Tourism Organisation/International Hotel and Restaurant Association, 2004). However, the United Kingdom (UK) is at the forefront in developing a 'unified' grading system that incorporates the major UK 'private sector', and also state sponsored, rating agencies. An examination of how this unified system has emerged, and continues to emerge, may well be of benefit to hotel star rating developments in other countries. This chapter explores the evolution of the UK hotel classification and grading systems and the movement towards a unified system. Firstly, the basis of the UK five point star rating system is reviewed and discussed alongside the potential for consumer confusion, inherent in the initially separate rating systems with their different rating criteria. The chapter continues by examining the evolution of the rating systems adopted by the main exponents, that is the Automobile Association (AA), Royal Automobile Club (RAC) and tourist boards. Although the basic rating systems they adopted have been consistent, the criteria used for measurement and grading have not always been equable. In latter years, the quality grading facet of the star systems has been enhanced with additional mechanisms, most recently by the AA percentage scores and the RAC blue, gold and white ribbon awards. The UK tourist boards evolved a separate and distinct system of rating hotels, the Crown classification system, then each of the three main tourist boards introduced a quality grading system as an addition to the crown system. The chapter then reviews the recent 'harmonisation' of the classification and grading systems, at least in the context of England, and considers whether harmonisation has been achieved in the eyes of the consumers. An examination of the AA, RAC and VisitBritain websites highlights that these organisations are now all using five point star rating systems. However, a review of the star rating descriptors published on their websites shows that these descriptors differ in both emphasis and depth of content and that the AA and RAC continue to operate different additional quality indicator mechanisms. In short, 'harmonisation' may not be apparent to the consumer.

Introduction

To reiterate: There is no European, or wider international, unified, consistently applied and sufficiently thorough hotel rating system. As Maternovsky, writing in the Moscow Times (2003, p. 8) confirms: "There is no real international hotel ratings system. Ratings of hotels in different countries, if they exist, typically come from government or quasi-government sources, independent ratings agencies or sometimes the hotel operators themselves…in France the government conducts a star rating system ranging from 1 star for simple accommodation to four star for de-luxe accommodation. Hotels in Germany and some Scandinavian countries have a one to five star rating." Bricker writing in the Prague Post (March, 2004) highlights the problem that exists in the Czech Republic and Prague in particular: "If you are looking for stars to predict your future stop now. According to Petr Divis of the Tulip Inn, the Czech Republic does not have a strict star rating system that governs hotel classifications. Prague has a number of five star hotels without swimming pools, for example, which are required for five star accommodation in most countries." Maternosky (2003, p. 8) notes that the Russian Department of Tourism of the Economic Development and Trade Ministry has developed and is promoting a 'unified' national hotel classification system to help bring to an end the star-rating lottery. However, as Maternosky (2003, p. 8) also confirms, the system is voluntary, on the part of hotels, and does not take into account subjective service factors.

It is with the above international context in mind that this chapter focuses on star rating developments for hotels in the UK where it is demonstrated that the development of a 'unified' star rating system is advancing. The system intends to incorporate the major UK 'private sector' rating agencies and also state sponsored rating agencies. An examination of how this unified system has emerged, and is still emerging, may well be of benefit to star rating developments in other countries. This chapter does not focus on the UK 'bed and breakfast' or 'lodge' hotel sectors although some of the discussion may well be applicable to those market segments.

The Context for the Development of a 'Unified' Hotel Rating System

A hotel classification and grading system is an important facility and, (sometimes), a quality indicator that enables potential hotel guests to select an hotel that is most likely to suit their budget, visitor purposes and needs. As Medlik and Ingram (2000, p. 11) state: "Whatever the criteria used in hotel guides and in classification and grading systems in existence in many countries, normally at least four or five classes or grades have been found necessary to distinguish adequately in the standards of hotels and these have found some currency among hotel users. The extremes of luxury and basic standards, sometimes denoted by five stars and one star respectively are not difficult concepts; the mid-point on any such scale denotes the average without any particular claims to merit. The intervening points are then standards above average but falling short of luxury (quality hotels) and standards above basic (economy)."

Bowie and Buttle (2004, p. 92) define more clearly, in a general international context but still in relatively basic terms, the five star system outlined by Medlik and Ingram (2000).

One star:

"A budget market hotel with limited facilities, offering bed, breakfast and evening meal, and characterised by informal standards of service to residents."

Two star:

"An economy market hotel with limited facilities, offering more extensive dining facilities, and characterised by informal standards of service to residents."

Three star:

"A mid-market hotel with more extensive facilities, offering a full range of dining and bar services, with professional standards of service, to residents and non-residents."

Four star:

"An up-scale hotel offering formal standards of service, with extensive facilities and services to residents and non-residents."

Five star:

"A luxury hotel offering 'flawless' service standards, with professional multilingual staff, and a full range of facilities of the highest quality."

The pattern of classification and grading systems historically and currently found in the United Kingdom (UK) fit the pattern and relatively simple five point concept outlined by Medlik and Ingram, however, from a consumer perspective, is the reading and interpretation of such systems that simple? Callan (1995, pp. 142-143) defines the terms 'classification' and 'grading': "Classification is where the stock of accommodation is divided into categories. Each category consists of specified facilities, such as the proportion of private bathrooms, minimum size of rooms, full length mirrors, etc. The term grading is often confused with classification by hoteliers, but it implies entirely different criteria. Grading is a qualitative assessment of facilities described under classification. Grading will assess how good or bad are the facilities or services offered". In short, 'classification' relates to a quantitative, factual, descriptive definition of hotel facilities, whilst 'grading' relates to a qualitative, arguably subjective, set of value judgements related to the described facilities.

If hoteliers are confused, what chance is there for the consumers? Since the early twentieth century a number of UK hotel classification and grading systems have emerged, based on a five point scale, most notably those established by the Automobile Association (AA), Royal Automobile Club (RAC) and the UK Tourist Boards. These systems have, to a degree, evolved independently of each other, have varying levels of complexity and most significantly, to a greater or lesser extent, mix the classification of facilities with quality indicators. David Wickers, writing in The Sunday Times (1997, p. 7) succinctly summed up the problem faced by consumers: "Anyone who has ever looked for an hotel in an unfamiliar destination must have been through a scenario like this: you need an hotel in Sodcaster for the weekend. You ask around for a recommendation, but none of your friends has been there. So you look in the hotel guides. And you find that some list a particular hotel in the town, but for others it doesn't appear to exist; some publications give it a hefty star rating, while others are sparing with their gongs. In the end, you are exactly where you were before you started consulting the guides – trying to find a pig in a poke." This chapter explores the evolution of five point UK hotel classification and grading systems, their meaning to consumers, and the likely future evolution of such systems. The main focus of the chapter is on the AA, RAC and UK tourist boards as it is these organisations which have been the principal participants in any move towards a common classification and grading system and the removal of the confusion articulated by Wickers.

The Automobile Association

The Automobile Association (AA) was formed in 1905 and is one of the oldest organisations in the UK promoting an hotel classification and quality grading system. On June 29th 1905, a group of motoring enthusiasts met in London at the Trocadero restaurant to form the AA. Their original aim was to help motorists avoid speed traps! (http://www.theaa.com). By 1912, the AA had progressed from erecting danger and warning signs, promoting road safety, offering legal advice to motorists and providing route advice to inspecting hotels and subsequently to reviewing restaurants (http://www.theaa.com). The AA produced its first Hotel and Restaurant Guide in 1967 (Automobile Association, 2004) and this has developed into an annual hotel guide that now assesses hotel facilities and awards star quality ratings to hotel accommodation throughout the UK.

In 1974, the AA adopted a black, white and red star classification system. Black stars related to service accommodation, white stars were associated with motor hotels and red stars were reserved for hotels that AA inspectors considered "to be of outstanding merit within their classification", Callan (1999, p. 38). Callan (1999) also confirmed that, as a consequence of the AA review of hotel classifications in 1984, the white star classification was removed. In 1981 the AA introduced its first quality awards, the subjective H, B and L (Hospitality, Bedroom and Lounge/Public areas) awards, as Callan (1999, p. 38) states: "These symbols were to indicate to the customer that a higher standard existed in each area (hospitality, bedroom and public areas) than would normally be found in the star classification...Red star hotels were those which were considered to be ahead of all three subjective awards and thus reflected an overall level of excellence."

By 1991, the AA had ceased the H, B and L awards and introduced a subjective percentage quality rating system which was included in its hotel guide alongside the star rating awarded to a particular hotel and was intended to enable guests to compare the quality of hotels. The percentage quality rating was claimed to enhance the qualitative facet of the star rating system. As Callan (1999, p. 38) states, this was the culmination of "a major research exercise which involved a strategic review of the relevance of the AA hotel classification system to consumer requirements."

From the early years of the involvement of the AA in hotel inspection, a system that incorporates assessments by peripatetic inspectors has evolved. The inspectors stay in an hotel, usually for one night, and assess the hotel, including its guest accommodation, restaurant and general service standards. The assessment takes place in the context of predetermined criteria, which are both qualitative and facility based, and results in a star rating and additional percentage quality rating. The latter is intended to enable guests to compare the quality of hotels "...within each star classification. So when using the guide, guests can see at a glance, for example, that a two star hotel with a percentage score of 69 offers a higher quality experience than a two star hotel with a percentage score of 59." (Automobile Association, 2004, p. 9). Additionally, "to gain AA recognition in the first place an hotel, must achieve a minimum quality score of 50 per cent."(Automobile Association, 2004, p. 9).

The star rating and percentage quality rating were designed to give [prospective] hotel guests an indication not only of the nature of the facilities but also the quality of the facilities and services on offer. Both the star rating and percentage quality score can also be used by an establishment as a marketing tool. The following star rating descriptors were published in November 2004 on the AA website (http://www.theaa.com):

One star:

"At this level, staff are polite and courteous and provide informal yet competent service. The majority of rooms are en-suite and there is a designated eating area with a reasonable choice of food and wines available."

Two star:

"Staff are smartly presented and provide competent, often informal, service. All rooms are en-suite and have a TV. There is at least one restaurant or dining room with a substantial choice of food and wine available."

Three star:

"Staff will be skilled in responding to guests needs, and there will be a dedicated receptionist on duty. All rooms are en-suite and have remote control TV and direct dial telephone. There is a restaurant open to residents and their guests and a bar or lounge serving drinks."

Four star:

"A formal, professional service is provided and staff anticipate and respond to guests needs. Reception is staffed 24 hours a day, with porters available on request. Bedrooms offer superior quality and comfort than at the three star

level; en-suite bathrooms have high quality toiletries and dry cleaning will be available, and the restaurant demonstrates a serious approach to cuisine."

Five star:

"Flawless guest service and professional, attentive staff are a must at this level. Accommodation throughout the hotel is spacious and luxurious, with impressive interior design and immaculate furnishings. En-suite rooms offer exceptional quality and provide extras such as bath sheets and robes and an evening turn-down service. The restaurant produces dishes created with a level of technical skill, complemented by superior wines."

It is of interest to note at this point that the AA Hotel Guide 2005 (Automobile Association, 2004, p. 11), published in book form, provides more extensive star rating descriptors than those provided on the AA website. For example, the explanation for an hotel with a three star classification requires:

> "Management and staff smartly and professionally presented and usually uniformed. Technical and social skills of a good standard in responding to requests. A dedicated receptionist on duty at peak times, clear direction to rooms and some explanation of hotel facilities. At least one restaurant or dining room open to residents and non-residents for breakfast and dinner whenever the hotel is open. A wide selection of drinks served in a bar or lounge, available to residents and their guests throughout the day and evening. Last orders for dinner no earlier than 8.00pm, full dinner service provided. Remote control television, direct dial telephone. En-suite bath or shower and WC."

The Royal Automobile Club

The Royal Automobile Club (RAC), a competitor organisation to the AA, was formed in 1897 and, as with the AA, began rating hotels early in its history. In common with the AA, a similar system of inspectors and inspections was adopted. Hotels were also rated in the context of a five star system and, although there were differences in the detail, there has been an overall chronological parity with the AA in the development of the RAC star classification and grading system. However, whereas the AA has developed a percentage rating system to enhance its quality rating of hotels, the RAC has followed a different path. In 1987 the RAC adopted the H, C and R (See below) 'blue letter merit awards' and the premier 'blue ribbon award' for exceptionally high quality hotels in the one to four star categories. As Callan (1999, p. 39) confirms: "'five star hotels were excluded from the scheme, as they were already expected to provide the highest standard." Callan (1999, p. 39-40) also defined the nature of the merit and blue ribbon awards:

Merit Awards:

"H   Hospitality and service granted to an hotel when the quality of hospitality and service is superior to that expected in its classification.

C   Comfort granted to an hotel where the overall comfort of the bedrooms and public rooms is superior to the general run of hotels within its classification.

R   Restaurant granted when the cuisine at an hotel is of higher standard than is normally expected within its classification."

Blue Ribbon Award:

"To be considered for a blue ribbon, an hotel must first receive the three merit awards. In addition, the hotel must have the almost indefinable quality of 'guest awareness' amongst management and staff."

The RAC awards' scheme has evolved into a three Ribbon Awards system: Gold, Blue and White. These awards are made to "the hotels ... that consistently provide superior standards of service" (http://www.rac.co.uk/travelservices/hotels, 2004). The Gold, Blue and White awards scheme includes one star through to five star hotels. The RAC website further defines these awards and the quality attributes that an hotel, in relation to its star classification, must exhibit to receive such an award:

Gold ribbon:

"RAC's Gold Ribbon Award is exactly that. An Award for the very best. Awarded only to hotels, townhouses and restaurants that offer and accept nothing less than the finest. Winners of a Gold Ribbon Award offer truly exceptional experience in comfort, cuisine, customer care and service."

Blue ribbon:

"RAC's Blue Ribbon Award recognises excellent hotels, townhouses and restaurants with rooms. These establishments strive for, and achieve, excellence in all aspects of comfort, cuisine, service and overall quality. Winners of the Blue Ribbon Award offer a level of commitment and service that will ensure you enjoy first class standards and a memorable stay."

White ribbon:

"This new award is given to hotels, townhouses and restaurants with rooms that are commended for achieving high standards of hospitality, comfort, service and cuisine. We're convinced that when you stay in an RAC White Ribbon establishment, you will be impressed by the commitment, enthusiasm, and warmth of service" (http://www.rac.co.uk/travelservices/hotels, 2004).

To provide a comparator with the AA rating star scheme, the following are the RAC star rating descriptors as published on the November 2004, RAC website (http://www.rac.co.uk/travelservices/hotels):

One star:

"Likely to be a small and independently owned with a family atmosphere. Services may be provided by the owner and family on an informal basis. Generally limited facilities and meals may be fairly simple. Lunch for example, may not be served. Some bedrooms may not be en-suite. Maintenance, cleanliness and comfort will always be acceptable."

Two star:

"Small to medium sized hotels with more extensive facilities than one star hotels. You can expect comfortable, well equipped overnight accommodation, usually with an en-suite bath/shower room. Reception and other staff will aim for a more professional presentation than at one star level, and offer a wider range of services, including food and drink."

Three star:

"Three star hotels are usually large enough to support higher staffing levels, and offer a significantly greater quality and range of facilities than one or two star hotels. Reception and other public rooms will be more spacious and the restaurant will normally also cater for non residents. All bedrooms will have fully en-suite bath and shower rooms and offer a good standard of comfort and facilities, such as hair dryer, direct dial telephone and bathroom toiletries. Some room service can be expected and some provision for business travellers."

Four star:

"Expectations at this level include a degree of luxury as well as quality furnishings, décor and equipment throughout the hotel. Bedrooms will usually offer more space than at lower star levels, with well designed, coordinated furnishings. En-suite bathrooms will have both a bath and a fixed shower. There will be sufficient staff to provide services such as porterage, 24 hour room service and dry cleaning. The restaurant will demonstrate a serious approach to cuisine."

Five star:

"In a five star hotel, you should find spacious and luxurious accommodation of the best international standards throughout the hotel. Interior design should impress with its quality, detailing, comfort and elegance. Furnishings should be immaculate. Services should be formal, well supervised and flawless in attention to guests needs without being intrusive. The restaurant will be technically excellent, producing dishes to the highest international standards. Staff will be knowledgeable, courteous and efficient, as well as being well versed in all aspects of customer care."

Unlike the 'AA Hotel Guide, 2005', the 'RAC Hotels, Bed and Breakfast Guide, 2004' (2005 guidebook not available at the time of writing) does not necessarily provide a more expansive explanation of what is meant by each star rating. However, it is to a degree, a different explanation than that contained on the RAC website. For example, the explanation for an hotel with a three star classification is:

> "Here you should find a receptionist, more spacious lounges, a restaurant and bar and professional staff who'll respond to your requests promptly and efficiently. All rooms should be en suite and offer extras such as remote control television, hairdryer, direct dial telephone, toiletries and room service. Fax or email services should also be available for business travellers. Last orders for dinner no earlier than 8.00pm" (RAC, 2003, p. 14).

The Evolution of UK Tourist Board Hotel Classification and Grading Systems and the Drive towards a Unified Classification and Grading System

The English, Scottish and Welsh Tourist Board were formed, along with the British Tourist Authority (BTA), as a consequence of the Development of Tourism Act, 1969. As an exemplar, one of the English Tourism Board's (ETB) key roles was to: "improve the quality and competitiveness of English holidays by setting and monitoring independent quality standards across accommodation provision and customer service training" (http://www.spinet.co.uk/careercompass, 1998). Thus, the Tourist Boards were charged with the key role of monitoring and improving the quality of guest accommodation a key factor in encouraging repeat business and ensuring the economic success of an hotel or guest house.

In 1974 a voluntary self classification scheme was introduced by the ETB. Callan (1999, p. 33) outlines the basis of this scheme and its most significant drawbacks: "It allocated numbers from one to six for each of three categories: bedrooms, services and meals, the higher the number in each category the wider the range of facilities. The system provided 216 possible classifications from 1.1.1 to 6.6.6. The system was not readily understood and did not lend itself to display signs for use on the premises, perhaps the most important means of making the public familiar with a classification system. The scheme did not contain a qualitative element." A further problem existed because the system was voluntary and did not facilitate routine inspection: hotels could exaggerate the level of facilities to enhance their classification level. In 1981 the ETB "rationalised the 3-way system and represented the bedroom category only with roses" (Callan, 1999, p. 34), to be displayed on a sign outside an establishment: but again the basis for the categorisation was information submitted by the hotelier.

In the 1970s the Welsh Tourist Board (WTB) also operated a system of self classification and the problem of 'exaggeration' also emerged in Wales, as Callan (1999, p. 37) states "When verification was introduced in 1981, 65% of establishments inspected did not have the facilities and services which they claimed". Then in 1982 the Scottish Tourist Board (STB) introduced a self classification scheme allowing establishments to evaluate facilities under three categories: "bedrooms, services and meals…As with the ETB scheme there was a maximum of six points in each category" (Callan, 1995, p. 176).

In 1985 the Crown classification scheme was implemented by the English Tourist Board, along with the Scottish and Welsh Tourist Boards. This was an annual inspection based scheme using "the same crown symbol, the same classification criteria and the same 'code of conduct'" (Callan, 1999, p. 33). Hoteliers who applied to participate in the scheme were awarded one to five crowns, depending on the level and type of facilities in the establishment. The ETB commissioned research in 1987 to test consumers' awareness of the scheme and the crown symbols. The results were not encouraging, as Callan (1995, p. 160) states: "Only 4% of adults in Great Britain were spontaneously aware that the ETB had a rating system for hotels and other accommodation, and 11% of those knew that the symbol used by the ETB was a crown". Moreover, the ETB was criticised for awarding five gold crowns to an excessive number of establishments. Callan (1995) confirms: the AA had awarded five stars to only 20 establishments whilst the ETB had recognised some 200 establishments with five gold crowns. As a consequence, the ETB initiated a new five gold crown category and the number of establishments to be awarded five gold crowns was restricted to 30 (Callan, 1999).

In 1986 the STB was the first of the UK tourist boards to adopt a quality grading system as an addition to the Crown classification system. The WTB adopted this system in 1988. Callan (1999, p. 36) outlines the fundamental principles of this system: "The grading officers worked from a 24 point assessment form, covering the six broad areas: exterior; bedrooms; bathrooms, washbasins and toilets; public rooms including bars; dining room and or restaurants; and hospitality and service." The ETB introduced the quality grading of hotels in 1989, following a similar model to that adopted by the STB. The ETB decided that quality grades "should be assessed separately" and presented "as an addition to the Crown classification" (Callan, 1999, p. 35) rather than as a fully integral scheme. This was largely, as Callan (1995, p. 165) states in his commentary on research conducted on behalf of the three national Tourist boards because "the integral scheme was found to be 'totally confusing' as the customer would not know on what basis the crowns had been awarded, and what were the quality standards. The classification only basis of the current scheme was viewed as misleading, as customers would assume that some quality standards were incorporated." Callan (1999, p. 37) also confirms that "a study commissioned by the STB in 1992 indicated better levels of performance by classified and graded hotels; bed occupancy in 1991 showed an increase of nine percentage points between classified and non-classified hotels, which rose to 10 in 1992. Graded hotels were 9 percentage points ahead of ungraded in 1991, rising to 11 in 1992." It was assumed that this increase had provided positive proof that classification and grading schemes were of benefit not just to consumers endeavouring to make an hotel choice but also to hoteliers in terms of hotel profitability.

Nevertheless, by the late 1990s, the differences in the grading systems, that is between the RAC and AA and between stars and crown classifications, were deemed to be unsatisfactory. As D'Arcy (1997, Sunday Times, Feb 9[th]p2) stated: "Currently, some organisations award stars to denote excellence while others feature crowns; furthermore, the criteria used to determine grades also differ, making it difficult for potential guests to compare properties." This comment further reinforces the observations by Wickers, previously highlighted, and publicly reflects the concerns of the Department of National Heritage and those of government ministers that were being expressed as late as 2002. As Kite (The Times, May 21st, 2002) states: "English Hotels are confusing their customers with signs carrying an incomprehensible array of stars and crowns, the Minister for Tourism said yesterday….The current combination of classifications, including the AA, RAC and various tourist boards, was incomprehensible…" As a consequence, in the late 1990s, discussions were promoted between the various UK Tourist Boards and the AA and RAC and other industry bodies, with a view to establishing a unified grading system. Yates and Winter in The Which? Hotel Guide 1999 (1998, p. 9) concluded optimistically: "Over the 12 month life of this guide we should see the fruits of the unified grading system (by the ETB, AA and RAC) in England." However, the drive towards a unified classification and grading system has not been easy and, even now, is not yet concluded. Yates and Winter (1998 p. 9), continued: "the Scottish and Wales Tourist Boards press on with their own variations of the star rating system."

The whole debate on a unified classification and grading system was made more difficult by the abolition of the ETB (but not the Welsh and Scottish Tourist Boards although the latter is now named: 'VisitScotland') and the merger of the English Tourism Council and The BTA into a unitary body: 'VisitBritain'. As a consequence of discussions between the ETB (and subsequently with 'VisitBritain'), the AA and RAC, the Crown systems were abandoned in September 1999 (Bartlett, 2002) and a common set of hotel quality standards was agreed. These new standards have resulted in a theoretically unified star rating system, at least in England. To provide a comparator with both the AA and RAC star rating schemes, the following are the 'VisitBritain' star rating descriptors, as published on the November 2004 'VisitBritain' website (http://www.visitbritain.com), in relation to any particular hotel advertised on this website:

One star:

"Practical accommodation with a limited range of facilities and services, but a high standard of cleanliness throughout. Restaurant/eating area for breakfast at least. 75% of bedrooms will have en-suite or private facilities."

Two star:

"Equipped bedrooms, all with en-suite/private bathroom and a colour TV. A lift is often available. Dinner available."

Three star:

"Higher standard of services and facilities including larger public areas and bedrooms, a receptionist, room service, laundry service."

Four star:

"Accommodation offering superior comfort and quality; all bedrooms with en-suite bath, fitted overhead shower and WC. Spacious and well appointed public areas. More emphasis on food and drink. Room service of all meals and 24 hour drinks, refreshments and snacks. Dry cleaning service available. Excellent customer service."

Five star:

"A spacious, luxurious establishment offering the highest international quality of accommodation, facilities, services and cuisine. A wider range of extra facilities. Guests are very well cared for by professional, attentive staff providing flawless guest services."

As with the AA Hotel Guide 2005, the 'Where to stay in England: Somewhere Special 2004' guide, published by 'VisitBritain' provides a more expansive explanation of the star rating classifications. For example, the explanation for an hotel with a three star classification states:

> In addition to what is provided at one and two star establishments "very good accommodation with more spacious public areas and bedrooms all offering a significantly greater quality and higher standard of facilities and services. A more formal style of service with a receptionist. A wider selection of drinks light lunch and snacks served in a bar or lounge with greater attention to quality. Room service for continental breakfast and laundry service."

Unification and Harmonisation of the Classification and Grading Systems operated by the AA, RAC and Tourist Boards: the consumers' perspectives

It is of interest to take the role of the consumer in comparing the previously highlighted AA and RAC star rating criteria with the above VisitBritain criteria. All three entries are the consequence of the harmonisation of the grades. It has taken over four years to reach a position where "from around September 2004, properties in England at least [should] not show three different grades outside their doors" (http://www.travelweekly.co.uk). This is a reference to a situation which existed prior to harmonisation where an hotel, if participating in the AA, RAC and ETB rating schemes, could "find itself classified as four crown, highly commended, from the ETB, but have three stars from the RAC and just two from the AA" (http://www.travelweekly.co.uk). In short, an hotel now participating in all three rating schemes should be rated the same in the context of all three schemes, that is, if it is a three star hotel then it should be rated three star by each of the AA, RAC and VisitBritain.

A search of the world wide web identified a number of websites that refer to the harmonisation of the AA, RAC and VisitBritain rating schemes, including websites related to the monitoring organisation websites: "In response to consumer demand, the AA, VisitBritain and the RAC have joined forces to create one overall rating scheme for serviced accommodation…" (http://www.wightindex.com/ratings_explained.asp). "The AA, English Tourism Council and RAC, in response to customer demand, have joined forces to create one new overall rating scheme for Hotels and Guest Accommodation" (http://www.faversham.org/wheretostay/ratings.asp). "All full participants in the AA-recognised accommodation schemes have been assessed under the quality standards agreed between the AA, The English Tourism Council and the RAC" (http://www.theaa.com/getaway/hotels/hotesl_explained.html). "In response to consumer demand, VisitBritain, the AA and RAC have joined forces to create one overall rating scheme for serviced accommodation…" (http://www.visitbritain.com/VB3-en-GB/productsearch/ratingsinformation.aspx).

The message that a unified ratings scheme is being implemented has clearly been promoted nationally and internationally. However, what may not always be so clear to consumers, as evidenced by the above exemplar website comments, and in the context of some of the fuller website entries, is that the scheme applies only to England. The other main UK tourist organisations, that is the Scottish and the Welsh, are still operating their own published ratings schemes. Although the AA and RAC schemes do cover the whole of Great Britain, the VisitBritain scheme covers only England. In fact, the term 'VisitBritain' is a misnomer, in the context of ratings, as this implies equivalent ratings coverage across all parts of Great Britain. In addition, it is evident from the current rating descriptors reproduced in this chapter that, whilst a unified star rating scheme may theoretically be in operation, supported by AA, RAC and VisitBritain hotel inspectors and assessors using common assessment criteria, the AA, RAC and VisitBritain website and book form published star rating descriptors differ in terms of emphasis and depth of content. As an example, the VisitBritain website three star descriptor is very brief, whilst the RAC three star descriptor is comparatively much fuller and combines quality issues with facility provision.

The handbook forms of the AA, RAC and VisitBritain hotel guides are all relatively costly and, as such, are unlikely to be purchased by the occasional hotel user. Although they may be available in libraries they are often 'for reference only'. They are also not always stocked in bookstores and may have to be ordered, with a subsequent time delay. Websites are an increasingly preferred consumer information source, not least because of low cost easy access for both national and international consumers. Many consumers now book through websites and are able to combine an hotel search with a booking process that is quick and convenient.

Scrutiny of the current website descriptors reveals significant differences in content. A one star AA hotel is required to have a "reasonable choice of food and wines" whilst the RAC descriptor cautions the reader that meals "may be fairly simple". The VisitBritain descriptor stipulates that there should be a "Restaurant/eating area for breakfast at least", suggesting that some one star hotels may serve only breakfast. The RAC cautions that: "Lunch, for example, may not be served" in a one star hotel, but there is no mention of breakfast or dinner. Some readers might be likely to assume correctly that breakfast is served but they may or may not expect a dinner option. The AA descriptor does not stipulate any breakfast, lunch or dinner restrictions; this lack of clarity is reinforced by the offer of 'wines' which could suggest that meals other than breakfast might be offered. The RAC and VisitBritain two star descriptors stipulate clearly that all rooms will be en-suite. However, the AA two star descriptor, states that rooms "will usually have an ensuite bath/shower room": this implies that some rooms will not have en-suite facilities. The VisitBritain two star descriptor is extremely brief, with no reference to quality of service. The four star descriptors in relation to dining appear to indicate variable standards; the AA and RAC stress a "serious approach to cuisine", whilst VisitBritain states there will "…..be more emphasis on food and drink. Room service of all meals….." and then emphasises "24 hour drinks, refreshments and snacks' provision" - not apparently a serious four star approach to 'cuisine' but perhaps more in common with motorway service stations which also have a 24 hour refreshment and snack priority. Equally, the AA four star descriptor does not mention room service. In short, some of the star rating descriptors provided by the AA, RAC and VisitBritain seem to remain contradictory from the consumer's perspective.

Has the confusion articulated by Wickers (1997), outlined in the first section of this chapter, been removed? Is it easier for consumers to compare hotels and make an informed choice of where to stay? In England, a very qualified 'yes' should be the answer. However, has the point of a fully harmonised and totally consumer friendly star rating system been reached? An unqualified 'no' is probably the answer even in the context of England.

The latest development in the drive towards a fully unified UK star rating system involves possible harmonisation with the Scottish (VisitScotland) and Welsh (VisitWales) systems. This will only be fully effective, in the eyes of consumers, if the rating descriptors provided by the different monitoring bodies are consistent in their language, meaning and interpretation. Such consistency must apply in the context of both website entries and published book forms. However, the question has to be asked: Why should there continue to be star rating descriptor and quality indicator differences if there is a claim that significant unification and harmonisation has been achieved? The AA and RAC, in particular, are commercially driven organisations and thus, the answer may lie with their respective publishing arms. Perhaps also the answer lies in considering the following questions: Are published star rating descriptor and quality indicator differences a commercial necessity to sell hotel guides? Are differences in additional quality indicator mechanisms necessary to attract hotels to pay for a particular organisation to grade their facilities and services and, as a consequence, for hotels to pay for marketing space in the hotel guide promoted by the grading organisation?

Student Activities

Student Activities (It is recommended that students work in pairs)

1. Use websites, text books and local information to make a list of criteria for rating hotels.

2. Divide the criteria into those attributes that can be assessed using a 'tick' list and those which require quality ratings.

3. Make a list of five local hotels and evaluate each hotel, from the consumer's perspective, using publicly accessible information.

4. Using your list of criteria for rating an hotel, make your own assessment of each of the five hotels and provide a justification for these assessments.

5. Critically evaluate the current 'unified' system of rating hotels from the perspective of a hotelier deciding on which organisation to employ to rate his/her hotel.

6. Explore the reasons for the continued differences in star rating descriptors and additional quality indicator mechanisms.

References

Automobile Association (AA) (2004). *The Hotel Guide 2005*, 38th edn., AA Publishing, Windsor.

Bartlett, M. J. (2002). *The New English Tourism Council Rating System,* [on-line] available from: http://www.cherwood-hotel.co.uk/ratings.htm [accessed March 30th 2005].

Bowie, D. and Buttle, F. (2004). *Hospitality Marketing: an Introduction*, Elsevier Butterworth-Heinemann, Oxford.

Bricker, M. K. (2004). It's not all in the stars, *The Prague Post*, March 11th [on-line] available from: http://www.praguepost.com/P03/2004/spsect/0311/sp1.php. [accessed March 28th 2005].

Callan, R. J. (1995). *An empirical study to determine the pre-eminent range of attributes of United Kingdom hotels as perceived by the hotelier and the customer and to educe how proficiently such ascriptions are measured by hotel classification and grading schemes*, PhD Thesis, University of Kent, Canterbury.

Callan, R. J. (1999). Hotel Grading Schemes. In C. S. Verginis and R. C. Wood (eds.), *Accommodation Management: Perspectives for the International Hotel Industry*, International Thomson Business Press, London.

http://www.faversham.org/wheretostay/ratings.asp.

http://www.rac.co.uk/travelservices/hotels.

http://www.spinet.co.uk/careercompass.

http://www.theaa.com.

http://www.travelweekly.co.uk.

http://www.visitbritain.com.

http://www.visitbritain.com/VB3-en-GB/productsearch/ratingsinformation.aspx.

http://www.wightindex.com/ratings_explained.asp.

Kite, M. (2002). Hotels to be given single national star rating, *The Times*, May 21st, p. 18.

Maternovsky, D (2003). Hotel Rating Seeks to End Lottery, *The Moscow Times*, December 9th, p. 8.

Medlik, S, and Ingram, H. (2000). *The Business of Hotels*, 4th edn., Butterworth Heinemann, Oxford.

Royal Automobile Club (RAC) (2003). *Hotels and Bed & Breakfast 2004*, BBC Worldwide Limited, London.

VisitBritain. (2003). *Where to stay in England: Somewhere Special 2004*. VisitBritain, London.

Where to Stay, [on-line] available from:
http://www.theaa.com/getaway/hotels/hotesl_explained.html [accessed November 12th 2004]

Wicker, D. (1997). A clash of symbols, *The Sunday Times*, Travel, January 5th, p. 7.

World Tourism Organisation/International Hotel and Restaurant Association (2004). *The joint WTO and IHRA study on hotel classification*, [on-line] available from: http://www.world-tourism.org/ [accessed April 2nd 2005].

Yates, P. and Winter, K. (eds.) (1998*). The Which? Hotel Guide 1999*, Which? Ltd., London.

Suggested Further Reading

Automobile Association (2003). *AA Quality Standards for AA Recognised Hotels*, Automobile Association Developments Limited, Windsor.

Callan, R. J. (1995). Hotel classification and grading schemes: a paradigm of utilisation and user characteristics, *International Journal of Hospitality Management*, Vol. 14, No. 4, pp. 271-284.

Callan, R. J. (1996). Attributional analysis of customers' hotel selection criteria by grading scheme categories, *Proceedings of the Fifth CHME Conference*, Nottingham Trent University, UK, pp. 116-143.

Israeli, A. A. (2002). Star rating and corporate affiliation: their influence on room price and performance of hotels in Israel, *International Journal of Hospitality Management*, Vol. 22, pp. 405-424.

Lopez Fernandez, M C. (2004) Is the hotel classification system a good indicator of hotel quality? An application in Spain, *Tourism Management*, Vol. 25, pp. 771-775.

VisitBritain, *Participation Benefits: VisitBritain National Quality Assurance Standards*, [on-line] available from: http://www.tourismtrade.org.uk [accessed March 29th 2005].

Chapter Five

Developing and Managing an Event

Catherine Feeney

Overview

In this chapter, the key issues for consideration in developing and managing an event are summarised. It aims to identify some of the skills required by an event manager and addresses the main elements required for the management of an event. Also, it examines the nature of events and considers their impacts on the organisers, consumers, participants and the host community. The role of the stakeholder is examined along with those of funding and sponsorship, which take into account legal considerations and their importance, particularly that of risk management. Then the practical applications of organising an event through the use of human resource management, financial management, marketing and merchandising, logistics, catering and corporate hospitality are outlined. Observation of the operational aspects of an actual event through managing the various components of theming, choice of venue, audience and guests, stage, power, lights and sound, audiovisuals and special effects catering, performers, crew, hospitality, production schedule, recording the event and the inevitable contingencies are also reviewed. The closing down of an operation through the 'shut down' process, along with the utilisation of the reporting, debriefing and evaluation, is also discussed. It is suggested that the framework from this chapter is used as a model for the development and management of events in Central and Eastern Europe.

Introduction

The emergence of the events' industry in the latter part of the twentieth century is a major growth area within the tourism sector, particularly in a hospitality context. The realisation by communities of the importance of events, and the increased co-operation between the public and private sectors, has enhanced and benefited the lives of the majority of stakeholders involved in such events. The concept of an 'event' produces variable definitions. For example, Collins English Dictionary and Thesaurus (1992, p. 341) defines an event as: "anything that takes place especially something important". The same thesaurus provides us with [an] adventure, affair, business circumstance, episode, experience, bout, competition, contest, game and tournament. Shone and Parry (2004, p. 3) attempt both a "definition and a means of classification": they summarise a special event as "that phenomenon arising from those non-routine occasions which have leisure, cultural, personal or organisational objectives set apart from the normal activity of daily life, whose purpose is to enlighten, celebrate, entertain or challenge the experience of a group of people". They imply that, by nature, all events fall outside daily routines, have a purpose and require group involvement.

Events have been celebrated globally since the beginning of time as can be seen in the predominance of events in our private and public lives. The observation of New Year, religious festivals, local and national events differ according to the importance attributed to the cultural and economic affluence and the influence of the beholder. In a personal context, such events progress through birth, birthdays and subsequent rites of passage, finally to death and are commemorated according to people's cultural heritages, usually within the domain of the family. If the numbers are sufficiently large then an event may be catered for by outside operators as exemplified by the large industry for the "Wedding Organiser/Facilitator", particularly in North America, which is fast developing through the more affluent communities of the world. In the public world, events have become more sophisticated within the last 25 years. Wood (1982) highlighted the birth of what is now becoming known as the events' industry. She identified that commercialising popular celebrations required wealth for people to participate. This identification of funding as being essential for the development of an event occurs at all levels and is threaded throughout public events' research.

As opposed to events being the focus of a gathering, they can also be utilised to promote gatherings such as those events that achieve 'cultural and social aims' as highlighted by Salem, Jones and Morgan (2004, p. 17). They note that such events "may focus on encouraging local participation to: increase awareness of a venue, occasion, tradition or socio-cultural value, increase 'civic' pride, heighten an area's profile, satisfy the needs of special interest groups or conserve local heritage". These gatherings can range from small local celebrations to the international mega-events of the Olympics or World Sporting cups. The significance of events to communities is acknowledged further by Derrett (2004, p. 40) who states: "Festivals and events provide an opportunity for community cultural development".

The development and understanding of urban and rural areas in the context of the utilisation and cultural value of events and festivals has grown in the last quarter century. City developers in particular are identifying these driving factors. Ali-Knight and Robertson (2004, p. 10) note that the "economic phenomena of cultural and cultural-driven festival and event strategies are global phenomena" and "consequently, investment and development of appropriate attractions, events and concomitant infrastructure have occurred rapidly". Progress of this type is evident in examples such as 'Glasgow's *City of Culture* in Scotland (1990), Madrid's *Year of Culture* and Seville's *Exposition,* both in Spain (1992) and Toronto's *Arts Week and International Film Festival* in Canada held annually throughout the 1990s.

All events, whether they occur regularly or 'once in a life-time', require detailed organisation. The successful management of an event demands an experienced management team of creative and resourceful experts who are adept in professional communication at all levels. They need to examine and plan the event from a strategic perspective and also to consider and incorporate plans for the implementation of the operation. A further key to success lies in developing a compatible theme and then, through the observance of detailed plans, launching the proposed event to the targeted potential attendees. It makes sense for all event management teams to establish economic viability before the event is launched so they need to possess a combination of highly developed operational skills to identify, co-ordinate and recognise the potential benefits for all of the possible stakeholders.

The Nature, Function and Purpose of Events

Events can be presented in different forms. Salem et al (2004, p. 16) state that an event aims to "fall into three main categories: economic, social and cultural, political". These categories are then incorporated into the various events and festivals, particularly those that are developed and funded by local and national governments. Larger events, referred to as mega-events or hallmark-events, have become a popular concept for urban areas that wish to profile and attract visitors to these destinations as noted by Robertson and Ali-Knight (2004). The Olympic Games are a typical example of a mega-event, which is not linked to a destination, but "affects whole economies and reverberates in the global media" (Bowdin, McDonnell, Allen and O'Toole, 2003, p. 16). The Athens Olympics (2004) was broadcast to 230 countries and 4 billion people (http://www.Athens2004.com). This amount of media coverage provides enormous potential for the chosen destination regarding the development of infrastructure which should reap benefits for the local community and in terms of tourism revenue. In contrast, hallmark-events revolve around destinations that have grown famous for such events. For example, Edinburgh (Scotland) now presents 10 festivals during the year and terms itself 'Festival City' (http://www.edinburghfestivals.co.uk), the Mardi Gras Carnivals of Rio de Janeiro in Brazil (http://www.brazil.org.uk) and the Carnivals of Venice (http://www.carnivalofvenice.com) are hallmark events.

Any attempt at a classification of events is bound to be complex as they may be grouped in various ways, for example, according to the nature of the participants (public or private), the stakeholders and/or beneficiaries (individuals, communities, private businesses or public organisations, charities) or access (ticket, invitation or free). In general, they comprise:

(i)   Civic celebrations and commemorations, local and regional community events, festivals, fairs and carnivals;

(ii) Arts, cultural and special interest events;

(iii) Sporting events;

(iv) Theatrical concerts and exhibitions;

(v)   Media promotions, charity and fundraising events; and

(vi) Industrial/workplace focus, for example: training, seminars and conferences; promotions and product launches; corporate hospitality and entertainment; and trade fairs and exhibitions.

However, these categories are neither mutually exclusive nor exhaustive. The term 'Special Event' is often used to identify an event that has a certain or special significance: "an opportunity for leisure, social or cultural experience outside the normal range of choices or beyond everyday experience" (Getz, 1997, p. 4). Such an event can be a celebration of a historical national occasion (for example, in the United Kingdom, the Queen's Jubilee of 2002) through to the global millennium celebrations. Events which are instruments for tourism development have gained "world wide momentum in recent years" (Felenstein and Fleischer, 2003, p. 385). The development of a series of events in a specific time period can be placed under the banner title of a 'Festival'. Both Special Events and Festivals have special significance for communities developing or maintaining their identities.

Developing Events

Allen, Harris and O'Toole (2003) identify a matrix for the initial stage of developing an event (See Figure 1):

WHY	What is the event trying to achieve?
WHO	At whom is it directed?
WHAT	What idea will best achieve the goal?
WHERE	What venue will add to/support the event?
WHEN	What is the best season, day and time to hold the event?

Figure 1: Event Development Matrix
Source: Allen et al. (2003, p.4)

Following the inception of the original idea or catalyst for the event, the most important initial planning step is that of conducting a feasibility study, including an environmental impact audit, to determine the viability and potential legacies of the project. This audit should be used when establishing the event's key aim and objectives, or the mission statement, or the statement of its purpose, or a combination of all of these.

Impacts of Events

The success, and indeed the failure of an event, can be affected if all the impacts have not been carefully considered. A model by Hall and Selwood (1989) outlines clearly the sphere of event and juxtaposes the positive and negative impacts that can occur during and after the event (See Table 1).

Sphere of event	Positive impacts	Negative impacts
Social and cultural	Shared experience Revitalising traditions Building community pride Validation of community groups Increased community participation Introducing new and challenging ideas Expanding cultural perspectives	Community alienation Manipulation of community Negative community image Bad behaviour Substance abuse Social dislocation Loss of amenity
Physical and environmental	Showcasing the environment Providing models for best practice Increasing environmental awareness Infrastructure legacy Improved transport and communications Urban transformation and renewal	Environmental damage Pollution Destruction of heritage Noise disturbance Traffic congestion
Political	International prestige Improved profile Promotion of investment Social cohesion Development of administrative skills	Risk of event failure Misallocation of funds Lack of accountability Propagandising Loss of community ownership and control Legitimation of ideology
Tourism and economic	Destinational promotion and increased tourist visits Extended length of stay Higher yield Increased tax revenue Job creation	Community resistance to tourism Loss of authenticity Damage to reputation Exploitation Inflated prices Opportunity costs

Table 1: The Impacts of Events
Source: Bowdin et al., (2003, p. 27), adapted from Hall and Selwood (1989).

The use of events can bring many benefits to a particular destination; however, negative impacts during an event can have serious adverse effects on communities. One of the main areas of discontent can be the 'crowd effect', whereby the local area suffers from traffic congestion, noise and other discomforts, perhaps for an extended amount of time. Furthermore, the behaviour of visitors may be anti-social and detrimental to continuation of the event. Such disruptions must be handled with great care; they may also be anticipated and so alleviated. By developing partnerships with all stakeholders, particularly residents, and then communicating information through updated briefings, negative impacts can be minimised and useful collaboration encouraged (Derrett, 2004).

Adoption of a culture of inclusivity in partnership with the local community is essential. In some cases giving benefits through discounted tickets and other means can help to appease and reduce complaints. When Manchester hosted the Commonwealth Games in 2002, the local community, from specialists including doctors, information technologists, and engineers through to retired persons, housewives and students, were invited to join a volunteer force (N=10,000) to support the event. Large areas were devoted to free suburban car parks and free transport was offered to residents and visitors throughout the city centre during the period of the games (See http://www.bbc.co.uk/manchester/2002/ for further information). Such identification and management of impacts considered to be sensitive is a core part of planning a successful event and lead to an enjoyable experience for all stakeholders. Salem et al (2004, p. 16) comment that: "Cultural and social aims may focus on encouraging local participation"; such participation is an important part of developing acceptability by the local community, and thus enhances their support of the event.

Stakeholders

The complexity of events necessitates participation at various levels of an assortment of individuals or groups who are known as stakeholders. These are the main players in the event process, all of whom have a personal and/or business interest in the event; they may range from the organiser who wishes for the event's success, to the local resident who requires a reasonably quiet time and ease of access, to the participants who may be seeking information, enjoyment, enlightenment or just a break from the daily grind. Bowdin et al, (2003, p. 50) identify the main stakeholders in Figure 2.

UK (United Kingdom) Sport (1998) identifies a list of key stakeholders for major sporting events: For example, Olympics' stakeholders comprise: athletes; The British Olympic Association; broadcasters; coaches; event organisers; the general public, international federations; local authorities the media; national government; national sports governing bodies; officials; sponsors; sports councils; and volunteers.

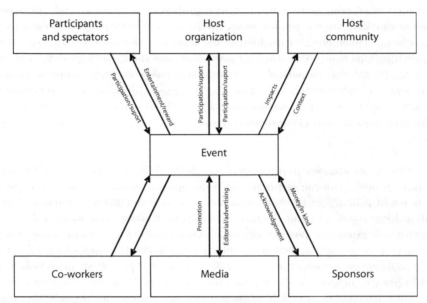

Figure 2: The Relationship of Stakeholders to Events
Source: Bowdin et al. (2003, p. 50)

In Table 2, Bowdin et al (2003, p. 52) present a model of event generators in relation to events' typology. These generators are the catalysts for developing events. As the main protagonists they are also identifiable as major stakeholders.

Event Generators	Types of Events
Government Sector	
Central government, e.g., National events	Civic celebrations and commemorations.
Public Space Authorities	Public entertainment, festivals, leisure and recreation events.
Tourism with the countries Tourist Board	Festivals, special interest and lifestyle events, destination promotions.
Visitor and Convention bureaux	Meetings, incentives, conferences and exhibitions.
Arts	Arts festivals, cultural events, touring programmes, theatre, themed art exhibitions.
Sport	Sporting events, hosting of national and international events (Olympics, World championships).
Economic development	Focus on events with industry development and job creation benefits.
Local government e.g.	Community events, local festival and fairs.
Corporate Sector	
Companies and corporate organisations	Promotions, product launches, incentives, corporate hospitality, corporate entertainment and image-building sponsorships.
Industry associations	Industry promotions, trade fairs /exhibitions, seminars, training, conferences.
Gaming and racing	Race meetings and carnivals.
Entrepreneurs	Ticketed sporting events, concerts and exhibitions.
Media	Media promotions, e.g. concerts, fun runs, appeals.
Community Sector	
Clubs and Societies	Special interest groups.
Charities	Charity events and fundraisers.
Sports organisers	Local sporting events.

Table 2: Event Generators in Relation to Event Typology
Source: Bowdin et al. (2003, p. 52)

Event generators are divided into 3 main sectors: government, corporate and community. Identification of an event with one of these sectors further aids understanding of who may be the main protagonists in establishing events. One of the main considerations for any event is the necessity to abide by local and government legislative regulations and by-laws. By their nature and according to the nature and purpose of the event, stakeholders are from a diverse range of backgrounds. One consequence of such diversity may be conflict which can arise quite suddenly and has to be resolved by the event management team as quickly and amicably as possible. The responsibility of the organisers to all stakeholders is paramount and can greatly assist in the success of the event.

There is a developing emphasis on partnerships, particularly through the public sector (representing local and national communities) working in conjunction with the private entrepreneur. Whilst planning an event, involvement of the host community is essential. It is an aid to creating harmonious relations; it can be a means of fulfilling local needs and creating opportunities for the community. Also working in collaboration with the media can make or break an event. Being positive and serving their needs will ensure good reportage. Israelewicz (1996, p. 4) wrote that several reporters working on the 1996 Atlanta Olympics, were displeased at the organisation of games. For example the reporter from 'Le Monde' suggested that events of this stature should be organised predominately by the public sector and dominated less by the politics of private funding; he particularly disliked "pandering towards the demands of the sponsors". Furthermore, he stated that the Atlanta games had two weeks of questionable efficiency, horrendous traffic jams and computer foul-ups. His article implied that the buses for the whole of the games were not coping with the schedules. The true story was different, only that their media bus did not arrive on time but the others were running according to schedule (http://slam.canoe.ca/Olympics/home.html).

Another major stakeholder is the host organisation, which may range from the Olympic Games Committee to the local community organisation. It is usually the catalyst for the event and has a vested interest in benefiting all stakeholders. In addition to any sponsor(s), the spectators (who may be referred to as the participants, punters, guests, customers, clients or consumers et al.) are usually the people who contribute, through the purchase of individual or batches of tickets, to the funding of some or most of the event. Sometimes even competitors are charged entry fees. Quite often the main income generated will stem from ticket sales and/or entry fees. All purchasers expect value from the price of their tickets; some purchasers also seek added benefits. If there is a scarcity of tickets (through limited numbers or high sales) then the prestige attached to attending and participating in the event may be sufficient in terms of added value. The supply of spectators can make or break an event and is an important element of the process in which stakeholders represent a myriad of elements from differing organisations and individuals. It requires great interpersonal skill by the management team to bring all of these groups together harmoniously not only for the benefit of all but also to contribute to the success of the event.

Funding and Sponsorship

Securing funding is an essential element of the event project process. Funding can be found in different guises. Sponsors are important stakeholders whose funding is usually essential to the continuation of an event. Depending on the type of event some government (local and national), corporate and/or community funding will probably be necessary to aid development from the embryonic stage. The Olympic Games Committee relies heavily on the host country to fund the development of any additional infrastructure required for the operation of the games (http://www.olympicgames.org). The strong emphasis of their argument is that the infrastructure development and stadium construction required for a mega-event, will benefit the local population subsequently with a legacy of new provisions.

Initial funding or investment may come from the person or organisation that has been the catalyst, or original generator or even the sponsor for the event. This money may be supplied from personal resources or by raising capital using various financial banking agencies and other means. The use of funding through sponsorship is highly sought after. Gardner and Shuman (1987, p. 16) suggest that "sponsorship is investing in causes and/or events to support overall corporate objectives or marketing objectives". This type of funding originates from the necessity of organisations, usually those with reputations for success, to have their products and services associated with a successful event. Equally events' managers only want to be sponsored by organisations that are commensurate with their own main aim and objectives. Walters and Raj (2004, p. 361) draw attention to the observance of sensitivity in this context: "sponsors must be aware of the ethos and ideology of the event and its customer bases". Getz (1997, p. 57) agrees that "the right sponsor enhances the event image through association with a positive corporate image and thus attracts better participants, customers and media coverage". Consequently sponsorship through certain products, for example from tobacco companies, has diminished particularly for many national and international sporting events.

Funding or resources from sponsors can be provided in different forms which normally comprise monetary benefits, the secondment or utilisation of experienced personnel or supply of relevant equipment or products, or combinations of these. Sponsorship has become a regular part of contributing to, or subsidising, the costs of the event. It is important to understand that without the guarantee of sponsorship funding the majority of events would not be able to progress beyond their inception. In return for sponsorship, the success of an event can reflect well on those who have contributed support and partnerships may be developed between sponsors and local, national or international events that can not reap immediate benefits but also may be ongoing for the future.

Legal Considerations

Within the feasibility study there must be provision for the fulfilment of the statutory and legal requirements necessary for the event. These vary according to the site and location of the event; different local and national authorities have their own requirements. Depending on the geographical location, those bodies who grant planning permission have to be consulted as early as possible before the event planning commences and any legal requirements at local government level must be noted and adhered to. The event manager has legal responsibility for applying for the required permits and licences to progress with the event, for example in relation to: public entertainment (music, performance and dancing); liquor; transmission (radio and television); video performance; food and hygiene; et al., all of which reflect the requirements of the current legislation of the country and the area in which the event takes place. The issue of these licences and permits can be contested and withheld by the local emergency services (police, fire and paramedics) if certain criteria pertaining to the event do not respond to legislation or safety requirements. Careful advanced research and organisation by the event managers, in collaboration with the emergency services, should increase the chances of a successful event in this context.

The issue of contracts in events' management is an important one. There are several types of requisite contract with: clients; the event site/venue/location; personnel; the performers;

merchandisers; and vendors amongst others. O'Toole and Mikolaitis (2002, p. 154) state that "contracts are the goals and objectives of the event frozen in time and are the responsibility of the event manager". Contracts must be printed and signed by the relevant stakeholders and should be legally binding. The areas of insurance for public liability, loss or damage to goods (materials, equipment, stands or exhibits), employers' liability and personal accident for participants have to be covered to reduce risk of negligence and of the organisers being sued by an aggrieved party. Contracts can be purchased under a collective indemnity policy and they are covered normally by one insurance company. Observance of the legislation regarding health and safety issues is an essential requirement for establishing events. They are identified in the following section on the management of risk.

Risk Management

Taking reasonable care or in legal terms 'the duty of care' is a principal responsibility of the event manager for all stakeholders concerned with an event. Bowdin et al. (2003, p. 199) identified it as "taking actions that will prevent any foreseeable risks of injury to the people who are directly affected by, or involved in, the event". The personal safety of all stakeholders during the creation, activation and breakdown of an event is of paramount importance. Risk management is an essential element of this process. It minimises the probability of damaging situations that could be detrimental to an organised event. It ensures that all stakeholders can operate within a predicted and measured level of safety.

The work experiences of the author suggest that there has been a marked increase in legislation and lawsuits in the UK over the last few years as the result of adverse circumstances when dealing with groups of people at events. It has increased the responsibility for managing all components of events in a safe manner. Risk or safety assessment of all aspects of the event provides a process that can be considered to aid the reduction of culpability in law of the event manager. The level of liability and accountability can be reduced through a process known in legal terms as "due diligence" or commonly known and mentioned previously as a 'duty of care' (Bowdin et al., 2003). When assessment for all aspects of the event has been documented and a risk management strategy has been developed, implementation of this strategy, with regular review and updates, should provide a suitable defence if an accident or an adverse situation does occur. Therefore, the risk assessment is an essential tool for predicting situations that could have a potential risk for those involved at an event; it shows that the event manager has exercised a duty of care and practised due diligence in the operational and strategic plans for an event. Depending on the size of the event, risk assessment can be conducted by the organiser, or delegated to external experts. The Olympic Games in Sydney 2000 had a team of risk assessors who, through their developed expertise, only worked subsequently on major sporting games events and they were seconded successfully to the Athens 2004 Olympics.

This risk assessment, although the ultimate responsibility of the organiser, must become by its nature a responsibility that cascades down through the management team to all stakeholders for their continuing safety. The Health and Safety Executive (1998, p. 3) provide five steps for risk assessment:

1. Identification: look for the hazards

2. Decision: decide who might be harmed and how

3.   Evaluation/control: evaluate the risks and decide whether the existing precautions are adequate or whether more should be done

4.   Recording: record your findings

5.   Review: review your assessment and revise if necessary

The implementation of these components aids the development of the risk management policy. The creation of a culture of shared responsibility from the event manager through to all stakeholders greatly assists and supports the safety of all. An example of this empowerment of stakeholders is often viewed at large popular musical events and is known as 'surfing the crowd'. Members of the audience may be utilised to pass individuals with problems, physically above them, to the front of stage safety zone. This procedure can work well in avoiding crushing incidents and to remove anyone who is having a panic attack due to the large number of people. Surfing the crowd has become a common occurrence and artistes appearing on stage can announce the contingency plans to the audience in advance of the event so that safety measures can be met. Hence, individuals are made aware of their own personal responsibility in this context.

The reduction of possible adverse circumstances, as identified by Allen, O' Toole, McDonnell and Harris (2002, p. 279), is achieved by planning strategies to "minimise losses and maximise opportunities". He continues to assert that risk management is as "much about identifying opportunities as avoiding and mitigating losses". Risk management is an area that should never be skimped. Therefore, an experienced and professional team, in collaboration with the events' management team, should conduct the risk assessment. During the event, the updating and constant surveillance of the risk assessment criteria must be adhered to. It is imperative to test that all systems are safe and effective. Such practices should enable any incidences to be dealt with expediently and maximise the safety, hence impact positively on the enjoyment, of all participants. Liaison with the emergency services (police, fire and paramedics) is essential. In some countries events can be cancelled if the support of these services is not provided, particularly if the event or parts of it are deemed unsafe. Correct reportage at the event debriefing is essential to test that all risk management systems are safe and effective. Also, it is useful in support or defence of any claims that are made through the legal system regarding incidences that have occurred at the event.

Organisation of Events

The event planning process may be broken into strategic and operational planning, as outlined by Bowdin et al. (2003, p. 67). Strategic planning develops from the setting of a mission and objectives and includes agreeing policies and examining funding culminating in an overall event strategy which will enable the mission to be achieved. Operational planning involves decisions about specific operational procedures and steps needed to undertake the event. It might involve single use plans for non-recurring events or standing stages/plans (for recurring events). When plans are developed the use of a checklist is useful. O'Toole (2003, p. 11) has developed such a list "from the experience of many event managers" as presented in Figure 3. This plan clearly identifies the main areas requiring detailed management. The utilisation of Gantt charts, critical path analysis and work breakdown schedules should provide "a consistent and visible framework" that "offers uniformity in definition and consistency of approach" (Getz, 1997, p. 175).

Organisational schedules are invariably peculiar to the event that is being developed but there are many lessons that can be learnt from previous operations, where examples of good practice can be carried forward. The use of networking and sharing of information with other experienced event managers has become a valuable part of developing good practices. O'Toole (2003) believes strongly in the development of good practice and the capability to make optimal decisions quickly. He further emphasises the importance of the management team's ability to communicate those decisions, and to execute them as a matter of urgency. Communication at all levels is essential. Dissemination of current information to all stakeholders is an integral part of the communication process, particularly for those who are working on its implementation. In the twenty first century, an essential part of this communication process is the development of a website to provide current information prior to, during and subsequent to the event; furthermore, immediate updating as the event progresses is paramount.

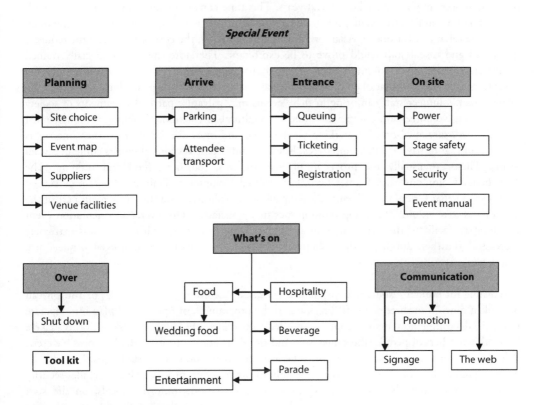

Figure 3: Event Financial Model
Source: O'Toole (2003)

Human Resource Management

The difficulty of recruiting human resources for events is more "complex than for other leisure organisations and differs between one-off events, events with a permanent home and peripatetic events" (Salem, Jones and Morgan, 2004, p. 25). Forecasting for staffing is complex, Armstrong (2003, p. 372) indicates that there are four main methods for forecasting human resources: "(i) managerial or expert judgement; (ii) ratio-trend analysis; (iii) work-study techniques; and (iv) forecasting skill and competence requirements". It is noted in Bowdin et al. (2003, p. 93) that "a combination of managerial judgement and one of the three other techniques would be used, probably because it is intuitive and easy to comprehend". The event manager is intrinsic in this process and s/he must have extensive events' experience with highly developed team leadership skills. One of the major requirements of an event rests on the building of a successful and experienced team. The diversity of the co-workers from various backgrounds means that interpersonal relationships may have to be handled carefully. Employees working on an event require good team skills along with the ability to be resourceful and the desire to succeed as a team, amongst other attributes. It is common for a significant number of staff to be employed on a casual basis, as and when required. Many event managers use recruitment agencies usually to reduce the time and costs associated with direct recruiting. Some students 'follow' events round the UK, working as casuls throughout the summer season.

The nature of an event is that it is activated usually during a short period of time, although the planning process might have taken several years. This time constraint can provide organisers with challenging human resource management situations. With mega-events, particularly sporting ones, such as the Olympic, European, Asian or Pan-American Games, the cost of paying all the requisite specialised and casual staff could prove to be exorbitant. Therefore the use of specially trained volunteers has become a common theme throughout mega-events. The challenge of employing volunteers is different to that of employing paid staff. Salem et al (2004, p. 17) have recognised the benefits that volunteer staff can bring in that "events may galvanise particular segments of society strengthening volunteerism, co-operation and intercultural interaction". Volunteers though must have the necessary attributes for working on the event and must also be afforded the same rights (other than that of pay) as other employees. Rewards and incentives for volunteers come in several forms. These are usually the provision of free uniform, transport, food and training. The Manchester Commonwealth Games (2002) specialised Volunteers' Training Programme started with a spectacular Orientation Evening, leaving all of the volunteers wanting to remain part of the Games and 'Crew 2002'. Ongoing training met many obstacles. However, "an orientation event was used to facilitate the integration of paid staff with volunteers. This event was extremely successful" (Leather, 2003, p. 10). Volunteers were also invited to join the medal winners at a 'thank you' party after the games.

Forecasting for human resources at an event is complex. According to Getz (1997, p. 186), it can be broken down into three steps: (i) break down the programme or operational plan into separate tasks; (ii) determine how many people are needed to complete the different task; and (iii) make a list of the numbers of people, the supervisors and the skills needed to form the best possible crew. When these steps are completed then the establishment of the budget for staffing is devised. The budget should comprise costs that relate not only to the selection process, which includes security clearance checks, but also for travel expenses, accommodation, uniforms, meals, on site staff accommodation, training and induction. The recruitment and selection should take place as geographically close to the event as possible. Staff who are working at an operative level are employed usually from the local area. Those who have specific areas of expertise may have to be recruited from outside of the local catchment area by utilising specialist recruitment agencies and advertising in relevant professional magazines. Legislation and statutory requirements for recruiting staff must be adhered to.

Induction and training of staff to help the team to understand the event, and how and where they fit in is a significant part of the event's process, which should fall in line with local and national agreements. Staffing is one of the most important components for enabling the success of an event. The staff's attitude and ability to work in teams is paramount. The quality of the recruitment process is demonstrated during the training period and any problematic issues must be resolved at this stage. Corporate identity through motivational instructions, good team leadership, the wearing of an identifiable uniform and the ability of the team members to operate as individuals within an event's organisation can contribute substantially towards the consumers' positive experience of the event itself.

Marketing and Merchandising of Events

The success of an event is highly dependent on arriving at the correct marketing formula for each occasion. Getz (1997, p. 250) advocates "the process of employing the marketing mix to attain organisational goals through creating value for clients and customers. The organisation must adopt a marketing orientation that stresses the building of mutually beneficial relationships and the maintenance of competitive advantages" utilising the classical seven Ps model: Product; Price; Promotion; Place; People; Physical evidence; and Process (Cowell, 1984). This model is contextualised to events' marketing by Getz (1997, p. 251) who has added 'Programming' and 'Packaging and distribution of tickets'. The component of programming is an important one for establishing major events, particularly if they have a festival base, with different venues and a variety of minor sub-events to co-ordinate. Examples of these major events are cultural, musical and other types of festivals as well as sporting tournaments including the Olympic Games, and World cup matches or competitions and certain regional multi-site events. Such events may (i) comprise a series which is contained physically in one venue (for example, a theatre's summer season) (ii) be contained within a local geographical area (for example, the city environment of the (htttp://www.edinburghfestivals.co.uk), Montreal (htttp://www.montreal.com/tourism/fests.html) or Montreaux Jazz Festival (http://www.montreauxjazz.com) which are spread across various city venues) or (iii) be spread across regional areas, such as the Olympic games, or even throughout or across several countries (for example, The Soccer World Cup 2002 event was hosted by Japan and Korea). When working with geographically dispersed organisations and cultures, the marketing of events can become very complex. Therefore strategic planning and extremely careful co-ordination of the programmes are essential.

The success of packaging and distribution of tickets is central to providing revenue for the financial success of the event. In the 2002 soccer world cup in Japan and Korea, filming of the matches showed half empty stadiums. When spectators tried to obtain tickets they were unavailable. The ticketing system became inefficient through computer systems failures and lost a considerable amount of revenue for the event. Tickets may be used as barriers or entrants into specific areas. Therefore prestigious 'perks', ranging from highly priced to complimentary tickets for select venues, to reduced entrance for locals, can provide perceived added value for both guests and key stakeholders. Such added value may present itself in other forms, one of which might be that a highlight for a guest is to meet a performer or sport's personality at the event.

The aims in marketing an event are very much dictated by the resources available. It is also crucial to identify the target market segment, i.e. the demographic and psychographic profile of the potential consumers. Attracting them to the event requires some knowledge and understanding of consumer behaviour. Normally, the consumer or participant goes through a decision-making process (Morgan 1996, p. 80) known as PIECE: Problem recognition; Information search; Evaluation of alternatives; Choice of purchase; and (if a purchase has been made) Evaluation of post-purchase experience. The results are presented in the actual purchase of a ticket and the merchandising with which it is associated.

Merchandising is an intrinsic part of the tangible products which often serve as a reminder of the event; it is a key revenue creator. This revenue can be negotiated by using different methods. A popular one is that of selling the rights of the event. These multimedia rights, sold through the mediums of broadcasting (television and radio) film, the world wide web, mobile/cellular telephones and CD-Roms are a major source of income for events, and in particular mega and hallmark-events. Clearly a mega-event such as the Athens summer Olympics (2004), with a television viewing population of 3.9 billion people in 220 countries, presents enormous potential for marketing products worldwide. Merchandising can fulfil several objectives for an event. Brassington and Pettitt (2003, p. 163) have identified these:

(i)   Income generation: branded products associated with the event, for example, programmes, clothing, CD-Roms etc.

(ii) Reward: given as gesture of thanks to participants; products that are an essential part of the event; bags, pens, clothing for identification at a conference as part of an event. Also famous or trend leaders, with whom the event wishes to associate its products

(iii) Brand/product awareness: products to promote awareness of brands

(iv) Integral component: product launches etc.

(v)   Experience enhancement: the ability to leave an event with something tangible

(vi) Experience memory: some artistes and highly sought after products offer limited edition articles so they actually become valuable reminders for the participants.

The utilisation of 'free' merchandising [possibly perceived by the reader as an oxymoron or contradiction in terms] to support the corporate identity of the event, through those actively involved in it, is a popular pursuit and may be perceived as a necessary requirement for some sporting events for example. Such merchandising is usually in the form of free clothing provision (an 'event' uniform) so that employees or volunteers are easily identifiable. Uniform can create a firm sense of identification with, and belonging to, the event, intrinsically through the team or extrinsically via the fans or supporters. With the right training and good leadership, a very strong loyalty can be built amongst employees and volunteers that can enhance the event considerably. The Manchester Commonwealth Games (2002) provided all volunteers with uniforms that easily identified them around the city. They felt that this raised their confidence and intrinsic profile and also helped with the 'reward' factor for their volunteering (Ralston, Lumsdon and Downard, 2003). Various organisations have found a rise in this loyalty and the ability for teams to be developed on the strength of this togetherness through branding. For example, Marta Maratchi (2004), managing director of her own career wear clothing company who has worked with different organisations, has consistently witnessed the natural development of teams and a gravitating of individuals towards each other when wearing clothing from a branded wardrobe.

Creating an image for the purposes of marketing an event to the consumer is important, particularly as participation in an event is an intangible product. The promotion of this image needs to be aimed at the right market segment and should match the customers' expectations. By utilising the image of the event, the creation of merchandising can be activated; mascots, logos and colours usually initiate this process. Examples of these images can be seen in the media exposure of launches given to uniforms for mega games events (the Olympic, various European, Asian, Pan-American and various sport world games). The various merchandising branded products, referred to as memorabilia, provide a tangible reminder, which is an integral part of the event experience. Sometimes, key revenue can be provided through selling the rights for merchandising, with a percentage going to the host organisation. The contract or concession for selling memorabilia can be extended after the event, especially if it has been a prestigious event whereby highly sought after merchandising can be continued with sales 'on-line' and by other traditional means such as mail order.

Financial Aspects

There are two main elements of the financial process to be considered whilst managing events: (i) identify financial resources to fund the event, i.e. the strategic element (as outlined previously in funding), and (ii) management of the budget and control of finance for the operational element of the event. Devising a budget is a necessary part of the event implementation. It is also necessary for the control of incoming and outgoing funds. Some source funding organisations will only provide funding when a budget has been presented. Salem et al (2004, p. 23) state that "most costs are incurred pre-event and most revenue is generated during the event". Financial control is a priority for the event manager. The appointment of an accountant or financial manager is essential. Initially, funding to conduct a feasibility study must be a priority for the event manager, in collaboration with the financial manager. When this study has established the viability of the event, these managers should devise event budgets, including contingency plans for supporting and controlling the financial aspects. Allen et al. (2003), in consultation with other event managers, have developed a model for the financial management process as shown in Figure 4.

Cost Classification	Estimating
Direct/indirect	Estimating methods
Unique and standard	Top down or analogous estimating
Fixed and variable	Bottom up
One off or recurring	Parametric
Opportunity costs	When to estimate
	Contingency
	Explanations

Cost control

Bookkeeping – cost control codes

Event project life cycle (cash flow)

Mark-up and passing on discounts

Problems

Procurement programme

Quotes

Team

Conclusion

Figure 4: Costing, Procurement and Cash Flow
Source: Allen et al. (2003)

The areas for consideration are outlined and present a coherent pathway for the development of the financial aspects for an event. At the actual event, systems need to be in place for the taking of cash, debit and credit cards and in particular their security on site, during transport and, during the transport of cash and documents for depositing off site.

Catering and Corporate Hospitality

Catering is the supply of food and beverages at the event, which may be provided in-house or contracted out. The majority of event management teams, particularly for medium sized to mega-events, do contract out. Unless it is for an event that is specifically food and drink orientated, the catering is not considered to be the primary business. However, catering is an important element of the event experience, especially if, as Salem et al (2004, p. 24) note, it "can provide a lucrative income stream". Using a professional, contract caterer who has expertise in the food and beverage area, has many benefits. Primarily, this approach gives the event manager the opportunity to concentrate purely on the nature and operation of the event per se and allows a company with specialist knowledge and expertise to provide, and take responsibility for, the catering. Normally, catering needs to be supplied to one or more of three distinct groups of stakeholders:

(i)   Staff, volunteers and participants (and/or back of scene personnel) at the event: They are catered for in an area known as the green room. This catering can be married with the provision of a useful communication centre, whereby information pertinent to the event can be passed on to these groups of personnel. Food and beverage should be provided during the set up, operation and break down of the event. The area needs to be managed carefully as it should provide staff with a place of respite from a busy operation.

(ii) For the (regular) punter or ticket holder, catering may be provided in-house or by contractors or through concessions. For large events the concessions are usually on-site vans or stalls, from which fast food and beverages are dispensed; ideally, the concession holders should be experts in dealing with large crowds, turn around customers speedily and have easy access to replenishments should supplies be threatened by high demand or unexpected weather conditions.

(iii) Corporate Hospitality is reserved usually for VIPs (Very Important Persons) or for those who have paid a premium/high rate for the whole event experience: VIPs expect premium seats for the event; they may be entertained by the sponsors, or be invited as guests of certain businesses, or by both groups. Corporate Hospitality can play a key role in raising revenue for the event and, therefore, this catering operation should be serviced by highly experienced personnel. The prestigiousness of the VIP area requires a relatively 'up market' approach to location, space, the design of the seating, food and beverage. Corporate sponsors as identified by Sodexho Prestige (2000, p. 5) "suggest that the main drivers for corporate hospitality are building relationships with potential customers, rewarding customers, raising corporate awareness, increasing business/sales and developing informal contact in a relaxed setting".

The catering manager, in consultation with the event management team, must obtain the relevant licences for the provision of food and beverages. The catering manager also has a responsibility with regard to procuring these licences and the dispensing of alcohol. It is common knowledge that recent problems with those who have imbibed excessively have become a cause for concern for event organisers. Behavioural problems from clients who have drunk excessive amounts of alcohol can be avoided, through observance of potentially difficult situations and the operation of a problem-solving contingency operational plan. Utilisation of the event safety stewards can further help to alleviate any difficult situations.

It is essential that the catering and corporate hospitality provision is a high quality product, especially if stakeholders have to rely on on-site provision; failure to meet their expectations may not only affect the current event adversely in terms of complaints and adverse press coverage but also can be sufficient to de-motivate people to the extent that repeat business is lost in terms of subsequent events. At some events, because of the huge numbers, catering has not been as professional as it should be. To counteract such problems, Anderson (in Bowdin et al., 2003) exemplifies the Glastonbury Festival, in England (http://www.glastonburyfestival.co.uk), where all caterers are scrutinised carefully before, and monitored during, the event to ensure that their provision meets the quality control standards. In addition, at the majority of international mega- (and some national and local) events, all vehicles and personnel that arrive on site must pass through a high security screening process due to the increasing threats of terrorism with events being used as focal points (cf. Bowdin et al, 2003).

Logistics

The logistics of supply and distribution to, and storage on, a site can be onerous if not managed correctly. Coyle, Bardi and Langley (1988) describe logistics as the planning, implementing and control of the flow and storage of products and their related information from production to the point of consumption, according to consumer requirements. Logistics are the backbone of the practical application of an event. Without consistent and easily identifiable logistical systems then the event can become difficult to manage. The logistics manager, as outlined in Bowdin et al. (2003, p. 232) "has to be a procurer, negotiator, equipment and maintenance manager, human resource manager, map-maker, project manager and party organiser". The logistics' plan is developed from the pre-planning stage, as identified in the feasibility study, in line with the operational plan. It is essential that the developer of the logistics' plan has an understanding of the infrastructure of the event and how it affects all stakeholders. The feasibility study should have identified the criteria for venue selection. It is essential that the relevant workforce has an understanding of what the logistics' plan requires. This workload communication and allocation is particularly pertinent for all types of event, including those with non-traditional temporary structures such as tents or marquees. Bowdin et al. (2003, p. 217) developed a model identifying a logistical system for events (See Figure 5): The model outlines the supply of customer, product and facilities that identify an event site logistics from initial conception through to event shut down.

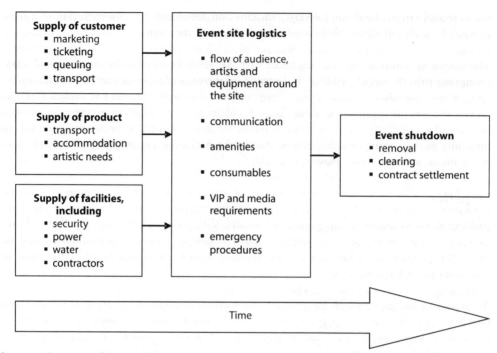

Figure 5: Elements of the Logistics System
Source: Bowdin (2003, p.217)

Harrison and McDonald (2004, p. 237) posit that "the logistics of event management requires a large degree of skilled communication, as it is the task of the event management professional to translate the often-complex conceptual information of the event into clear and specific guidelines and directions". The management of logistics from conception through to completion and break down is at the core of the event and essential to the success of the venture. The use of Gantt charts, critical path analysis and work breakdown schedules, as mentioned earlier in this chapter, can facilitate the logistical management of the event. Constant communication and updates can be presented on the event's dedicated website and through other predetermined means, such as local, national or international media, to ensure that all relevant personnel are informed. The development and co-ordination of all elements of the logistical plan by the relevant stakeholders, aids the understanding and progress of a cohesiveness that is beneficial in the context of the event's profile of success.

Staging the Event

This chapter has emphasised the substantial activities that require consideration prior to the staging of an event. McDonnell, Allen and O'Toole (1999, p. 248) identify the elements of staging an event as follows: "theming; venue; audience and guests; stage; power, lights and sound, audiovisuals and special effects; catering; performers; crew; hospitality; the production schedule; recording the event and contingencies". This list is explored further below. The theming of an event utilising a design element brings the creative process from the original concept onto a firm basis that can be shared with others (McDonnell et al., 1999, p. 245). The culmination of ideas developed during this phase is identified in Salem et al (2004, p. 19) and includes the following: "name, logo, venue décor, staff uniforms, performers' costumes, activities, entertainment, lights, music special effects, food and beverage, mascots and merchandise". The nurturing of a theme provides for a cohesive brand that is easily identifiable with the event.

The choice of venue should be determined by the feasibility study; the venue should always complement the theme. Depending on the nature of the event, the venue may be one location or a series of locations with permanent and/or temporary buildings. The venue has a substantial effect on how the event is staged. For example, during the investigation of the various cities competing to host the Olympic Games great emphasis is placed on local transport, international access and the proximity of the geographical location of the venues. McDonnell et al (1999, p. 249) provide a useful list of considerations regarding venue choice: location; matching the venue with the theme of the event; matching the size of the venue to the size of the event; venue configuration, including sight lines and seating configuration; history of events at that venue, including the venue's reputation; availability; what the venue can provide; transport to, from and around the venue; parking; access for audience, equipment, performers, VIPs staff and the disabled; toilets and other facilities; catering equipment and preferred caterers; power (amount available and outlets) and lights; communication, including telephone; climate, including microclimate and ventilation; and emergency plans and exits.

The audience and guests are an integral part of the event. Without their support the event cannot take place. Bowdin et al. (2003, p. 251) outlines the position of entrances and exits, arrival times – dump[many people together] or trickle (gradual flow of people), seating and sight lines, facilities including disabled access and sufficient toilets to cater for the number of participants.

Usually the central event occurs on a stage or in an arena. In a festival or mega-sporting event there may be several stages or performance areas at different venues. There are many health and safety issues associated with raised stages or platforms. One is that of height, and the indication of where the stage ends, so that artistes do not fall over the edge and risk hurting themselves and/or spectators. Risk assessment enables the consideration of strategies for the prevention of accidents in the stage area. The technical team operating the staging requirements needs to be inducted carefully. If the induction is by an in-house team, in collaboration with an external operator, then contracts maybe necessary to facilitate teamwork and smooth out any foreseeable problems regarding territorial issues.

The use of power, lights and sound, audiovisuals and special effects is fundamental to many performances and their management and operation requires highly specialised personnel. Access to sufficient power to accommodate the full requisite capacity should be ensured from the outset. Replacement and spares, or contingency plans, should be in place in case of any failure and access to back up power is vital.

Catering, by its nature, quality and quantity, can vary enormously depending on the event; when offered as a perk of the job, food provision can be a great motivator for food and beverage staff. As noted previously, food and beverages can be major income generators and, if agreed and monitored by the event manager, they can be of benefit to the operation through the selling of concessions or receipt of a percentage of sales. The Glastonbury Festival (http://www.glastonburyfestival.co.uk) holds food tasting sessions for all prospective event operators annually in January before any licences are granted for the following June.

The performers may be specialists or amateurs; they are specialists who can make or break the event. Some professional performers require specific contracts of employment. Contingency plans should be in place in case any of the advertised performers cannot appear on the advertised date(s). Taking out insurance against such problems is advisable.

The crew organise all aspects of the staging and they need to work as a coherent group. Co-ordination of, and communication amongst, to and from this group are vital to ensure smooth running of the event.

Hospitality packages encompass sponsors and corporate or individual guests, who may be specially invited or may have paid a premium for being in an exclusive area. Normally, the hospitality package includes entry to the most prestigious spectators' area of the event with catering, merchandising and in some cases access to meet with the celebrities of the event.

The production schedule is the main document for outlining the requirements and procedures, that is 'what to do' and 'when to do' it, in staging the event. Rehearsals usually precede the performance per se.

Recording the event may be important for immediate broadcasting or for future reference, either from a historical perspective or for review by managers, staff and, in particular, prospective clients. When working on several events it is easy to forget what, how and where things were done so recordings serve as valuable reminders. Recordings can also help in the debriefing process by highlighting difficult and excellent areas; they can be a lucrative source of future income if sold through commercial outlets.

Contingency plans, of which all key personnel must be aware, are an integral and essential part of the risk management process. If they have been brought into play, they test the resourcefulness of the event manager. Some incidences are resolved easily but others might take much more time, effort and acumen.

Although the above elements are interrelated, the nature and diversity of events mean that, according to the size, venue, site and importance of an event, some elements might require more consideration than others. For example, an event in the local town hall for 250 participants would not require the same resource input for staging as a city festival or a mega-international sports event. The staging of the event is the part that most people will remember and it is indeed the focus of any events' project.

Event Shut Down

Allen et al. (2003) suggest that events' management should follow the project management process which is a systematic procedure covering all areas and they provide a checklist for filed formal and informal reports including: finance; contractors; site management; crowd management and dispersal; marketing and promotion; human resources; equipment; liability; sponsors and grants. The information from these reports feeds into the final report to the client. Allen et al. (2003) recommend establishing timelines; issuing task responsibilities and developing reporting procedures from all participating areas. The event shut down team has its own set of responsibilities that have been delegated to the various protagonists at the commencement of the event; it is their duty to initiate the breakdown. Allen et al (2003, p. 233) provide a useful checklist (See Table 3) that outlines tasks to be performed for the event shut down.

Allen et al. (2002, p. 402) state that "event evaluation is a process of measuring and assessing an event throughout the event management cycle" and subsequently Allen et al. (2003) reaffirm the belief that constant evaluation can help to develop the event manager's practice and increase his/her professional status. At shut down a collation of the evaluation of the activities and operation of all the different departments should take place. On the completion of the event, closure procedures are equally important and essential for a successful closure. Table 3 identifies these major areas and presents a list of necessary requirements that will prove useful for the shut down.

Crowd Dispersal	**Onsite/Staging Area**
Exits/transport	Cleaning
Safety	Back to normal
Related to programming	Environmental assessment
Staggered entertainment	Lost and found
Equipment	Idiot check
Load-out schedule including correct exits and loading docks	Site/venue hand-over
Shut down equipment using specialist staff (e.g. computers)	**Contractors**
Clean and repair	Contract release
Store – number boxes and display contents list	Thank you
Sell or auction	**Finance**
Small equipment and sign off	Pay the bills
Schedule for dismantling barriers	Finalise and audit accounts – best done as soon as possible
Entertainment	Thanks donors and sponsors
Send-off appropriately	**Marketing and Promotion**
Payments – cash	Collect press clippings/video news
Thank you	Reviews of the event – use a service
Letters/awards/recommendations	Market research on community reaction
Human Resources	**Sponsors and Gants**
The big thank you	Release grants: prompt reports
Final payments	Meet sponsors and enthuse for the next time
Debrief and gain feedback for next year	Government politics
Reports	Thank services involved
Celebration party	Report to councils and other government organisations
Liability	**Client**
Records	Glossy report, video, photos
Descriptions	Wrap up and suggestions for next time
Photo/video evidence	

Table 3: Requirements for Event Closure
Source: O'Toole (2003)

Reporting, Debriefing and Evaluation

Debriefing and reporting are an essential and integral part of the events' process. Reporting provides all interested parties with information regarding their area and the whole event. The final report is supplied to nominated stakeholders, especially those who provided sources of funding for the event. Provision of online reports has become common, particularly for mega-events. Reporting should be conducted throughout an event and contributes towards debriefing which may be a 'hot one', that is immediately after the event or, as usual, especially if the crew and cast are tired, a 'cold one'. The latter should be carried out with all worker participants and within a reasonable period of time, ideally as soon as possible after close down. Debriefing is about learning from the event. Many issues will arise from the debriefing session. Event evaluation is a process used after gathering together all the information and data acquired during the event and analysing it for the benefit of 'your' client and developing 'your' event management practice. Many lessons can be learned from this analysis. The evaluation should be an outcome of the debriefing session, which should identify the extent to which the main aim and objectives of the event have been met. The evaluation exercise is a major learning tool that can be utilised for the next event. Positive outcomes can be taken forward and the negative outcomes can be rectified or eliminated for the benefit of a new event.

Conclusion

This chapter has indicated that events, by their very nature, are multi-disciplined and unique projects. The event manager requires considerable expertise and experience in many areas to create successfully a memorable event. Goldblatt (1990) identifies such expertise and experience in part of the the the title of his book as 'the art and science of celebration'. The event organiser has enormous responsibility for any event. Carlson (2004, p. 251) states that: "event organisers spend a great deal of time and effort in creating the right 'atmosphere' and festive spirit to encourage 'joyfulness (even revelry)', freedom from routine constraints and inversion of normal roles and functions". Developing a creative product, originating from an informal idea through to the event and its conclusion, can be extremely rewarding, especailly if a professional event management team can be involved.

There is an apparent increasing interest in festivals and events from organisations through to participants. Derrett (2004) notes that events can assist in providing an image or identity for communities and destinations, products or services; in fact, destinations can be 'married' to events in the support of local and national tourism. There is a rise in non-traditional tourist areas utilising festivals and events as a primary attraction method and so the destinations are being associated with certain images. For example, Manchester, as the venue for the 2002 Commonwealth Games developed a new provision portfolio, which offers more diverse accommodation and facilities for visitors than ever before.

Events are about benefiting all stakeholders and even enhancing their lives. The legacy of events has become a key consideration for the events' manager, in particular the leaving behind of physical assets that are of value to both locals and visitors, especially when a large investment has been made. Venues such as sports arenas can be utilised by the local community and volunteer resources can be provided for subsequent events. The legacy can create an identity for areas that previously had a relatively low profile and so benefit the local community. Sydney (Olympic Games 2000, Australia) and Manchester (Commonwealth Games, 2002, England) are two examples of cities that raised their profiles internationally and have subsequently attracted international visitors although they were not considered previously to be international tourist destinations. Sydney is now portrayed as a 'world city' (Waitt, 2004, p. 393) and it might be argued that, in addition to shops, Manchester's main assets are its cultural facilities and events.

Events are a positive tool for developing communities and economies. They are a way of creating a collective emotion (Waitt, 2004). From small to mega-events, they offer a means by which people are bound together by a common theme and provide a lasting impression that can be recreated through the support of businesses, local authorities and governments. There is a tradition of local events and festivals in Central and Eastern European countries and such events may be seen as vehicles for developing international tourism. As the popularity of Central and Eastern European destinations increase, they can be made more durable not only through the utilisation of local events and festivals but also by examining their potential as venues for hallmark and mega-events. Specialised regular events and festivals, especially if they take place annually in the same location in the same month or season, can provide an excellent source of repeat business and reap economic benefits for the area. It is worth the while of tourism managers to examine the viability of even more frequent, regular events that could provide a steady income for a developing area. For example, on a recent trip to Slovakia, the author noted a need for the development and marketing of local festivals. Countries taking such opportunities to share cultural exchanges, and to develop them for the potential of the residents and visitors, could see great benefits for all concerned.

Student Activities

1. Several mega-events pertaining to Games have been mentioned in this chapter. Identify one such recent event and look at the relevant website (For example, http://www.olympicgames.org or http://www.thecgf.com)

    Outline 10 important points for each of the following areas:

    (i)   Preparation for event

    (ii) Theme

    (iii) Staging

    (iv) Breakdown

    (v)   Debriefing

2. Identify a small event or festival in your home area, which is normally attended by about 1000 people in an existing controlled park or field (usually used for festivals), that appears to have opportunities for further development. Plan the development of the upscaled event by itemising requirements in the one or more the following areas:

    (i)   Preparation for event

    (ii) Theme

(iii) Operation of the event

Determine the requirements for each area and state whether it is a profit or non-profit making event. Identify the stakeholders and say what consideration must be given to maintaining their interest and commitment. In your initial seminar paper and/or presentation, identify who should benefit from the event and how their contribution might be measured.

References

Allen, J., Harris, R. and O'Toole, W. (2003). *Executive Certificate in Event Management, course material.* Course delivered by Australian Centre for Event Management, University of Technology Sydney at Napier University, Edinburgh.

Allen, J., O' Toole, W., McDonnell, I. and Harris, R. (2002). *Festival and Special Event Management,* 2nd edn., John Wiley, Sidney.

Ali-Knight, J. and Robertson M. (2004). Arts, leisure, cultural concepts and experience. In I.Yeoman, M. Robertson, J. Ali-Knight, S. Drummond and U. McMahon-Beattie, *Festival and Events Management: An international arts and culture perspective,* Butterworth-Heinemann, London, pp. 4-13.

Armstrong, M. (2003). *A Handbook of Human Resource Management Practice,* 9th edn., Kogan Page, London.

Bowdin, G., McDonnell, I., Allen, J. and O'Toole, W. (2003). *Events' Management,* Butterworth and Heinemann, Oxford.

Brassington F. and Pettitt S. (2003). *Principles of Marketing,* 3rd edn., Financial Times, Prentice Hall, Harlow.

Carlson, J. (2004). The Economics and evaluation of festival and events., In I. Yeoman, M. Robertson, J. Ali-Knight, S. Drummond and U. McMahon-Beattie. *Festival and Events Management: An international arts and culture perspective,* Butterworth-Heinemann, London, pp. 246-259.

Collins Dictionary and Thesaurus (1992). Harper Collins, London.

Cowell D. W. (1984). *The Marketing of Services,* Heinemann, London

Coyle, J. J., Bardi, E.J. and Langley, C.J. (1988). *The Management of Business Logistics* 4th edn., West Publishing Company, St Paul, MN.

Derrett, R. (2004). Festivals, Events and the Destination. In I. Yeoman, M. Robertson, J. Ali-Knight, S. Drummond and U. McMahon-Beattie (2004). *Festival and Events Management: An international arts and culture perspective,* Butterworth-Heinemann, London, pp. 32-50.

Felenstein, D. and Fleischer, A. (2003). Local festivals and tourism promotion: The role of public assistance and visitor expenditure, *Journal of Travel Research,* Vol. 41, No.4, pp. 385-392.

Gardner, M. P. and Shuman, P. J. (1987). Attitudes towards Sponsorship, *Journal of Advertising* Vol. 16, No. 1, pp. 11-17.

Getz, D. (1997). *Event Management and Event Tourism,* Cognizant, New York.

Goldblatt, J. (1990). *Special Events: The art of science and celebration*, Van Nostrand Reinhold, New York.

Hall, C.M. and Selwood H. J. (1989). Hallmark Events and the Planning Process. In G.J. Syme, B. J. Shaw, D.M. Fenton and W.S. Mueller, *The Planning and Revaluation of Hallmark Events*, Avebury, Aldershot, pp. 20-39.

Harrison, L. and McDonald, F. (2004). Events Management in the Context of New Zealand's Art, Leisure and Cultural Sectors. In I. Yeoman, M. Robertson, J. Ali-Knight, S. Drummond and U. McMahon-Beattie (2004). *Festival and Events Management: an International arts and Culture Perspective,* Butterworth-Heinemann, Oxford, pp. 232-245.

http://www.Athens2004.com/.

http://www.bbc.co.uk/manchester/2002/.

http://www.brazil.org.uk.

http://www.carnivalofvenice.com.

http://www.edinburghfestivals.co.uk.

http://www.glastonburyfestival.co.uk.

http://www.montreal.com/tourism/fests.html

http://www.montreauxjazz.com.

http://www.olympicgames.org.

http://slam.canoe.ca/Olympics/home.html.

http://www.thecgf.com/games.

Izraelewicz, L. (1996). Atlanta Ganes, *Le Monde Reporter*, 4 August1996, New York Times, p. 4.

Leather, D. (2003). *Manchester 2002 The XVII Commonwealth Games: Post Games Report*, Vol. 3, Commonwealth Games Federation, [on-line] available from: http://www.thecgf.com/games/2002reports.asp?yr=2002 [accessed March 23rd 2004].

Marta Maratchi (2004). Managing director of Marta Maratchi clothing company, personal communication, June.

McCarthy, E.J. (1960). *Basic Marketing*, Irwin, Homewood, IL.

McDonnell, I., Allen, J. and O'Toole, W. (1999). *Festival and Special Events' Management*, John Wiley and Sons, Brisbane.

Morgan M. (1996). *Marketing for Leisure and Tourism*, Prentice Hall, London.

O'Toole, W. J. (2003). *Events' Project Management System,* [on-line] available from: http://www.personal.usyd.edu.au/~wotoole/epmspage1.html [accessed January 8th 2004].

O'Toole, W. and Mikolaitis P. (2002). *Corporate Event Project Management,* John Wiley and Sons, New York.

Ralston, R., Lumsdon, L. and Downard, P. (2003). *Study of Volunteers (pre-Games) Sport Development Impact of the Commonwealth Games,* (CD ROM) International Centre for Research and Consultancy, Manchester Metropolitan University, Manchester.

Salem G., Jones E., and Morgan N. (2004). An overview of Events' Management. In I. Yeoman, M. Robertson, J. Ali-Knight, S. Drummond and U. McMahon-Beattie, *Festival and Events Management: An international arts and culture persepective,* Butterworth-Heinemann, London, pp. 14-31.

Shone A. and Parry B. (2004). *Successful Event Management,* Thomson, London.

Sodexho Prestige (2000). *Corporate Hospitality Guide 2000-01: Best Practice Guide,* Sodexho Prestige, Alperton.

The Health and Safety Executive (HSE) (1998). *Five Steps to Risk Management,* HSE, London.

UK Sport (1998). *Public Opinion Survey: Importance and Measure of UK Sporting Success.* UK Sport, London.

Waitt G. (2004). A critical examination of Sydney's 2000 Olympic Games. In I. Yeoman, M. Robertson, J. Ali-Knight, S. Drummond and U. McMahon-Beattie, *Festival and Events Management: an international arts and culture perspective,* Butterworth-Heinemann, London, pp. 391-407.

Walters, P. and Raj, R. (2004). Sponsorship, funding and Strategic function: Carling Festival and V-Festival. In I. Yeoman, M. Robertson, J. Ali-Knight, S. Drummond and U. McMahon-Beattie, *Festival and Events Management: an international arts and culture perspective,* Butterworth-Heinemann, London, pp. 358-370.

Wood, H. (1982). *Festivity and Social Change: Leisure in the Eighties,* Research Unit. Polytechnic of the South Bank, London.

Suggested Further Reading

Hall, C. M. (1997). *Hallmark Tourist Events,* John Wiley, Chichester.

Masterman, G. (2004). *Strategic Sports Event Management,* Elsevier Butterworth-Heinemann, Oxford.

O'Toole, W. (2002). *Corporate Event Project Management,* John Wiley, New York, (Also translated into Chinese).

Vasey, J. (1998). *Concert Tour Production Management,* Butterworth-Heinemann, Boston.

Vasey, J. (1999). *Concert Sound & Lighting Systems,* Butterworth-Heinemann, Boston.

Chapter Six

The Development of Tourist Attractions and Entertainment

Crispin Dale and Neil Robinson

Overview

This chapter examines the provision for tourist attractions and entertainment utilising various academic models to aid the reader's comprehension of the attractions and entertainment concept; this understanding is underpinned further with reference to the wider European and global environment. The utilisation of characteristic examples reinforces further understanding of the role played by attractions and entertainment in aiding economic well-being and national prosperity. Attention is drawn to the position of Central and Eastern Europe whose environmental setting has become a catalyst in which new and existing attractions and entertainment have been developed following the expansion of the European Union (EU). This experience has led to increased international participation and therefore facilitated consumer consumption and enjoyment so that both developers and participants are provided with an appropriate level of satisfaction, leading to their increased understanding and appreciation of the attractions and events phenomenon.

Introduction

The provision for tourist attractions and entertainment is fundamental to the development of any destination and it could be argued that, without their presence, many countries would find it hard to sustain any kind of tourism industry (Cooper, Fletcher, Gilbert and Wanhill, 1998). Central and Eastern European countries, in particular the new EU member countries, are taking advantage of new markets in promoting their tourist attractions and entertainment provision, with a view to attracting investment and developing their economies. Indeed, Central and Eastern European countries have a wealth of potential and under-utilised attractions, both man-made and natural, that if rejuvenated and marketed properly could act as catalyst for generating tourist demand.

The Nature of Tourist Attractions

Tourist attractions and entertainment are by nature tourism facilitators that generate tourism demand and create incentives for tourists to travel. Although there is a general consensus that defining tourist attractions is fraught with difficulties (Leask and Yeoman, 1999), Swarbrooke (2000) offers a typology of tourist attractions that includes natural, man-made and event phenomena as illustrated in Table 1. Swarbrooke (2000) recognises that natural and man-made buildings (non-tourism and tourism specific) are static and generally permanent in nature, whereas special events are temporary and often have a limited life span.

Attraction	Examples
Natural	Beaches, forests, wildlife, lake, caves, farms
Man-made buildings (non-tourism)	Churches, stately homes, gardens
Man-made buildings (tourism specific)	Theme parks, museums, galleries
Special events	Sporting events, historical events, religious events

Table 1: Classification of Attraction Types
Adapted from Swarbrooke (1995 p.5)

However, it can be argued that Swarbrooke's (2000) classifications are possibly over-simplistic (Leask, 2003) and too limited in scope to recognise the different attraction types that have emerged within the tourism industry. Table 2 presents a wider classification of attraction types that reflects more truly the diversity and breadth of attractions that exist in today's global tourism industry; in due course, this model will be applied to attraction types in Eastern Europe.

Nature of Attraction	Examples
Heritage	Hadrian Wall, Northumberland UK, Albert Docks, Liverpool UK, Iguazu National Park, Argentina, Roman Walls of Lugo, Spain, The Old City of Acre, Israel.
Natural	Grand Canyon, USA Niagara Falls, Canada
Religious	The Blue Mosque, Istanbul, Turkey St Paul's Cathedral, London, UK
Entertainment and festival	Glastonbury Music Festival, Glastonbury, UK Reading Music Festival, Reading , UK
Industrial	Ironbridge Gorge Museum, Ironbridge, UK Wigan Pier, Wigan, UK
Coastal	Blackpool, UK Costa Del Sol, Spain
Spa	Bath Spa, UK, Baden-Baden, Germany, Vichy, France; Bagno Vignoni, Italy.
Arts and cultural	Tate Gallery, Liverpool, UK The Lowry, Salford, UK
Sport	British Grand Prix, Silverstone, UK Wimbledon Tennis Championships, London, UK
Dark	Jim Morrison's Grave, Pere Lachaise, Paris JFK assassination – The Sixth Floor, Dallas Texas

Table 2: Diversity of Attraction Types
(Dale and Robinson, 2005)

Leask (2003) extends Swarbrooke's (2000) classification further (Figure 1), based upon whether the attraction is built, natural, free or paid, whether it is publicly or privately owned and whether it operates in the local, regional, national or international arena. Leask argues that this model offers a better understanding of different stakeholder expectations and the subsequent management objectives that need to be satisfied. At the heart of the model is the attraction's product itself and the associated resources that are required to produce additional revenue streams and increase the viability of the attraction such as catering and retailing, for example. The interpretation of the attraction is also important to encourage the potential target market and in consideration of the costs involved in its presentation. For example, the Science Museum in London (http://www.sciencemuseum.org.uk) is targeted primarily at school children but requires a significant amount of technological resources for its interpretation of science. The next stage of the classification determines whether the attraction is built or natural and this will influence the management approach taken. For example, the management approach for the Lake District in the UK (http://www.lake-district.gov.uk) is predominately focused upon conservation and visitor management issues to ensure impact minimisation. In contrast, in a man-made theme park like Alton Towers (http://www.alton-towers.co.uk), management is focused on human resources that underpin the delivery of the service experience and visitor enjoyment of the attraction.

Whether the attraction is free or paid will vary depending upon whether the attraction is publicly or privately owned; without doubt, this element does influence the resources and management of the attraction. For example, to widen market appeal and participation the UK Government has aimed to ensure that free entry is given to all publicly funded museums and art galleries. Offers of free entry mean that these attractions need to be subsidised heavily. Although donations may be requested from visitors, they rely predominantly on additional revenue streams, such as the national lottery in the UK and EU funding in certain geographical areas, for income. The final part of the model focuses on the target market (local, regional, national, international) at whom the attraction is aiming and this focus will depend significantly on the marketing resources at the attractions disposal. For example, the Disney Corporation has a massive marketing budget to promote its theme parks around the World, whereas the publicly funded Museum of Cannock Chase, for example, (http://www.cannockchasedc.gov.uk/museum) only has enough resources to promote locally and regionally.

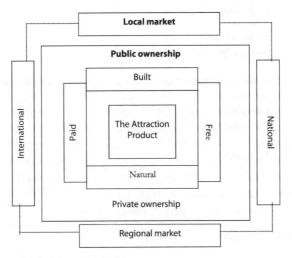

Figure 1: Classification of Visitor Attractions
Adapted from Leask, 2003, p.7

In determining the tourist attraction product, which is central to the classification model, Wanhill (2003a) puts forward the notion of "imagescape", a term used to describe the specific theme or image upon which the context of the attraction is based. He maintains that imagescape is crucial in being able to "convey the essence of the visitor experience to the potential market" (Wanhill, 2003a, p. 19). Both the attraction's tangible features and the support services it offers assist in conveying its imagescape. The challenge for many destination marketers is the need to develop a coherent and co-ordinated tourism product that articulates a consistent imagescape not only for the individual attractions themselves but also for the destination as a whole. It is argued that such development should result in a well-positioned product, which can be differentiated clearly from competitors' products and does not lead to confusion in the eyes of the consumer.

In developing the visitor attraction products that a destination has to offer, Wanhill (2003a) offers the market-imagescape mix as illustrated in Figure 2. It can be argued that a 'me-too' attraction is one that involves least risk by embracing tried and tested imagescapes, for example, the coal mining attractions in Wales such as the Big Pit National Mining Museum in Blaenavon (http://www.nmgw.ac.uk/bigpit). However, the development of 'me-too' attractions should be based upon evidence that demand is not only sufficient but also ongoing for the attraction to be viable and does not cannibalise the visitor demand for other attractions. 'Grand inspiration' attractions are new attractions that are based upon a creative idea and are subsequently developed. For example, the Disney concept was launched in California and was based upon the vision and aspirations of Walt Disney (http://www.disneyinternational.com). 'New version' attractions are existing imagescapes that can be established in a different location to appeal to a new market and to rejuvenate the product. For example, the extension of the Disney theme park brand to Paris and Tokyo. 'Wonder attractions' are major projects that can act as catalysts to the economic development of an area and enhance its image. Examples are the London Eye (http://www.ba-londoneye.com) and the Eden Project in Cornwall (http://www.edenproject.com).

Market	Image	
	Current	New
Current	Me too attraction	Grand inspiration attraction
New	New version attraction	Wonder attraction

Figure 2: The Attraction Market-imagescape mix
Source: Wanhill, 2003a, p.27

In many cases the characteristics of such attractions help to define a location and create avenues for its marketability. For example, Bermuda (http://www.bermudatourism.com) has a number of man made attractions in the form of its old forts and Docklands and natural attractions such as its beaches and special events, including the Gombey dancers and military marching bands (beating the retreat). Whilst numerous tourists visit the island to experience its many attractions, it could be argued that it is the augmented tourist product, comprising the attractions and entertainment provision, which acts as the catalyst in facilitating tourist demand. Nevertheless, Bermuda itself has an extensive tourist product and offers a multitude of related tourist activities (Dale and Robinson, 1999).

Product Differentiation

As tourist attractions and entertainment provision develop further, the need for differentiation from competitors becomes a priority. The intangible nature of many attractions plays a key role in maintaining their existence and is often utilised to facilitate their marketability. Take for instance the historical attraction of Buckingham Palace in London, England (http://www.royal.gov.uk). The attraction itself uses its intangible historical past to reinforce its presence with the utilisation of images and themes in an attempt to tangibilise the intangible. This tangibility may be operationalised and communicated through the utilisation of physical objects, dummies, animatronics (automated characters), live people in costumes, sound and even smell effects (such as Jorvik Viking Centre in York (http://www.jorvik-viking-centre.co.uk/trialsplash2.htm) and the Scotch Whisky Heritage Centre in Edinburgh (http://www.whisky-heritage.co.uk) in an attempt to bring to life the past and in many cases to legitimise and give meaning to history. This 'edutainment' approach enables the visitor to appreciate the historical origins of the attractions and at the same time disseminates key factual information in a format which is manageable, accessible and interesting to people of all ages and nationalities. The Disney corporation has been a market leader in employing this kind of technique by using technological systems which aid presentation and bring to life subject matter (Wanhill, 2003b).

Entertainment Defined

Hughes (2000, p. 13) encapsulates the notion of entertainment by stating that "the word entertainment is used to include a wide variety of activities such as watching television or playing computer games at home, listening to compact discs, cinema visits, watching sport and visits to theme parks and going to discos. In addition it is applied to live performances of musicals, variety shows and band concerts".

Entertainment itself is arguably one of the most important components of any tourism destination and, without it, the need to visit a destination can be diminished greatly. Imagine the impact on visitor numbers if the entertainment facilities or peripheral superstructure were to be removed from Las Vegas, (http://www.vegas.com), which is in the heart of a desert. Likewise, the City of Liverpool's successful bid for European City of Culture 2008 hinged on its Maritime history and musical legacy, such as the Beatles (http://www.liverpool.gov.uk).

Entertainment Characteristics of Global Destinations	
Location	**Entertainment**
Las Vegas (USA)	*Gambling & performance entertainment,* theatre productions, events, musicals, hotel themes (MGM Grand, Bellagio).
London (UK)	*Historical entertainment,* Changing of the Guard, opening of Parliament, Buckingham Palace, theatres, musical events /tours.
Liverpool (UK) European City of Culture 2008	*Historical & musical entertainment,* Mersey River Festival, the tall ships, Beatles museum, Titanic Exhibition, Cavern tours, Magical Mystery Tours.
Amsterdam (Netherlands)	*Historical & musical/nightlife entertainment,* Anna Frank Museum, Van Gogh museum, Heineken museum, Blues café, Brown café, red light district.

Table 3: Entertainment Characteristics of Global Destinations
Source: Robinson, 2005

By way of an example, Table 3 enables clarification to be established in relation to the entertainment characteristics that might exist in global destinations. Indeed it can be argued that some geographical locations such as Las Vegas (gambling and entertainment related) offer a collective of associated attractions and entertainment products; others such as Liverpool offer themed (historical & musical entertainment related) products and some, for example; Amsterdam appear to provide a compendium of the historical, cultural, nautical within an entertainment based periphery. The entertainment commodity often acts as financial catalyst for locations which have yet to exploit their historical legacy fully, or do not have the pre-requisite funds available to 'kick start' a tourism economy. For example, before the last decade, the City of Dublin (Republic of Ireland, http://www.dublin.ie) had very little organised tourism infrastructure in the form of tours and excursions. By utilising its existing transport infrastructure and the inner city superstructure, a tourism product has been packaged around its entertainment provision and nightlife. This City has been successful over recent years in attracting tourists to experience its growing entertainment provision, which in turn has promoted growth in visitor numbers. Hence its greatly increased revenue, in the form of tourist spend, can be further reinvested to aid tourism development.

In many cases, entertainment provision acts as a tourism facilitator and is often instrumental in creating tourism demand. Looking historically at the development of tourism in Europe, one can often identify prerequisite levels of entertainment long before the development of any tourism concepts. Tourist destinations such as Pamplona in Spain have benefited greatly from the international appeal of traditional local cultural events such as 'The festival of San Fermin – running of Bulls' (http://www.red2000.com/spain/Pamplona/fest.html) in terms of increased visitor numbers and have seen the development of a tourism industry, on the back of an entertainment activity which greatly predates any local tourism industry. This entertainment spectacle was in existence well before the tourism boom of the early 1960s and now acts as a magnet for visiting tourists. The activity draws a large number of visitors to the northern Spanish town in early July and sees locals and visitors alike, running through the streets of Pamplona, pursued by a group of bulls. As one might expect this entertainment show has been incorporated into a week long collective of activities, with the purpose of extending the product lifecycle. It may be noted that entertainment can be a fairly inexpensive way for locations to develop the seeds for the newly born tourism economy and one which limits any adverse financial impacts associated with opportunity costs (Cooper et al., 1998).

When looking at entertainment provision in Central and Eastern Europe, it is clear that not only is provision plentiful but also there is a multitude of opportunities for further development. However, the development, marketability and quality of the entertainment entity needs to be managed carefully and, in some destinations, better managed. In the same way that most Western European countries have developed tourist economies out of entertainment manifestations, other European countries are following suit. The next part of this chapter examines the chronology of attractions and entertainment development.

Pre Fall of the Iron Curtain: Problems and Potential

After World War II and the development of Stalinist economic policies across Eastern Europe, a period of economic growth followed (Hall, 1991), characterised by intense industrialisation and collectivism, with little attention being paid to the role of the service industries such as tourism. Under these conditions the notion of tourism, particularly that characterised by the influx of foreign tourists, was virtually non-existent. (Arefyev and Mieczkowski, 1991).

The first real development of international tourism within Central and Eastern Europe, and more specifically in the Soviet Union, began in the late 1950s (Hall, 1991). This period was characterised by some improvement in East-West relations and further improvements came with the recognition that hard currencies such as Sterling and US Dollars could be very beneficial and with this a carefully designed tourism policy was constructed (Hall, 1991). Burns (1998) has commented that the main reason for the design of such a policy, was to promote Eastern European countries to their Western adversaries and to legitimise their socialist ideals. It is worth noting at this stage that only carefully selected locations and attractions were made available to foreign visitors, such as Red Square in Moscow, Russia.

Despite some of these minor changes in tourism policy, Central and Eastern Europe remained fairly inaccessible and thus international tourism and visits between fellow Central and Eastern European countries were limited. This limited tourist flow was due largely to currency inconvertibility and hard exit visa policies (Hall, 1992). The policy of encouraging a form of state tourism (often referred to as social tourism) in which domestic tourism was advocated under a socialist order, promoted the well being of the working populace and further supported the socialist cause (Hall, 1991). Organisations such as trade unions sponsored many of these state tourism policies and in some cases part contributed towards hotel developments and superstructure components required for domestic, group oriented tourism and recreation (Hall, 1991). The state also supported domestic health tourism, for example, in Bulgaria, Hungary, Czech Republic, Poland and the former Soviet Union; See Chapter 7 for further details) The role of trade unions was the key to the development of social tourism within Central and Eastern Europe with the utilisation of health spas and treatment facilities being made available for convalescent union members (Burns, 1998). In addition to this the Ministries of Health and Social Welfare operated a voucher system (Burns, 1998) which entitled workers to participate in tourism activities emphasising sport and recreational development in the pursuit of building healthy socialist members. This ideology shares commonalities with the Hitler Youth movement during the 1930s, which placed great emphasis upon outdoor pursuits and well being of mind and body (Keeley, 2000).

Recent Tourism Developments in Central and Eastern Europe: A Micro/Macro Perspective

As early as the 1980s, political changes aligned with growing economic and social leniency from the ruling Communist system in Moscow, in part facilitated the development and growth of a service sector by attracting international partnerships and superstructure development (Hall, 1991). Following this period a number of important developments facilitated the increase of foreign tourists. The initial fear and scepticism often held by Central and Eastern Europeans had almost evaporated and given way to a belief in tourism and a philosophy predisposed to profit maximisation and wealth. The impacts of these issues are discussed further by Hall (1992) who comments upon the benefits of having tourism opportunities within a socialist environment including the creation of employment and the ongoing promotion of the country to the outside world. In contrast the perceived image and cultural characteristics of socialism, for example, centralisation, collectivisation, unionisation, poor production and management techniques, bureaucracy and a general dislike of private enterprise, did have the effect of limiting tourism development further (Hall, 1990).

From the mid-1980s, and with the emergence of Glasnost a new form of optimism emerged and with it fundamental transformations to the political makeup of Central and Eastern Europe. These changes re-energised the service sector and with this came greater economic elasticity and internationalisation in the form of trade and increased European co-operation (Hall, 1991). Hall (1998) noted that much of [Central and] Eastern Europe's tourism provision was dated and fell greatly behind westernised standards. Infrastructure in the form of transportation links, communications networks and utility supplies had suffered greatly from years of under investment and poor management. In addition to this superstructure, provision in the form of attractions lacked many of the pre-requisites which many Western tourists have come to expect. The emergence of the private sector with entrepreneurs developing service products, has had some success in developing a non-governmental tourist sector. In consequence, services are moving rapidly away from the traditional socialist ideologies to one which embraces predominantly private sector enterprises.

Attractions and Entertainments Post Communism: Opportunities and Challenges for Development

The recent developments taking place in the form of hotel growth and superstructure creation come at a time when further Eastern European countries are seeking entry to the European Union. This move is a long way from the origins of Eastern Europe's beginnings, which were characterised by the Communist ideology of often shunning privatisation and restricting individual entrepreneurship. However, although they shared the 'generic' definition 'communist countries', there have been historical fundamental country specific differences, for example, between the Czech Republic and Albania. Since the fall of communism a growing number of tourist attractions have emerged in Central and Eastern Europe; however many potential tourist attractions within some Eastern European countries remain underdeveloped and under-utilised. These can be the focus for the regeneration of Eastern European economies whilst also acting as a flagship to the development of the wider augmented tourist attractions' product, including restaurants, hotels, souvenir production and so on.

Countries in Eastern Europe need to ensure that they embrace a diversity of attraction and entertainment opportunities so as to maximise the benefits of tourism activity whilst concurrently minimising the negative consequences that tourism can bring. By utilising the existing infrastructure and cultural resources, Eastern European countries can employ tourism as a means for regenerating areas of social deprivation and bring about economic prosperity that many of these areas desire. Indeed the attractions and entertainment commodity, whilst requiring much in the provision of financial support, has the potential to change tourism development in Eastern Europe fundamentally and at the same time create a tourism legacy from which all can share and benefit. The key to such a strategy is the notion of sustainable development (as advocated in Chapter 8), which itself must be controlled by those stakeholders who have most to gain from such developments, that is, the host and the visitors. By establishing such a working relationship between the host and the visitors, a positive/cooperative and mutually beneficial product can be developed. Table 4 exemplifies some individual attractions that Central and Eastern European countries have to offer.

Nature of Attraction	Examples
Heritage	Amphitheatre, Pula, Croatia;
	Diocletian's Palace, Split, Croatia;
	Toompea Castle, Tallinn, Estonia;
	Statue Park, Budapest, Hungary;
	Peninsula Castle, Trakai, Lithuania;
	Wawel Castle, Krakow, Poland;
	Spissky Hrad, Spisske Podhradie, Slovakia.
Natural	Vidova Gora mountains, Bol, Croatia ;
	Danube Bend and Tihany Peninsula, Budapest Hungary;
	The Tatras, Zakopane, Poland;
	The Carpathians, Transylvania, Romania;
	High Tatras, Poprad Plain, Slovakia;
	Lake Bled, Slovenia;
	Durmitor, Lovcen, and Durmitorska Gora, Montenegro.
Religious	Rila Monastery, Bulgaria;
	Bone Church, Sedlec, Kutna Horá, Czech Republic;
	Church of the Holy Ghost, Raekoja Plats, Estonia;
	St John's Church, Bernardine Church, Church of the Holy Spirit, Vilnius, Lithuania.
Entertainment and festivals	Summer Festival, Dubrovnik, Croatia;
	Szentendre's Summer Festival, Budapest Film Festival, Sziget Festival and BudaFest Opera Festival, Hungary;
	Festival of Mountain Folklore, Zakopane, Poland.
Industrial	Kutná Hora Silver-mining Centre, East Bohemia, Czech Republic;
	Leevaku Village, South-East Estonia;
	Industrial Museums and Old Mines of Southern Poland.
Coastal	Mariánské Lázne and Karlovy Vary, West Bohemia, Czech Republic;
	Pärnu Resort, Pärnu, Estonia;
	Nida, Lithuania;
	Budva, Yugoslavia;
	Bol, Croatia.
Spa	Tabán, Rác and Rudas Baths, Hungary;
	Jurmala Spa, Latvia;
	Beauty Farm Hotel Group, Slovenia.
Arts and culture	Szentendre, Hungary;
	Black Madonna of Czestochowa, Poland;
	Theatres and Galleries of Prague.
Sport	Hungarian Grand Prix, Budapest, Hungary;
	Golf Courses and Sea Sports of Croatia;
	Lithuania Winter Sports centre.
Dark	Salaspils Concentration Camp, Salaspils, Latvia;
	Genocide Museum, Vilnuis, Lithuania.
	Auschwitz Concentration Camp, Poland;
	Bran Castle (Dracula), Bran, Romania.

Table 4: Examples of Attractions in Central and Eastern Europe
Source: Dale and Robinson, 2005

Eastern European countries need to present a collective brand identity (Morgan, Pritchard and Pride, 2002) which embraces the diversity of attractions on offer. This brand identity needs to incorporate the core values that reflect the Central and Eastern European tourism attraction product and should be communicated consistently to the target markets. However, relative to many of their well established tourism destination competitors in Western Europe, it could be argued that Central and Eastern European countries are presented with a unique set of challenges and opportunities that could make this a difficult exercise to complete, as outlined in Table 5.

Opportunities	Challenges
Development of an holistic Central and Eastern European brand identity	Fragmented public sector co-ordination of the tourism industry
Promoting the diversity of attraction products targeting niche tourism markets	Fragmented marketing approach
Natural tourism resources	Limited financial resources
Rich cultural history	Poor infrastructure (for example, transport, accommodation, hospitality)
Novelty value of visiting Eastern Europe	Lack of service standards and quality benchmarks
Target markets ➤ Short breaks market ➤ Touring vacations ➤ Affluent couples and independent travellers	Management of the economic, social and environmental impacts of tourism Seasonality Encouraging repeat visits

Table 5: Opportunities and Challenges for Attraction Development in Eastern Europe
Source: Dale and Robinson, 2004

Stevens (2003) puts forward a number of trends relating to tourist attractions that have already emerged in North America and Western Europe and are anticipated to impact globally over the next decade. Firstly, the emergence of a new 'geography of destination' attractions, which are developed in partnership with other sectors of business and tourism, such as those funded by the CTC (Canadian Tourism Commission) that is described as a "unique public/private sector partnership ... that delivers and funds marketing and research initiatives in partnership with provincial and regional tourism associations, government agencies, hotel-keepers, tour operators, airlines and attractions' managers" (Small Business BC, 2005. p. 14). The on-line guide offers advice in particular for potential small and medium sized enterprise (SME) developers. Secondly, the creation of all-inclusive, multi-faceted, year round destination attractions, such as Las Vegas and the Canary Islands, targeted at different markets simultaneously; to suggest that. Stevens (2003) argues that this kind of attraction development is crucial to [Central and] Eastern European economies seeking to use tourism as a catalyst for the regeneration of redundant land stock and for the benefit of local communities.

Thirdly, the closer integration of shopping and entertainment as a core feature of the attraction product. Fourthly, due to the further private capital investment in destination attractions, there will be the need for the professionalisation of the attraction sector and its management approach. The latter will result in a number of destination management companies (DMCs) operating on a global basis. Central and Eastern European countries should utilise these DMCs for positioning themselves relative to their global competitors and for communicating their brand image to target markets. With the lack of economic resources at the disposal of many of the smaller independent states, such as Estonia and Latvia, a joint marketing effort would generate a positive "imagescape" (Wanhill, 2003a) for the region as a whole. A collective brand identity is, to some extent, already apparent but its focus needs to be centred on a core set of attraction products that will act as a catalyst to further tourism and infrastructure development in surrounding areas. Joint ventures and promotion require a well-coordinated approach by the public and private sector in the management and marketing of the diversity of attractions as a coherent whole. For example, England (in partnership with the national tourist boards in Northern Ireland, Scotland and Wales) is marketed under the brand "Visit Britain" (http://www.visitbritain.org) which acts as a honeypot to attract inbound tourism into the country. Further marketing efforts are then devolved locally to the private and public sector to attract tourists to the respective destination attractions. Though this approach can be fragmented, it enables greater marketing control and facilitates competitiveness amongst the individual attractions than would be possible if either sector tried to operate alone.

In terms of Wanhill's (2003a) market-imagescape mix as presented earlier, Central and Eastern European countries are advised to begin by developing their existing 'me-too attractions' which include their city culture and heritage where there is high density of available accommodation and relatively good transport links. Cultural and heritage attractions might be developed with relative ease into 'new-version attractions' in different locations, particularly heritage attractions which are based upon the common cultural and political heritage of the former communist states and which have the potential to be themed. Such innovative developments can have great potential in terms of their cultural and historical interest for Western visitors. The entrepreneurial spirit of Central and Eastern Europeans also needs to be nurtured to enable the growth of 'Grand inspiration' attractions that can act as a flagship enterprise for further tourism development, maybe in the form of small-scale, sport tourism entertainment events such as the European Football Championships or the European Athletic Championships. Though the initial requisite financial investment is likely to be fairly significant, the resulting regeneration of local areas and the remaining infrastructure can act as a catalyst for further economic development. "Wonder attractions" also require substantial economic investment and are often built on a large scale in order to offer a variety of experiences to a diversity of visitor types. Therefore, this type of attraction development may be realistically beyond the present reach of the majority of Central and Eastern European countries. Nevertheless, all of these developments are dependent on a satisfactory and acceptable transport and accommodation infrastructure and the free movement of people through independent states without visa restrictions.

The Future

The successful development of Central and Eastern Europe's attractions and entertainment infrastructure is dependent upon the creation of a product which is at least comparable with that of Western European countries. Furthermore, the rising expectations of the target markets of short break and touring vacationers, which Central and Eastern European countries are attracting, demand standards that are commensurate with their own country of origin. Therefore, the particular challenge for these is being able to deliver a tourist attraction and entertainment product based upon the highest standards of service provision, quality and continuity which are essential for the development of a sustainable tourism industry. In addition, Central and Eastern European countries will have to confront and develop strategies to minimise the consequences of operating in a seasonal industry (Goulding, 2003) and will need to encourage repeat visits to their visitor attractions (Wanhill, 2003b) once the novelty value of travelling to Central and Eastern Europe has subsided. Thus, Central and Eastern Europe need to embark on a co-ordinated and strategic approach to the development and marketing of its visitor attraction product, embracing the diversity of attractions that they have to offer to ensure their ongoing appeal to international markets. In line with the above comments, it is clear that whilst Western travellers seek reinforcement of the 'norm', in terms of quality and service provision, it is of paramount importance that entertainment specifications are comparable with alternative competing tourism providers. In conclusion, all attractions and entertainment provision should be planned, centred on a long-term developmental model, have strategies in place to aid and facilitate fiscal advancement and, at the same time, enhance the lives and standards of living for host providers.

Student Activities

1. Select and research two attractions in two contrasting Central or Eastern European countries (or other geographical areas as appropriate). You can use Internet search engines to find relevant information on the attractions.

2. Using Table 2, identify the nature of the attractions.

3. How would you classify the attractions based upon Leask's (2003) Classification of Visitor Attractions (Figure 2)? Are they natural or built? Are they free or paid? Are they publicly or privately owned? Are they targeted at local, regional, national or International markets?

4. Apply the Wanhill (2003a) attraction market-imagescape mix to both attractions. What implications does this pose for the development and management of the attractions?

5. Conduct a SWOT analysis (see below) for each attraction. How closely do these attractions reflect the opportunities and challenges presented in Table 5?

6. Make recommendations on the development of both attractions considering the issues of target markets, promotion, improving service quality, encouraging repeat visits, countering seasonality and obtaining funding sources.

SWOT analysis A SWOT or SWTO (**S**trengths; **W**eaknesses, **O**pportunities; **T**hreats) analysis is a simple structured approach to evaluating information to produce a systematic appraisal of a strategy, a place, an individual, a group, a business, research findings et al. It is often used in strategic (long-term) planning to evaluate a destination prior to the formulation of a development plan. The analysis is completed by gathering data in four areas:

Strengths: Advantages in terms of positive features such as product, location, skills, competences, funding/costs etc. which may form the basis of future recommendations, decision making, framework development, planning.

Weaknesses: Disadvantages, current or potential problems which require action, assistance or training to remove them or to minimise their impact. Costs need to be considered in this context.

Opportunities: May occur in relation to shifts in external environment; routes to exploitation of strengths.

Threats: May be economic or political, internal or external, source may be people or situations (For example, competitors, lack of investment capital).

References

Arefyev, V. and Mieczkowski, Z. (1991). International Tourism in the Soviet Union in the Era of Glasnost and Perestroika, *Journal of Travel Research*, Vol. 29, No.4 pp. 2-6.

Burns, P. (1998). Tourism in Russia: Background and Structure, *Tourism Management*, Vol. 19, No. 6, pp. 555-565.

Cooper, C. Fletcher, J. Gilbert and D. Wanhill, S. (1998). *Tourism Principles and Practice*, Longman, London.

Dale, C. and Robinson, N. (1999). Bermuda, Tourism and the Visiting Cruise Sector: Strategies for Sustained Growth, *Journal of Vacation Marketing*, Vol. 5, No.4. pp. 333-339.

Factbook.net (2000). *Bulgaria country commercial guide for the year 2001*, [on-line] available from: http://www.factbook.net/countryreports/bu/Bu_Tourism.htm, [accessed March 18th 2005).

Goulding, P. (2003). Seasonality: The Perennial Challenge for Visitor Attractions. In A. Fyall, B. Garrod and A. Leask, *Managing Visitor Attractions: New Directions*, Butterworth-Heinemann, Oxford, pp. 140-158.

Hall, D. (1990). The Changing Face of Tourism in Eastern Europe, *Town and Country Planning*, Vol. 59, Issue 12, pp. 348-351.

Hall, D. (1991). Tourism and economic development in Eastern Europe and the Soviet Union, Belhaven Press, London.

Hall, D. (1992). The Challenge of International Tourism in Eastern Europe, *Tourism Management*, Vol. 13, No.1, pp. 41-44.

Hall, D. (1998). Central and Eastern Europe: Tourism, Development and Transformation. In A. Williams and G. Shaw (eds.) *Tourism and Economic Development: European Experiences*, 3rd edn., John Wiley & Sons, Chichester, pp. 345-374.

http://www.disneyinternational.com.

http://www.jorvik-viking-centre.co.uk/trialsplash2.htm.

http://www.royal.gov.uk.

http://www.visitbritain.org.

http://www.whisky-heritage.co.uk.

http://www.sciencemuseum.org.uk.

http://www.lake-district.gov.uk.

http://www.cannockchasedc.gov.uk/museum.

http://www.nmgw.ac.uk/bigpit.

http://www.ba-londoneye.com.

http://www.edenproject.com.

http://www.bermudatourism.com.

http://www.vegas.com.

http://www.liverpool.gov.uk.

http://www.dublin.ie.

http://www.red2000.com/spain/Pamplona/fest.html [accessed January 25th 2005].

Hughes, H. (2000). *Arts, Entertainment and Tourism*, Butterworth Heinemann, Oxford, pp. 13-14.

Keeley, J. (2000). *Life in the Hitler Youth*, Lucent Books, San Diego, CA.

Leask, A. and Yeoman, I. (1999). *Heritage Visitor Attractions: An Operations Management Perspective*, Cassell, London.

Leask, A. (2003). The Nature and Purpose of Visitor Attractions. In A. Fyall, B. Garrod, and A. Leask, *Managing Visitor Attractions: New directions*, Butterworth-Heinemann, Oxford, pp. 5-15.

Morgan, N., Pritchard, A. and Pride, R. (2002). *Destination Branding: Creating the unique destination proposition*, Butterworth-Heinemann, Oxford.

Small Business BC (2005). *Destination resort: business sourcing guide,* [on-line] available from: www.smallbusinessbc.ca/pdf/resort.pdf [accessed March 18th 2005].

Stevens, T. (2003). The Future of Visitor Attractions. In A. Fyall, B. Garrod and A. Leask, *Managing Visitor Attractions: New Directions,* Butterworth-Heinemann, Oxford, pp. 284-298.

Swarbrooke, J. (2000). *The Development and Management of Visitor Attractions*, Butterworth-Heinemann, Oxford.

Wanhill, S. (2003a). Interpreting the Development of the Visitor Attraction Product. In A. Fyall, B. Garrod and A. Leask, *Managing Visitor Attractions: New directions*, Butterworth-Heinemann, Oxford, pp. 16-35.

Wanhill, S. (2003b). Economic Aspects of Developing Theme Parks. In A. Fyall, B. Garrod and A. Leask, *Managing Visitor Attractions: New Directions*, Butterworth-Heinemann, Oxford, pp. 29-57.

Suggested Further Reading

http://www.roughguides.com/.

http://www.hadrianswall.com/.

http://www.londontourist.org/.

http://www.attractions.com/.

Beaver, A. (2002). *A Dictionary of Travel and Tourism Terminology.* CABI Publishing, Oxon, UK.

Richards, G. (2001). *Cultural Attractions and European Tourism*. CABI Publishing, Oxon, UK.

Shackley, M. (2000). *Visitor Management,* Butterworth-Heinemann, Oxford.

Vospitannik, N., Littlejohn, D. and Arnot, R. (1997). Environments, Tourism and Tour Operators: 1985-1995 in Central and Eastern Europe, *International Journal of Contemporary Hospitality Management,* Vol. 5, No. 5/6, pp. 209-214.

Chapter Seven

Health Tourism: new opportunities for destination development

Philippa Hunter-Jones

Overview

The objectives of this chapter are to explain the meaning of health tourism, to classify different types of health tourist, to compare the significance of health tourism around the world and to consider the current and future opportunities for health tourism development in Central and Eastern Europe. The term health tourism is often used interchangeably with spa tourism, thermal tourism and health-care tourism. Existing definitions frequently include reference to health facilities and natural resources such as mineral springs and spas. Four types of health tourist can be identified: tourists seeking a rest from illness (respite); tourists seeking recovery from illness (recuperation); tourists seeking to enhance their general wellbeing (prevention); tourists seeking a holiday experience with health needs of secondary significance (incidental). Health tourism promotion worldwide is not uniform. Germany, Italy, France, the USA, Canada, the Caribbean and Israel provide examples of established health tourism destinations. In Central and Eastern Europe the situation is less clear cut for whilst Hungary and the Czech Republic are already capitalising upon the market, places such as Slovakia, Bulgaria, Poland and the former Soviet Union remain to be discovered. Financing and public sector support are keys to the future development of health tourism in such destinations.

Introduction

To survive within an increasingly competitive marketplace, tourism destinations need to search constantly for new markets, often captured through the promotion of new or niche tourism products. The health-tourism relationship offers one such opportunity for destinations upon which to capitalise. Yet, despite having roots within many of the earliest forms of tourism, this relationship is currently one of the least understood areas of tourism demand. Part of the reason for this situation is that understanding the meaning of health is complex. Two common approaches to defining health exist: *negative definitions; and positive definitions. Negative* definitions are those which relate to *the absence of* disease or illness whilst *positive* definitions are reflected through *the presence of* certain qualities, physical and mental fitness for instance (Aggleton, 1990). Traditionally, the negative end of the health spectrum has been the most extensively documented. Today, however, a consensus is emerging that health should be acknowledged as a positive concept emphasising social and personal resources as well as physical capacities. Many of the original contributions of the World Health Organisation (WHO) are founded in this belief including the frequently quoted WHO definition of health, documented in the constitution of the Organisation (WHO, 1948, p100): "Health is a complete state of mental, physical and social wellbeing and not merely the absence of disease or infirmity".

The most commonly reported area of the health-tourism relationship, and the focus of this chapter, relates to the health tourism product. Such a product has been linked traditionally and quite specifically to the presence of mineral springs and spa activities and socially to the leisured elite (see for example Goodrich and Goodrich, 1987; 1991; 1994; Hall, 1992; Horner and Swarbrooke, 1998; Smith and Jenner, 2000). Yet the narrowness of such an interpretation is problematic. To date, only a limited proportion of tourists have been recognised and hence classified as health tourists and only a limited number of destinations have been in a position to take advantage of marketing themselves to this growth sector of tourism activity. This chapter aims to extend the debate. Initially it provides an overview of the range of definitions and products associated with health tourism. Next the health tourism consumer is considered alongside the supply of related activities. Utilising case studies from a range of destinations, the chapter concludes by outlining the key factors which support the future development of this market with particular reference to Central and Eastern Europe.

Health, Leisure and Tourism Inter-Relationships

In the developed world the nature of ill-health is changing. In developed countries, degenerative or life style diseases are now much more common than infectious diseases such as tuberculosis which have been associated previously with epidemics. Life style diseases can give rise to a distinct range of medical problems including obesity, heart disease, anxiety and depression, with poorer psychological health in general extending throughout populations. To accommodate such changes, responses to ill-health have evolved. Alongside traditional treatments a range of therapies, including alternative, complementary and supportive therapies have taken on increasingly prominent roles. Many examples link improvements in health to leisure pastimes. Such studies refer to both *active* and *passive* leisure pastimes.

Active: The Royal College of Physicians (1991), investigating the medical aspects of exercise, provided evidence demonstrating the influence of exercise on good health and in the treatment of some diseases and disabilities.

Passive: Studies focusing upon passive leisure pastimes (see for example Forgas and Moylan, 1987; Hull, 1990; Driver, Brown and Peterson, 1991) have indicated that leisure experiences induce positive moods, improve cognitive functioning in humans, especially the elderly, reduce depression, improve self esteem and self concept and can have a beneficial effect upon various medical problems commonly associated with the sedentary lifestyles of modern industrialised society, for example, hypertension, obesity, diabetes, anxiety and asthma.

Holiday-taking has also long been recognised as having a positive role to play in enhancing health and wellbeing. The health tourism product provides one example of this relationship incorporating both active and passive leisure pursuits.

Health Tourism Product

There is no single clear-cut definition of the health tourism product. Definitions often reflect stages of product evolution with distinctions frequently made between *health tourism, spa tourism, thermal tourism and health-care tourism.* Ultimately the term health tourism is used as an umbrella term incorporating each of these different products.

Health Tourism: The International Union of Official Tourist Organisations (IUOTO) (now subsumed in the World Tourism Organisation (WTO)) provides a narrow definition of health tourism: "the provision of health facilities utilising the natural resources of the country, in particular mineral water and climate" (IUOTO, 1973, p. 7). This definition was extended subsequently by Mathieson and Wall (1982) to include rest homes and health farms. Van Sliepen's classification is much broader: "(1) staying away from home, (2) health [as the] most important motive, and (3) done in a leisure setting" (cited in Goeldner, 1989, p. 7).

Spa Tourism: "Spa. A Belgium town that has given its name to health resorts around the world" (Starr and Norwood, 1996, p. 199). In contrast, Wightman and Wall (1985, p. 395) opt for a more general approach: "Spa ... a thermal or cold mineral spring that has been exploited for medical or recreational purposes ... range in size and reputation...". A common feature of research in this area is to define a spa by the mineral content evident. Sodium, calcium, magnesium, carbon, sulphur, iodine and iron are often found to play a central role. Aside from this, it is the United States America (USA) based International Spa Association (ISPA) definition of spa tourism which is particularly useful. This latter definition differentiates amongst seven different categories of spa: club; cruise ship; day; destination; medical; mineral springs; resort/hotel (see Table 1).

The International Spa Association Definition of Spa Tourism

Club Spa

A facility whose primary purpose is fitness and which offers a variety of professionally administered spa services on a daily-use basis.

Cruise Ship Spa

A spa aboard a cruise ship providing professionally administered spa services and spa cuisine (healthy eating) menu choices.

Day Spa

A spa offering a variety of professionally administered spa services to clients on a daily use basis.

Destination Spa

A spa whose sole purpose is to provide guests with lifestyle improvement and health enhancement through professionally administered spa services, physical fitness and training courses on a full-board, live-in basis. Generally only spa-cuisine is available.

Medical Spas

Where an individual or group of medical and spa professionals has set up a spa, the primary purpose of which is to provide comprehensive medical and wellness care in an environment which integrates spa services, as well as conventional and complementary therapies and treatments.

Mineral Springs Spa

A spa offering an on-site source of natural mineral, thermal or seawater, for use in hydrotherapy treatments.

Resort/Hotel Spa

A spa located within a resort or hotel, providing professionally administered spa services, fitness and wellness programmes and spa cuisine menu choices.

Table 1: The International Spa Association Definition of Spa Tourism
Source: Smith and Jenner (2000, pp. 42-43)

Thermal Tourism: Becheri (1989) argues that a broader concept of health tourism exists which includes thermal spring tourism as an integral component. Such a tourism form may include massage centres, health clubs and centres, fitness, marine therapies, diet therapies and physiotherapies, beauty treatments, detoxicating treatments, sports and exercise, steam bath, hydrotherapies, health education and relaxation techniques (Hall, 1992).

Health-Care Tourism: is suggested to provide an alternative to medical treatment offering positive side effects, such as relaxation and enjoyment coupled with the holiday experience. It is defined by Goodrich and Goodrich (1991, p. 107) as: "the attempt on the part of a tourist facility (for example, hotel) or destination (for example, Baden, Switzerland) to attract tourists by deliberately promoting its health-care services and facilities, in addition to its regular tourist amenities. These health-care services may include medical examinations by qualified doctors and nurses at the resort or hotel, special diets, acupuncture, injections, vitamin-complex intakes, special medical treatments for various diseases such as arthritis, and herbal remedies".

Health Tourism Consumer

Reasons why people visit a health tourism location differ widely and have been shown to change over time. Following the Industrial Revolution, for instance, many Western European countries (West Germany, Austria, France, Italy etc) promoted the development of *egalitarian healing centres* where certain health treatments (spa-related) were incorporated into the health service obligations of the country. More recently, societal trends indicate a shift in patterns of health resort consumption from health to pleasure: "the tide appears to be turning against the traditional spa [i.e. based on natural mineral springs], as the US concept of spa (see Table 2) becomes ever more popular among customers, doctors and health insurers" (Smith and Jenner, 2000, p. 41). These authors argue that unless the international marketplace recognises and reacts to this shift in emphasis, in the long term, traditional spas will lose their market share to the 'health and fitness' consumption which emerged strongly in the early part of the twenty-first century. Such a widening of the health tourism consumer base suggests that today four types of health tourist can be identified:

> ➢ Those seeking *respite*, (an interval of rest or change during illness), intent upon discovering alternative treatments for ailments alongside a desire for relaxation within the holiday environment

> ➢ Those seeking *recuperation*, (to recover from illness), motivated by the need to treat a specific ailment, rheumatism for instance

> ➢ Those seeking *prevention*, (to avoid illness by maintaining and/or enhancing fitness), utilising health tourism related products to enhance health and fitness without any reference to a specific ailment

> ➢ Those seeking a holiday where any health issues are secondary, *incidental*, to the holiday experience

It is clear that none of the above depends necessarily upon the resources of any specific destination. Consequently such categories present an increasing range of destinations with an expanding number of consumers to target. Those destinations able to offer the springs and spas traditionally associated with health tourism may well benefit from an additional market advantage and be better equipped to deal with changing consumer preferences than those without such natural resources.

Saratoga Springs, USA	
Location:	New York State, USA
Population:	25, 000
Area:	2, 000 acres (State Park)
Spas first opened to the public:	1935
Current Spas:	Roosevelt Baths
	Lincoln Baths
	Crystal Spa
Current Target Market:	Respite
	Recuperation
	Prevention
	Incidental

The Saratoga Springs Commission, prompted by the New York State Authority, placed Saratoga Spa under medical supervision for the first time in 1932. Through legislation, money was appropriated to develop the spa for medical purposes. Designation was founded on a scientific study which had investigated the various health attributes the mineral waters offered and concluded that they could provide a source of health and wellbeing for the population of New York State and beyond. Research programmes into the health attributes of the spa began with an investigation into the effects of the waters upon blood pressure and continued with a range of initiatives for a period of approximately 20 years. In the initial stages, the development was encouraged by the Jewish community, many of whom had emigrated from Europe where spa therapy enjoyed an established tradition. During the 1930s through to the 1950s the spa was seen to be a place of all round therapy consisting of the natural therapeutic agents found in the area, drink halls, fountains and bath houses, with facilities for physical exercise such as gradual walks, golf courses and tennis courts part of the spa therapy. Such thinking remains the case today, even during a period of decline, with continuing integration of the mineral waters, recreation and entertainment facilities considered essential for health and wellbeing.

Table 2: Saratoga Springs, USA
Source: Adapted from Swanner (1998)

Destination Case Studies

Studies detailing the supply of health tourism facilities have tended to concentrate upon both the locations offering health-tourism facilities (see Goodrich and Goodrich, 1991; Gilbert and Weerdt, 1991; Smith and Jenner, 2000) and the type of facilities on offer (see Bywater, 1990; Bacon, 1997). Marked differences between continents can be identified with the European industry, specifically that located in Western Europe, being the most dominant in the global marketplace.

Gilbert and Weerdt (1991) examine the *health-care* tourism products of the principal countries of Western Europe, tabling the product on offer country by country. Three groups of health-care products are identified: the classical health-care product; the specialised health-care product; the remise en forme product (developed by the French in the 1970s). Such products include medical check-ups, special diets, vitamin-complex treatments, herbal remedies, hydrotherapy, and balneotherapy. Germany has a formalised, relatively well developed *health-care* tourism industry. The German Kur *(taking a cure)* industry operates four main types of health resort:

> *Kneipp Kurorte* based on the Kneipp (Sebastian Kneipp (1821-1897)) treatment, is characterised by alternating warm and cold hydrotherapeutic applications which are found to strengthen and improve the body's own immunity system

> *Mineral und Moorheilbader* are mineral water and mud treatments

> *Heilklimatische Kurorte* treatment is based on the therapeutic properties of the climate

> *Seeheilbader* treatments are based on sea-water, seaweed and the sea climate and are also referred to as thalassotherapy

In each instance mineral springs and waters are central to the product, with consumption motivated significantly by health factors.

In contrast to Germany, the mineral springs and spas of North America have experienced a decline since the turn of the century with many established businesses losing public favour. Today the better known mineral springs may be found at Saratoga Springs, New York State (see Table 2), Hot Springs, Arkansas and French Lick, Indiana. Research conducted by Wightman and Wall (1985) considered Radium Hot Springs, a spa developed originally by English businessmen to serve the needs of tourists, situated on the western slope of the Rocky Mountain in British Columbia, Canada. Analysing spa consumption over five time periods in relation to the environment, strategies and institutions, perceptions and attitudes and technology these authors demonstrate that Western Canadian spas share similar traits to US spas. Resource based activities such as camping, hiking, horse riding, fishing and skiing, in contrast to urban attractions, are one of the key distinguishing features of Canadian spas.

According to Goodrich (1994, p230), "...Caribbean Islands (...) such as Cuba, Jamaica, St Lucia and the Bahamas also have mineral springs and health resort facilities". Goodrich (1994) during 1990 and 1991, researched the concept of health tourism via interview and content analysis of brochures. Key research findings indicated that only seven Caribbean resorts were found to advertise health facilities to tourists (specifically through brochures and booklets). Facilities advertised included body wraps, massages, sauna, weight room, facials, beauty salon, special diets for weight loss, and workshops on health and nutrition. Primary tourist users tended to be younger adults between the ages of 25 and 45 years old, white, and predominantly from the USA. Furthermore it was suggested that the concept had spread to many cruise lines hopping between the Islands, indicating the growth of the industry not just on a geographical basis but also on an industry sector basis.

Further afield, interest in Israel's health tourism industry has been considerable. The rapid growth in the *health-cure industry* is linked to the discovery that minerals from certain quarries and springs have special properties which can cure or ease the symptoms of various ailments. Health resorts have been established in two main geographic regions: (i) Dead Sea; and (ii) Tiberius and Kinneret. The healing properties of the Dead Sea, the saltiest body of water in the world, are often a focus for attention: "the Dead Sea for psoriasis and related conditions ... rheumatism and other arthritic conditions ... The relaxing air, the hundreds of other patients who tell of their success in controlling their disease ... provide 'group therapy'" (Bar-On, 1989, p. 13-14). Recognition of the economic potential of the health industry has led to the setting up of a network of balneological centres and special tour packages in Israel which combine medical treatments of various kinds, tours around the country and recreation. Such a package is perceived to be of benefit to psychological wellbeing offering cure-seeking visitors the feeling of a real vacation while attending to health matters.

Central and Eastern Europe

The situation in Central and Eastern Europe is less clear-cut. Currently some parts of the region are benefiting significantly from health tourism whilst other parts remain to be 'discovered'. The development of the health tourism industry in Hungary is comparable to many found in Western Europe: "the promotion of the medicinal baths in Budapest and the associated development of a range of health hotels in the city has opened up the market for tourism in Budapest as a whole" (Horner and Swarbrooke, 1998, p. D43). Here health hotels exist which provide both traditional 'medicinal' services such as drinking the 'cure', dentistry, specialist internal and rheumatological examinations and also health services promoting feelings of wellbeing such as refreshing massage, mud pack and electrotherapy. The Czech Republic in resorts such as Karlovy Vary (Carlsbad), Marienbad and Podébrady and to a lesser extent Slovakia (For example see http://www.sunflowers.sk/index-en.php) are also beginning to tap this market. However, in many remaining parts of Central and Eastern Europe the potential for development has yet to be recognised. Destinations such as Bulgaria, Poland and the former Soviet Union, for instance, despite having the advantage of natural springs and spas are currently failing to make the transition from focusing upon treating the local community to attracting the domestic and international health tourism market.

In Bulgaria, the health resorts of Velingrad and Sandanski currently operate a closed, traditional approach to health tourism offering services, primarily to the local population, which would be classified elsewhere as 'health tourism' services. Velingrad resort for example, 140 kilometres away from the capital Sofia, is known for over 70 mineral springs. Conditions treated include:

> Functional and neurological disorders of the locomotory system, for example, rheumatism

> Diseases of the nervous system, for example, stress

> Disease of the respiratory system, for example, bronchitis, asthma

> Other conditions, for example, skin complaints and allergies

In addition, the town is equipped with two medical centres providing a range of treatments including hydrotherapy, massage, acupuncture. Sandanski resort, 160 kilometres away from Sofia, also contains approximately 20 mineral springs located in two regions. Conditions treated are similar to those treated at Velingrad, classified into the same areas. This resort has one medical centre.

Poland has a wealth of natural mineral springs and spas many of which have a considerable history of state support. However the practice of encouraging employment contracts which included welfare clauses that entitled workers to spend specified periods of time at spas in order to relax and refresh the mind and body is now no longer in place. The impact of this appears to be twofold. Firstly, the consumer loses out as such activities were commonly recognised as making a valuable contribution to health and wellbeing. Secondly, the spas themselves suffer as they no longer have a defined market, instead needing to commercialise their facilities in order to survive.

Detailing the changing fortunes of spas in the former Soviet Union, Oddy (1999) noted that by 1990, 2,500 sanatoria existed in the former Soviet Union, many equipped with hydrotherapy rooms, mineral baths alongside a range of 'cures'. Under the former political system such facilities were accessible to the whole population via government policy and trade union subsidies. As such, the practice is no longer widespread; today many exist in variable states of disrepair. Those that have survived, Mishkor Sanatorium near Yalta for instance, have done so with the continuing support of trade union subsidies, although such examples are the exception rather than the rule.

Conclusions

The evolution of health tourism to date has been assisted by many factors including improvements in transportation and accommodation "...more convenient travel and accommodation have made the spas, seaside resorts, and mineral springs more accessible to the expanding population of travellers" (Babcock, 1983, p. 230) and a more open acceptance of the contribution 'holistic' medicine may make to a healthy life. Opportunities exist to extend the recognised health tourism map further into Central and Eastern Europe. For such destinations to make the transition to successful international health tourism destinations certain support factors need to be in place. Significantly there are two inter-related factors which underpin health tourism success elsewhere: financing and public sector support.

The financing of spas and health resorts worldwide varies from destination to destination. Some spas are owned publicly and financed by a local spa authority whilst others are part of the commercial sector, often linked to hotels. In Italy, Gilbert and Weerdt (1991) found approximately 160 hotels had their own treatment sections in the region of Abano and Montegrotto and, in each resort, a spa association which receives funds from the Government and often additional funding from local hotel associations or mineral water industries. In France it is the government funded Chambres de Commerce who assist frequently in the construction and development of spas whilst thalassotherapy centres are often run in conjunction with large hotels. In the former West Germany, approximately 80% of the spas were community run (wholly-owned by the local authority), 10% were operated by the state (owned by the state but operated as a separate company) and 10% by the private sector (limited companies) (Gilbert and Weerdt, 1991). Further a field, Wightman and Wall (1985) found the Canadian federal government playing a major entrepreneurial role at Radium Hot Springs. Here policy dictated that recreational facilities should be available at low cost, that the use of the springs should be subject to a small fee and that inexpensive accommodation should be available to accommodate a wider range of tourists.

In most developed societies, governments provide substantial subsidised medical care and health services. Tourism is recognised generally as being beneficial to health. Yet public sector support, at an individual level, through a health tourism industry varies from country to country. Bar-On (1989) and Mesplier-Pinet (1990) document the financial assistance with treatment offered by *some* governments as a component of the health service delivery. Austria, Belgium, Denmark, Germany and the Netherlands, as well as Israel, are cited as countries whose governments cover most or all of the costs for suitable patients to be treated at spas and health resorts, in some cases paying also for a parent to accompany a child. Such support, traditionally evident also in areas of Central and Eastern Europe, is currently under threat. For such destinations to capitalise upon the opportunity presented by health tourism a fundamental change in the perception and promotion of health services within a tourism industry framework is necessary. Such a change will include the need for the present systems to be prepared to encourage and accommodate the international consumer market. Recognising the role that health tourism may play in the regional development of such destinations may help to substantiate the public sector support and financing necessary to underpin such developments.

Student Activities

Table 1 provides seven different categories of spa tourism.

1. In which countries/regions of the world might examples of each category be found?

2. Which type of health tourism consumer may each category be best placed to attract?

3. Select one category of spa tourism that you feel has the potential to be developed further in your chosen country. Discuss the opportunities for developing this type of spa tourism in a named destination of your choice.

References

Aggleton, P. (1990). *Health*, Routledge, London.

Babcock, J. (1983). *The Spa Book: A Tour of Health Resorts and Beauty Spas*, Crown Publishers, New York.

Bacon, W. (1997). The Rise of the German and the Demise of the English Spa Industry: A Critical Analysis of Business Success and Failure, *Leisure Studies*, Vol. 16, No 3, pp. 173-187.

Bar-On, R. (1989). Cost-Benefit Considerations for Spa Treatments, Illustrated by the Dead Sea, Israel, *Revue de Tourisme*, Vol. 44, No 4, pp. 12-15.

Becheri, E. (1989). From Thermalism to Health Tourism, *Revue de Tourisme*, Vol. 44, No 4, pp. 15-19.

Bywater, M. (1990). Financial Services/Leisure Industries. Spas and Health Resorts in the EC, *EIU Travel and Tourism Analyst*, No 6, pp. 52-67.

Driver, B. L., Brown, P. J. and Peterson, G. L. (eds.) (1991). *Benefits of Leisure*, Venture Publishing Inc, Pennsylvania.

Forgas, J. and Moylan, S. (1987). After the Movies: Transient Mood and Social Judgements, *Personality and Social Psychology Bulletin*, Vol. 13, pp. 478-489.

Gilbert, D.C. and Van De Weerdt, M. (1991). The Health Care Tourism Product in Western Europe, *Revue de Tourisme*, Vol. 46, No 2, pp. 5-10.

Goeldner, C. (1989). 39th Congress AIEST: English Workshop Summary, *Revue de Tourisme*, Vol. 44, No 4, pp. 6-7.

Goodrich, J. N. and Goodrich, G. E. (1987). Health-Care Tourism - An Exploratory Study, *Tourism Management*, Vol. 8, No 3, pp. 217-222.

Goodrich, J. N. and Goodrich, G. E. (1991). Health-Care Tourism In S. Medlik, (ed.) *Managing Tourism*, Butterworth-Heinemann, Oxford, pp. 108-114.

Goodrich, J. N. (1994). Health Tourism: A New Positioning Strategy for Tourist Destinations. In M. Uysal, (ed.) *Global Tourist Behavior*, Haworth Press, London, pp. 227-238.

Hall, C. M. (1992). Adventure, Sport and Health Tourism. In B. Weiler, and C. M. Hall, (eds.) *Special Interest Tourism*, Belhaven Press, London, pp. 141-158.

Horner, S. and Swarbrooke, J. (1998). The Health Tourism Market, *Insights. The Tourism Marketing Intelligence Service, BTA/ETB*, London.

http://www.sunflowers.sk/index-en.php.

Hull, R. (1990). Mood as a Product of Leisure: Causes and Consequences, *Journal of Leisure Research*, Vol. 22, pp. 99-111.

International Union of Official Tourist Organisations (IUOTO) (1973). *Health Tourism*, United Nations, Geneva.

Mathieson, A. and Wall, G. (1982). *Tourism. Economic, Physical and Social Impacts*, Longman Group Ltd, Essex.

Mesplier-Pinet, J. (1990). Thermalisme et Curistes: Les Contraintes, *Revue de Tourisme*, Vol. 45, No. 2, pp. 10-17.

Oddy, J. (1999). Soviet Sanatoriums, *The Independent Magazine*, November 6th, pp. 28-33.

Royal College of Physicians (1991). Medical Aspects of Exercise: Benefits and Risks, *Journal of the Royal College of Physicians*, Vol. 25, pp. 193-196.

Smith, C. and Jenner. P (2000). Market Segments: Health Tourism in Europe, *Travel and Tourism Analyst*, No 1, pp. 41-59.

Starr, N. and Norwood, S. (1996). *The Traveler's World. A Dictionary of Industry and Destination Literacy*, Prentice-Hall Inc, New Jersey.

Swanner, G. M. (1988). *Saratoga. Queen of Spas*, North Country Books, New York.

Wightman, D. and Wall, G. (1985). The Spa Experience at Radium Hot Springs, *Annals of Tourism Research*, Vol. 12, No 3, pp. 393-416.

World Health Organisation (WHO) (1948). *Constitution,* World Health Organisation, Geneva. Preamble to the Constitution of the World Health Organization as adopted by the International Health Conference, New York, 19-22 June, 1946; signed on 22 July 1946 by the representatives of 61 States (Official Records of the World Health Organization, No. 2, p. 100) and entered into force on 7 April 1948. [on line] available from: http://www.healthpromotion.act.gov.au/whatis/history/default.htm.

Suggested Further Reading

Douglas, N., Douglas, N. and Derrett, R. (eds.) (2001). *Special Interest Tourism*, Wiley, Chichester.

English Tourism Council (ETC) (2002). *Health Benefits Factfile*, English Tourism Council, London.

Hunter-Jones, P. (2000). Classifying the Health Tourism Consumer. In Robinson, M., Long, P., Evans, N., Sharpley, R. and Swarbrooke, J. (eds.) *Reflections on International Tourism: Motivations, Behaviour and Tourist Types*, Business Education Publishers, Sunderland, pp. 231-242.

http://www.experienceispa.com.

http://www.who.int/en/.

Chapter Eight
Developing Sustainable Tourism

Jarmila Indrová and Zdenka Petrů

Overview

Forecasts concerning the development of sustainable tourism from the present until 2020 anticipate continuing expansion with positive effects on national economies and regional development. However, apart from the positive effects, uncontrolled tourism developments are likely to have a negative effect on the environment. Therefore, it is essential to concentrate on issues pertaining to the sustainable development of tourism in all areas of management and to support environmentally friendly forms of tourism. The aim of this chapter is to underline the importance of sustainable tourism. The chapter provides some information about the major international organisations, whose expertise is sustainable development in general, and also reviews key documents concerned with problems of sustainable development in tourism. Definitions of specific forms of sustainable tourism such as agrotourism, ecotourism and ecoagrotourism are provided and particular attention is given to the attitudes of tourism enterprises to environmental protection. A case study outlines the findings from a pilot study in accommodation facilities in the Czech Republic. The framework for this research can be adapted and used for ecological audits of tourism industry enterprises in other countries.

Introduction

The issues of sustainable development started to appear in professional magazines and literature in the 1980s. Gradually, a number of other publications addressing this issue began to appear. With the evolution of the concept of sustainable development also came changes in the perception of economic development at not only regional but also national levels.

Sustainable development is now a global problem. For the past few years, national governments, non-government agencies and various civic organisations have all been trying to find the most appropriate, co-ordinated approach to resolving this problem, which is on the agendas of the meetings of many world-wide organisations. There exist numerous special commissions and agencies with agendas which focus on sustainable development; invariably, the conclusions from conferences and meetings suggest that sustainable development within societies comprises the interaction of economic, environmental and social aspects as indicated in Figure 1. In the implementation of this concept of sustainable development, it is therefore essential to take into account the cultural, legal and ethical principles that prevail in different countries.

The idea of upholding environmental principles in the development of different sectors of national economies is increasingly becoming a significant part of important documentation produced by world organisations; this issue is also a part of legislation in the majority of countries. "Agenda 21 is a comprehensive pln of action to be taken globally, nationally and locally by organizations of the

United Nations System, Governments, and Major Groups in every area in which humanity impacts on the environment" (United Nations, 2003). Listed below, in chronological order of their set up/founding, are some international organisations whose programmes include issues pertaining to sustainable development, particularly in the context of Agenda 21.

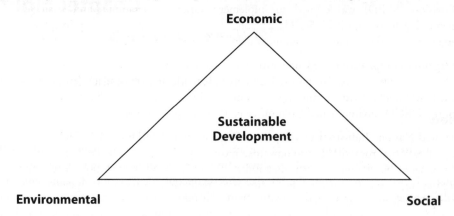

Figure 1: Sustainable Development
Source: European Commission, 2002, p.2

> **Food and Agriculture Organisation (FAO)** – founded in October 1945 with the main aim of reducing poverty and the malnutrition of people in developing countries. The principles of sustainable development provide the basis of most its activities. FAO acts as a co-ordinating agency in implementing a number of chapters of Agenda 21 (http://www.fao.org)

> **United Nations Educational, Scientific and Cultural Organisation (UNESCO)** – established in November 1945 and became an official agency in 1946. It may be said that issues dealing with sustainable development are to be found practically in all of the documents of this organisation. As regards tourism, it is worth mentioning, for example, the World Heritage Agreement with the aim of identifying and protecting unique cultural and natural sites. The organisation is involved in implementing a number of chapters of Agenda 21 (http://www.unesco.org)

> **World Meteorological Organisation (WMO)** – created in 1947 but did not commence operations until 1951. A large proportion of the WMO's activities are connected closely with the issues of sustainable development. The organisation is responsible for implementing several chapters of Agenda 21 (http://www.wmo.ch)

> **International Maritime Organisation (IMO)** – formally established in 1948 but, with the IMO Convention not coming into force until 1958, the organisation commenced operations in 1959. Principles of sustainable development are implemented in practice, particularly through the organisation's engagement in preventing pollution of the world's seas, which is also one of the aims of Agenda 21 (http://www.imo.org)

> **International Atomic Energy Agency (IAEA)** – started in 1956 but formally established in 1957. The concept of sustainable development is the underlying principle, particularly through projects for development aid. The agency is the author/co-ordinator of chapter 22 of Agenda 21 (*Safe and environmentally acceptable radioactive waste management*)(http://www.iaea.or.at)

➢ **United Nations Development Programme (UNDP)** – established in 1965. From the 1980s, particularly as a response to the conclusions of the 'Rio' conference in 1992. UNDP has engaged in the problems of human development focusing on the issues of sustainable development. Furthermore, its Sustainable Energy and Environment Division (SEED) was created to implement various programmes and strategies pertaining to the spirit of Agenda 21 and, also, to help to incorporate principles of Agenda 21 in the national development plans (http://www.undp.org)

➢ **Organisation for Economic Cooperation and Development (OECD)** – established in December 1961. A positive approach and attitude to sustainable development provides the basis for all activities of this organisation. Specific activities led to the establishment of the OECD Environmental Committee in 1970 (http://www.oecd.org)

➢ **United Nations Industrial Development Organisation (UNIDO)** – UNIDO was set up in 1966. From the 1980s onwards, most activities have been connected with sustainable development, with practically all of the UNIDO's major documents addressing this issue. The current resolutions respect Agenda 21 (http://www.unido.org)

➢ **United Nations Environment Programme (UNEP)** – created in autumn 1972 as a result of the resolution of the UN General Assembly. The aim of the programme is to assist with the development of international co-operation in caring for the environment. The activities of this organisation led to the acceptance of a number of global conventions and agreements. At present UNEP has a specific responsibility for implementing several chapters of Agenda 21 (http://www.unep.org)

➢ **United Nations Commission on Sustainable Development (CSD)** – created in 1992, CSD is a functional commission of the UN Economic and Social Council (ECOSOC) (http://www.un.org/esa/sustdev)

Other organisations with agendas related to sustainable development include:

➢ Council of Europe (CE) (http://www.coe.int)

➢ European Bank for Reconstruction and Development (EBRD) (http://www.ebrd.com)

➢ International Monetary Fund (IMF) (http://www.imf.org)

➢ International Union for Protection of Nature (IUCN) (http://www.iucn.org)

➢ North Atlantic Treaty Organisation (NATO) (http://www.nato.int)

➢ United Nations Economic Commission for Europe (UN ECE) (http://www.un.org/esa/sustdev/)

➢ World Bank (WB)(http://www-esd.worldbank.org/)

Non-governmental Organisations (NGOs)

There are also many non-governmental organisations that play increasingly important roles in promoting and enforcing rules pertaining to sustainable development in individual countries. Apart from their activities, which include consultation services and active involvement of their representatives at various conferences, NGOs are presently also increasing their political influence. Their present activities suggest that there is a significant shift in their role – from passive observers to active creators; to developers of proposals and to makers of recommendations. The most important NGOs' activities are under the umbrellas of organisations such as, for example:

> Friends of the Earth International: federation of independent environmental organisations of the world (http://www.foei.org)

> Greenpeace: organiser of international actions to protect environment (http://www.greenpeace.org)

> International Institute for Sustainable Development: advances policy recommendations to make development sustainable (http://www.iisd.org)

> National Councils for Sustainable Development: assist in enforcing principles of sustainable development on the national level (http://www.ncsdnetwork.org)

> Natural Resources Defence Council (NRDC): assist in protection of natural resources (http://www.nrdc.org)

> The Worldwatch Institute: conducts interdisciplinary research addressing global environmental issues and formulates proposals and suggestions for industry, agriculture and other sectors of national economy (http://www.worldwatch.org)

> World Wide Fund for Nature (WWF) – an organisation engaged in the protection of nature (http://www.wwf.org)

An essential part of the strategy for continuing improvement of the environment, and promoting principles of sustainable development in human society, is maintaining a high level of awareness of environmental conditions and issues among the general public by providing high quality information. A system of environmental indicators has been developed to implement this strategy. These indicators of environmental conditions and sustainable development have been developed at both international and national levels, with the national level considered to be the basic one. Apart from providing information to relevant bodies and organisations, this system also helps to provide support in the development of long-term national strategies, addressing the issues of environmental improvement and assisting with the regular assessment and evaluation of the implementation of these strategies. The system should also help to improve the quality of information required in adopting the short- and, particularly, long-term decisions concerning environmental issues at all levels of management.

The environmental indicators are divided into three categories: environmental; social; and economic. The indicators of sustainable development have been dealt with in numerous documents by global through to national and local organisations: worldwide documents (UN); European documents (OECD); national documents; and local documents. On the basis of the environmental indicators it is therefore possible to compare environmental situations and developments in different parts of the world. A list of environmental indicators may be found in Table 1.

Environmental	
Global agreements (1)	Emissions of greenhouse gasses (5)
Emissions of acidifying substances (9)	Emissions of solid particles (3)
Air quality (2)	Intensity of water use (3)
Water abstraction (4)	Biochemical oxygen demand in surface waters(2)
Phosphorus and nitrogen (3)	Waste water treatment (4)
Agricultural area and organic farming (4)	Use of fertilisers (4)
Use of agricultural pesticides (3)	Wood harvesting intensity (4)
Protected areas (3)	Threatened species (2)
Waste generation and treatment (5)	Hazardous waste generation and treatment (5)
Waste recycling (3)	Intensity of non-renewable resources mining (3)
Build-up area (3)	Total forest area by tree species (6)
Salvage [tree] fellings (2)	Expenditures for the environment conservation (4)
Social	
Unemployment rate (4)	Dependency ratio of non-working inhabitants (3)
Urban population (3)	Population density (3)
Life expectancy at birth (3)	Health expenditures (3)
Communication infrastructure (4)	Registered crimes (4)
Household expenditures (3)	Expenditure on research and development (5)
Economic	
Tourism (5)	Direct material consumption (5)
Passenger transport (5)	Gross domestic product (5)
Public debt (7)	Foreign debt (3)
Inflation rate (6)	Foreign trade balance (8)
Annual energy consumption (4)	Intensity of material use (4)

Table 1: Sustainable Development Indicators

Source: Ministry of Environment of the Czech Republic, 2002, p.1

Note: The number of sub-indicators in each indicator group is given in parentheses. Further detail may be found at: http://indikatory.env.cz/?main_group=IUR

Tourism and Sustainable Development

According to the World Tourism Organisation (WTO) forecast, it is anticipated that by 2010 the global number of international tourism arrivals will exceed 1 billion and that by 2020 this figure will increase to just over 1.56 billion (http://www.world-tourism.org/frameset/frame_ statistics.html). This 50% increase will have a massive impact on tourism development, which will require a sensitive approach to environmental protection on the part of all businesses involved in the industry. There is not just one definition of sustainable development, but quite a few. Typically, definitions of sustainable development stress the need for development that permits the use of currently available natural, economic and socio-cultural resources to meet the vital needs of present generations without compromising the ability of future generations to use those same resources to meet their needs (for example, http://europa.eu.int/comm/enterprise/services/tourism/studies/ecosystems/heritage.htm). This form of definition is related closely to recent perceptions of economic development that take into account the principles of environmental protection, at the same time aiming to minimise environmental pollution whilst preserving basic living standards. Increasingly, the principle of sustainable development is becoming an essential part of many international agreements, conventions or declarations, with the most important including the Rio Declaration on Environment and Development (www.un.org/documents/ga/conf151/aconf15126-1annex1.htm) – a plan defining a number of initiatives concerning the environmental protection adopted at the United Nations Conference on Environment and Development (UNCED) held in Rio de Janeiro in 1992. The Rio Declaration contains 27 principles of sustainable development defined by the World Commission on the Environment and Development[1] and Agenda 21 (http://www.un.org/esa/sustdev/agenda21.htm) which stresses the importance of economic, political, social and cultural aspects in relation to regional development.

Through time there have been other documents and materials dealing with the principles of sustainable development in relation to the regional development, including the publications such as, Studie Europa 2000+ (European Commission, 1997a; 1997b; 1997c), Directive for Sustainable Development Planning and Management (1996), The United Nations Istanbul Declaration (1996) and the European Spatial Development Perspective (2000). The concept of sustainable development has been afforded new dimensions with ecologically suitable economic development of a region being no longer the main factor. What is now also regarded as being equally important is balanced regional development. The economic requirements for regional development must be brought into harmony with the ecological and, in particular, the social and cultural functions of a given region. Therefore, the main aims of the European policy on sustainable development may be defined as follows:

➢   economic and social cohesion;

➢   conservation of natural resources and cultural heritage; and

➢   a more balanced competitiveness of the European regions.

Tourism plays an important role in regional development. However, it has to be said that the environmental impacts of tourism development had been underestimated for a long time. Initially, attention was concentrated on other industries such as mining, energy production, chemicals or agriculture. It was only the recent huge development of tourism as an industry, together with

---

[1] See Appendix 1 – *Report of the United Nations Conference on environment and development.*

increasing living standards in developed countries, that have brought about the necessity to deal with the problems of sustainability of the growth of tourism.

The Contributions of Tourism to Regional Development

Tourism creates new employment opportunities, either through the need to provide essential tourist services or other supporting services and makes a significant contribution to the development and growth of other industries, often described by academics as the 'multiplier effect' of the growth of tourism (See Chapter 10, p. 178 for further details).

> ➢ Income from tourism is an extremely important factor in the balance of payments of nations or regions or the other types of administration areas

> ➢ Tourism provides incentives for discovering other parts of the world, protecting the environment and cultural heritage; it aids the discovery and understanding of the mentality and habits of other nations and peoples, thereby promoting the idea of peace and peaceful coexistence

In contrast, the massive development of tourism as an industry in certain areas or regions can lead to destruction or damage to the preconditions for development in the regions, with negative effects including:

> ➢ increased environmental impact (for example, of the uncontrolled tourism, cyclotourism, new pistes or lifts in winter resorts) causing devastation of flora and fauna in a region

> ➢ increased pressure on the natural resources, i.e. increased water consumption, quantity of waste, pollution (for example, increased levels of exhaust fumes in protected natural areas or cities)

> ➢ increased noise or dust levels, which may antagonise the local population (http://europa.eu.int/comm/enterprise/services/tourism/studies/ecosystems/heritage.htm)

Considering the negative effects of tourism, it is inevitable that the problems of sustainable development must be addressed in the field of travel and tourism. The World Tourism Organisation (2001) defined a sustainable tourism development as meeting "the needs of present tourist and host regions while protecting and enhancing opportunities for the future. It is envisaged as leading to the management of all resources in such a way that economic, social and aesthetic needs can be fulfilled while maintaining cultural integrity, essential ecological processes, biological diversity and life support systems" (http://www.world-tourism.org/frameset/frame_sustainable.html). This definition implies that it is essential for tourism developers to plan for the reduction or, ideally, the elimination of the negative environmental effects of tourism. Furthermore, positive contributions to regional/local development, through the increased involvement of local population, should become a part of the concept of regional development. Local government agencies can make significant contributions in this respect by implementing the principles of Agenda 21. The local Agenda 21 initiatives were introduced by International Council for Local Environmental Initiatives (ICLEI), an international association founded at the World Congress of Local Governments for sustainable development in 1990 (http://www.iclei.org). Substantial support for national campaigns is provided also by several regional campaigns such as the European Campaign for Sustainable Towns and Cities which produced, among others, the Aalborg Chart that proposed a sustainable city development strategy. To provide methodological assistance to implement principles of Agenda 21 at local government level, the ICLEI issued a number of practical manuals based on the results of international research to establish methods and tools for the local Agenda 21 planning. These include, for example, The *Local Agenda 21 Planning Guide* or *An Introduction to Sustainable Development Planning*.

Environmentally Friendly Forms of Tourism

Environmentally friendly forms of tourism are those that do not cause environmental impact. The term 'green tourism' may be defined as an active form of tourism in open, natural and relatively sparsely populated areas that respects and protects natural environment (Indrová, Malá, Munzar, Patočka, Petrů, Ryšlavý, Slámová and Vaško, 1995). Western European examples of such highly specialised developments may be found in the Italian regions of Tuscany and Umbria, where guests can find hospitable, comfortable farm houses and feel in direct contact with nature. Specific forms of this type of tourism are referred to as 'ecotourism' and 'country tourism', which involves travel outside the main tourist centres, such as to colonies of weekend houses, villages or agricultural estates and farms (Indrová et al., 1995).

Ecotourism

In 1991 the International Ecotourism Society (p. 1) defined ecotourism as "responsible travel to natural areas that conserves the environment and improves the well-being of local people". In the same year, Ecotourism Australia was formed and has adopted the following definition: Ecotourism is: "ecologically sustainable tourism with a primary focus on experiencing natural areas that fosters environmental and cultural understanding, appreciation and conservation" (Ecotourism Australia, 2005, p. 1). The World Conservation Union (1996) maintained that: "Ecotourism is environmentally responsible travel and visitation to relatively undisturbed natural areas, in order to enjoy and appreciate nature (and any accompanying cultural features – both past and present), that promotes conservation, has low negative visitor impact, and provides for beneficially active socio-economic involvement of local populations." More specifically, ecotourism has been described as tourism or travel in natural areas, specifically nature reserves, national parks, protected areas or other natural sites that conserves the environment, i.e. areas with important and attractive natural sites such as landscapes and scenery with footpaths, cycle tracks and ski-tracks being in common usage for tourist transport (Paskova and Zelenka, 2002). Ecotourism is now a global concept with the implication that those persons who implement and participate in ecotourism activities should support local participation, ownership and opportunities and follow the following principles:

> ➤ Allow for the sharing of economic benefits with local community

> ➤ Build environmental and cultural awareness and respect

> ➤ Work towards the conservation of biodiversity

> ➤ Emphasise nature-based activities

> ➤ Include an interpretation/learning experience

> ➤ Stress the importance of responsible business

> ➤ Rely on an infrastructure that has been developed in harmony with the environment

> ➤ Minimise impact; require the lowest possible consumption of non-renewable resources

> ➤ Provide positive experiences for both visitors and hosts

> ➤ Provide direct financial benefits for conservation

> ➢ Provide financial benefits and empowerment for local people

> ➢ Raise sensitivity to host countries' political, environmental, and social climate

> ➢ Support international human rights and labour agreements

Adapted from The Institute of Ecotourism (2004, p. 1) and The International Ecotourism Society (2004, p. 1)

Country Tourism

The main form of country tourism is agrotourism, which includes a wide variety of activities, ranging from typical summer farm holidays or visits to 'wild-west' towns or fruit picking excursions to visits to specialised animal farms (for example, deer, ostrich or fish breeding farms). Agrotourism can mean different things to different people and for this reason there are various definitions of this type of tourism. Agrotourism (Paskova and Zelenka, 2002) is a specific form of country tourism characterised by the tourist's close relationship with countryside and the natural environment. It is ideal for family holidays as the provision of accommodation and catering on agricultural estates/farms allows visitors the hands-on experience of agricultural production or animal husbandry (especially horses which may be used for transport). The lodgings are owned and operated mostly by farmers and primary agricultural producers either as a main or subsidiary part of their business operations (i.e. agricultural production or animal husbandry) and their locations include agricultural estates, family farms and holiday homes (such as cabins, log-houses, cottages, converted barns and purpose-built holiday houses). The availability of their own products (for example, potatoes, milk, cheese, vegetables and fruit) and livestock allows operators to offer fresh, home-produced or local food (either for sale or as part of a package) and recipes to produce local country-style food dishes. Typical examples of agrotourism events include traditional harvest-time, pig-roasting or wine-picking feasts. Some visitors may take advantage of self-catering accommodation or eat in local restaurants and public houses. A special feature of agrotourism is education. The tourists move freely in a working agricultural environment which means that they have the opportunity to learn directly about the operation and maintenance of agricultural estates or farms by coming into contact with farm animals (such as cats, dogs, horses, cows, pigs, sheep, goats, poultry, etc.) and exploring agricultural buildings (for example, barns and stables) and working with or observing the operation of agricultural machinery and tools. Agrotourism is gathering strong support from small communities around the world as rural communities realise the benefits of sustainable development. Iakovidou and Turner (1995) commented on the role of the females in cooperatives in such tourism in Greece whilst recent developments include the setting up of local promotional companies such as the Cyprus Agrotourism Company (2004), which is supported by the Cyprus Tourism Organisation, who aim to attract visitors to the rural villages of Cyprus through websites. An example of such a successful project may be found in the basque region of Spain where argotourism led to an annual increase of 4% in visitor numbers and 16% in overnight stays in 2004 (Eustat, 2005).

A specific form of agrotourism is eco-agrotourism (Paskova and Zelenka, 2002), which is hosted on ecologically managed farms located in a healthy, natural environment and producing organic or organically grown food. The ecological or environment friendly farms do not use any synthetic chemicals and fertilisers, hormone-based agents, artificial food colouring or preservatives. Animals are kept in their natural environment and are not fed with any artificial or processed fodder. Products of environment friendly agriculture are subject to stringent controls. They must comply with the requirements of international standards and can use the official BIO trademark in the Czech Republic, which originated in 1993 (See Zidek, 2002). In typical eco-agrotourism schemes visitors live closely with the farming family, take part in the agricultural production process and consume the products of environmentally friendly agriculture. An example of a European initiative in this field may be found in the South Caucasus Cooperation Program (SCCP), which is a unique regional initiative established by the Eurasia Foundation in 1998 to facilitate greater contact and cooperation among leading organisations in Armenia, Azerbaijan and Georgia (See: http://www.eatsc.com/for_all/about_project.html). Its aims are to "promote the development of the interconnected eco-agrotourism Industry in the region, thus stimulating the progress of private businesses all over the territory of the Southern Caucasus" and to create a "common favourable image of the Southern Caucasus for the successful integration into the international Eco-agrotourism Community (p. 1). It is managed by staff in all three countries and "provides grassroots organisations in the Caucasus with financing to implement cross-border projects that address regional concerns. SCCP grants are awarded exclusively to support cross-border projects in three mandate areas:

1.   Private Enterprise Development

2.   Civil Society

3.   Public Policy Development" (The Eurasia Foundation, 2005, p. 1)

"Though Armenia, Azerbaijan, and Georgia share a geographically compact area, political conflicts and economic strife in the past decade have greatly diminished cross-border ties and relations. While reintegration at a state level remains dependent on a complicated array of political factors, it was argued that the re-establishment of cross-border contact and exchange between individuals and organisations could go a long way towards overcoming obstacles to regional stability and prosperity... Since the program's inception, SCCP has awarded over €3.474 million (4.458 million USD) in grants to support unique cross-border initiatives that address issues of concern to the entire region" (Eurasia Foundation, 2004, p. 1).

Approach and attitudes of tourism companies and businesses to environmental protection and sustainable development

There are many different companies and businesses providing specific services to the tourism industry. In particular, these are transport providers, airlines, travel and tourist agencies, accommodation facilities of different categories, catering businesses, tourist information centres, establishments operating heritage sites and sites of cultural importance, et al. Given the vast scope of this topic, it would be impossible to deal in this chapter with the approach and attitude of all the above agencies and businesses to environmental protection and sustainable development. As an example, the following case study focuses on the application of these principles in relation to accommodation and catering facilities.

Case Study:

The development of a framework for the construction of accommodation and catering facilities implementing the principles of environmental protection and sustainable development

Problems of sustainable development and practical guidelines for the operation of accommodation and catering facilities and businesses were not addressed and implemented to any significant degree until the mid-1990s. Gradually, a number of specific actions in this area were introduced in various countries including, for example:

> ➤ Green Hotelier & Restaurateur, an annual award for environmental management (1996) (http://www.greenhotelier.com/);

> ➤ Courtesy of Choice, a programme for support and designation of both smoking and non-smoking areas in hotels and restaurants (1996)(http://www.ih-ra.com/courtesy/);

> ➤ developing training programmes for students in hotel schools; and

> ➤ publishing professional literature to assist practical implementation of principles of sustainable tourism.

An important year in terms of providing a further boost to the implementation of the principles of sustainable tourism was 1999 when representatives of the Committee for Sustainable Development and the International Hotel & Restaurant Association met in New York. This meeting confirmed the interest of the Hotel and Catering Industry in addressing the problems of sustainable tourism and provided further guidelines to implement programmes of Agenda 21 in the industry. Practical implementation of the principles for construction of accommodation and catering facilities, together with the requirements of environmental protection and sustainable development, is the task of hotel and restaurant project design and engineering planners and contractors. Their main task is to balance the investment demands with sensitive siting of the building or facility in a given locality. Equally important is the need to provide an optimal design, appropriate to the future operational needs and functions of the building or facility. The main areas that have to be considered when developing a project for construction of a combined accommodation and catering establishment include:

Building and its surroundings (exterior design):

> ➤ carefully consider the number of stories; vertical transport in a multi-storey building is expensive;

> ➤ provide access to facilities for all (include disabled access);

> ➤ determine the requisite size and type of entrance doors to suit the proposed customers; further consider security and comfort (include maintenance of ventilation and temperatures inside the building);

> ➤ create the best possible conditions to maximise use of daylight;

> ➤ assess the need for and location of external lighting, also the lighting of adjoining parking areas to be controlled by sensors; and

> ➤ control watering of external landscaped areas by automatic switches.

Internal space of the building (interior design):

> design size and type of entrance hall and reception area to suit the proposed number and type of customers; give consideration to security of guests, employees, facilities, goods and money;

> provide access (including disabled access) to rooms and all areas designated for guests;

> provide air-conditioning in higher category facilities;

> control internal temperature and energy consumption (section by section of the building);

> provide adequate lighting in passageways during daytime, evening light sensors and night time emergency lighting; and

> locate all main production and operational areas, and public social amenities, on the ground floor.

Accommodation:

> employ a separate temperature control in individual rooms;

> install central control (turning out) of lights on leaving the room by an electronic locking card;

> control all lights in the room (including the bathroom) by a switch/switches beside the bed;

> minimise the number of ceiling and wall lights; control individual lights separately;

> dispose of the 'expensive trouser press'; provide a suitable vertical compartment for ironing board and iron (suitably in the wardrobe);

> replace minibars in the rooms by automatic drink dispensers in the passageways; equip rooms in higher category hotels with minibars without their own cooling component which should be fitted with a cooling plate that is operative for 24 hours and may be replaced daily when checking the minibar;

> equip bathrooms with liquid soap and shampoo dispensers; make guests aware of savings on replacement of towels in bathrooms (positive effects: minimises wear and tear, decreases water consumption, decreases use of washing powder, decreases water pollution, etc.); and

> saving on the lighting in bathrooms is not recommended.

Catering:

> ➢ design and select the size and equipment of production and service areas to match the accommodation section in terms of the occupancy rates, proposed events offered and expected numbers of guests and external customers;

> ➢ design the capacity of service areas to suit the capacity (including size and equipment) of the production areas; consider the delivery needs (i.e. 'needs of the supplier–client relationship');

> ➢ use dispensers for washing and cleaning agents; and

> ➢ check regularly the energy consumption and make use of the results when purchasing electrical appliances (appliances should be assessed regarding their energy consumption).

Waste management:

> ➢ match the waste management technology and systems so that they conform to the waste management systems used in the locality;

> ➢ sort out the waste for recycling; and

> ➢ reduce the quantity of waste generated.

(Adapted from: Stetina and Lambojova, 2002)

Conclusion

The sustainable development of our planet is a global issue which must be addressed at an international level through negotiations, agreements and regulations. However, positive results can be achieved only if the principles of environmental protection and the implementation of these principles become an integral part of the activities of all commercial and business organisations and also if they are reflected in individual actions so that they become the responsibility of every member of human society. Nevertheless, the main responsibility lies with politicians and economists involved in decision-making processes regarding the development and the directions for development of national economies, specific industrial sectors and specific administrative regions.

Student Activities

A Case Study

Example: An assessment of the attitude of companies and businesses in the tourism industry to environmental protection and sustainable development.

Specific environmental impacts of operating tourist facilities/hotels including the approach and attitude of management and employees to sustainable development was the subject of a thesis presented at the University of Economics Prague in 2000.[2]

Data gathering method and design of questionnaire

Face-to-face interviews, incorporating a structured questionnaire (See Ecological Audit pp. 143-147), were used to gather data. Eight different types of accommodation facilities, from pensions to five-star hotels, were selected for the research and divided into three groups:

(i)   Small accommodation facilities and hotels (one-star and two-star category)

(ii)   Medium-size accommodation facilities and hotels (three-star category)

(iii) Luxury hotels (four-star and five-star category)

Because of the complexity and the scope of the questionnaire, the semi-structured face-to-face interview method was employed. Although this method is very time-consuming it does, nevertheless, allow researchers to probe the responses and to discuss means of improving the company's approach and attitude to environmental protection and sustainable development. Personal visits allowed the researchers to view and assess the accommodation facilities, equipment and furnishings, whilst also providing opportunities to assess the management of the facilities and the behaviour of staff, and to obtain any pertinent company literature. This methodology, comprising direct interviewing of the management combined with personal inspection of rooms and review of operational methods, provided opportunities for establishing a relatively clear picture of the level of environmental management of the facility. It has to be said that the research itself presented some difficulties because Czech hotels/accommodation facilities, unlike many hotels abroad, do not publish any information regarding the implementation of environmental measures and their effect on the economics of the management. Also, some respondents found some of the questions 'annoying' as they thought that they might be divulging 'secret' information and did not want to answer the questions. Therefore, it was necessary to preserve their anonymity. A general assessment of the three categories of accommodation facilities/hotels in terms of equipment and standard of services is provided below.

---

[2] Novotny, J. *Hotel Management and Ecology.* A thesis presented to Prague University of Economics, 2000; Supervisor: doc. Ing. Indrova, CSc.

Results of the pilot research

(i)   Small accommodation facilities and hotels (one-star and two-star category)

The research demonstrated that small accommodation facilities and hotels generally had a low environmental impact on the surrounding area. The facilities visited as part of this research were tastefully and sensitively renovated and well insulated thermally. Mostly local materials were used for the construction and any later renovation; the work was carried out by the local companies. The external areas were well planted and tastefully landscaped. Although for interior furnishing and decoration not much use was made of natural materials, there was an apparent tendency to keep the style of the rooms uniform, with fittings and furnishings reflecting the category of the facility. As for the waste management, materials were sorted consistently before collection, although the quantity of waste produced had not been monitored. Soap dispensers were used irregularly. Bed linen was changed as needed or at the guest's request. There were no specific environmental measures taken to save energy in the facilities visited; in one case, the warm exhaust air from air-conditioning was used for heating the drying room. All of the facilities visited took measures to reduce water consumption by installing appropriate water-saving devices. There were no measures taken to restrict or discourage the use of individual transport by the guests. On the whole, cooperation with local government agencies was lacking; the proprietors/managers of the facility were largely disinterested in specific activities related to tourism development. The small accommodation facilities/hotels do not implement principles of sustainable development formally. The proprietors/managers were making only occasional, informal checks; the main concern was the economical operation of the facility.

(ii) Medium-size accommodation facilities and hotels (three-star category)

These types of accommodation facilities/hotels have ideal opportunities for implementing environmental management measures because they are not required to provide high level (luxury) services, but many of their guests are ready to accept such measures. However, the research demonstrated that, in most cases, they did not take this opportunity. The accommodation facilities/hotels in this category were mostly in character with the area and the local style of architecture but generally no use of local and natural materials was made in the restoration of those facilities. The external areas were landscaped but used mainly for car parking. Mostly artificial materials were used for interior finishes and the main aim during reconstruction/renovations was to comply with health and safety regulations. There is evidence to suggest that waste management is improving gradually, mainly due to the introduction of the Waste Materials Management Act Number 185/2001 (further detail at: http://www.czso.cz/eng/edicniplan.nsf/o/2001-03-2002-metodicke_vysvetlivky) including practical recommendations, in the Czech Republic. The facilities in this category were generally well thermally insulated and the heating in individual rooms can be regulated to some extent. Normally, bed linen is changed on request; washing/laundering is done by external companies. In one case it was found that the hotel reception staff were involved actively in conserving energy consumption (heating in the rooms). No energy saving measures regarding transport were adopted. About one-third of the personnel were provided with training on environmental protection and sustainable environmental management. The main concern was saving or keeping costs down regardless of the environmental perspective of the method used.

(iii) Luxury hotels (four-star and five-star category)

The majority of luxury hotels are part of international chains which are managed from abroad or franchised. Only imported materials are used in renovation and decoration. The external areas were landscaped. In terms of architectural design, the luxury hotels generally attract attention but the structures are not always sensitive to the surrounding area and urban fabric. Interior decoration and furnishing is generally very expensive with largely natural materials being used. Rooms all have minibars. Sorting of waste materials is the normal practice; emphasis is given to purchasing most of the products for daily use from recycled materials. Any saving measures adopted in the rooms must not reduce the quality of service and comfort of the guests. It was found that there has been no cooperation [with other agencies] regarding wider implementation of the principles of sustainable development. About 50% of the specific measures for implementing the principles of sustainable development are employed.

Because of the small study sample of accommodation facilities/hotels used in this research, it was not possible to reach clear, unambiguous conclusions regarding the awareness of environmental management of the operators in the tourism industry in the Czech Republic. The results of this pilot research show that in many hotels in the Czech Republic the level of awareness of environmental management is relatively low. The upside in this situation is that the legislation is exerting increasing pressure to reduce water and energy consumption and this move is having a beneficial effect on the behaviour and attitudes of tourism companies and businesses.

Instructions: Discuss the implementation of policies to promote environmental measures by tourist agencies in your country. Adapt the following ecological audit framework to match the profile of a pre-specified (agreed with tutor) tourism company or business in your country, complete the agreed audit and evaluate the extent to which the practices of the unit contribute to the development of sustainable tourism management.

Ecological Audit

I.   General Information about the Unit/Attraction:

Name: Location:

Nature of business/Category/Sector: Quality rating:

Number of rooms	Total bed spaces
Average occupancy rate	
Number of restaurants	Number of cafes and bars
Other social facilities	
Number of accommodation buildings	Number of other buildings
Total accommodation area	Total site area
Number of full time staff	Number of casual staff
Number of part time staff	Number of externally contracted staff

II.   Activities and Attitude Towards Sustainable Management

A.   Building

Is the building in keeping with the local style?	
Were the local companies employed for the construction of the building?	
What materials were used for building?	- nature
	- origin
Façade and roof insulation	- heating insulation
Windows	- noise prevention
	- size; heat loss prevention
	- placement; use of solar energy
Surroundings	- green/park site
	- quiet (silent) areas
	- outdoor leisure facilities
Additional notes	

B.   Indoor facilities

Materials employed	Natural	Man-made	
Traditional/regional style			
Are goods/services/facilities produced by local suppliers?			
Energy saving - lighting			
- appliances			
- dryers			
Luxury facilities: - for example, mini-bars			
Number of rooms for families with children			
Separate space for smokers and non-smokers	Guest rooms	Dining rooms	Public areas
Additional notes			

C.   Waste management

Activities to reduce waste (supplying policy, facilities)	Rooms	Dining	Behind scenes	Additional Notes
Waste sorting				
Waste recycling				
Cleaning and washing (linen change frequency), washing and cleaning detergents				
Company strategy				

Waste management plan, monitoring of its production						
Type of waste	Paper	Plastics	Glass	Aluminium/ metals	Organic	Mixed
Total amount of waste/year						
Percentage recycled						
Additional notes						

D.   Energy management

General energy policy				
Heating energy				
Heating resources				
Monitoring of heating consumption				
Control of heating, regulations				
Regular maintenance		Frequency		
Minimisation of losses, recuperation				
Education and motivation to savings	Staff:		Guests	
Use of alternative resources				
Cooling facilities - type	Nature of coolant		Age:	
Electric energy				
Monitoring of consumption				
Central switches in rooms (may be card operated)				
Saving systems for lighting and electricity				
Educating and motivating guests and staff to save energy	Staff:		Guests	
Use of alternative resources				
Investments in saving methods and plans	EUR		Nature of investments	
Achieved saving	EUR		During period	
Additional notes				

E.   Water consumption management

General policy for water consumption management			
Protection and maintenance of drinking water resources			
Protection and maintenance of utility water resources			
Monitoring of water consumption			
Reducing water consumption	Saving ventilation Information signs		
Waste water	Saving/automatic flushing Purifying station Recycling and how re-used		
Investment in saving methods and plans	EUR		Nature of investments	
Achieved saving	EUR		During period	
Notes				

F.   Transport

Facility for/support of communal transport of guests and staff			
Optimal usage of supply		Time	Local supply
Staff transport	Car-pools	Public transport	Bicycle/walk
Nature of own means of transport			
Offering holiday programmes which promote concern for the environment/sustainability			
Notes			

G. Support of 'green' activities in company and cooperation with locals for sustainable development

Cooperation with local governments in planning of regional tourism development	
Choose suppliers who apply principles of sustainability in their management and offer 'green' products	
Education and training for local inhabitants and guests	
Other forms of cooperation	

III. Activities used for Application of Sustainability Principles in Individual Internal Operational Centres

H. Food and beverage

Activities	Notes
Elimination of non-replaceable and non-recyclable food and beverage transport containers	
Supply of beverages only in replaceable or 100% recyclable containers	
Offering beverages produced by natural technologies, giving priority to local resources (beer, wine, fruit, juices)	
Offering fresh local products	
Purchasing raw materials from local resources to minimise transport costs	
Offering organic meals using local resources (healthy) kosher and/or vegetarian cuisine	
Planting own vegetables, fruit, spices, flowers etc.	
Information for staff and guests about principles of healthy nutrition and sustainable production of food	
Other activities	

I. Housekeeping

Activities	Notes
Staff training in sustainable methods of cleaning and ways of preventing waste accumulation	
Regular control of adherence to prescribed principles	
Other activities	

J. Laundry

Activities	Notes
Washing with energy saving programmes and minimum temperatures	
Use of waste heating for drying	
Elimination of use of disposable packaging of clean linen	
Use of natural detergents; restriction of their consumption	
Other activities	

K. Reception

Activities	Notes
Control of individual guest rooms with respect to optimisation of heating and hot water supply (hotel room segmentation)	
Management of energy supplies to rooms with respect of rooms utility (central regulation)	
Other activities	

L. Maintenance and garages

Activities	Notes
Regular control and maintenance of all facilities with respect to minimisation of resources' consumption	
Immediate repair of defects which cause losses or contamination and prevention of their occurrence	
Elimination of possible earth and water contamination and outflow of dangerous materials from vehicles and enclosed car parks	
Motivation for guests to minimise use of individual transport	
Other activities	

M. Hotel management and offices

Activities	Notes
Monitoring of energy consumption	
Activities for reducing energy consumption	
General planning and provision of 'ecological' investments	
Production and implementation of educational programmes for employees	
Production and implementation of motivational programmes for employees	
Formation of sustainability strategies and motivation to adhere to prescribed systems	
Formation of 'green teams' responsible for ecological hotel behaviour	
Consistent use of recycled paper	
Limitation of the consumption of paper	
Consideration of ecological issues as a part of total marketing strategy	
Support of 'green' guest behaviour through pricing	
Implementation of own ecological strategy in external business relations	
Other activities	

Adapted from: Novotny (2000).

Appendix 1

United Nations   **A/CONF.151/26 (Vol. I)**

General Assembly

Distr.   GENERAL

12 August 1992

REPORT OF THE UNITED NATIONS CONFERENCE ON ENVIRONMENT AND DEVELOPMENT* (Rio de Janeiro, 3-14 June 1992)

Annex I   RIO DECLARATION ON ENVIRONMENT AND DEVELOPMENT

The United Nations Conference on Environment and Development,

Having met at Rio de Janeiro from 3 to 14 June 1992,

Reaffirming the Declaration of the United Nations Conference on the Human Environment, adopted at Stockholm on 16 June 1972, and seeking to build upon it, with the goal of:

Establishing a new and equitable global partnership through the creation of new levels of cooperation among States, key sectors of societies and people,

Working towards international agreements which respect the interests of all and protect the integrity of the global environmental and developmental system,

Recognizing the integral and interdependent nature of the Earth, our home,

Proclaims that:

Principle 1

Human beings are at the centre of concerns for sustainable development. They are entitled to a healthy and productive life in harmony with nature.

Principle 2

States have, in accordance with the Charter of the United Nations and the principles of international law, the sovereign right to exploit their own resources pursuant to their own environmental and developmental policies, and the responsibility to ensure that activities within their jurisdiction or control do not cause damage to the environment of other States or of areas beyond the limits of national jurisdiction.

Principle 3

The right to development must be fulfilled so as to equitably meet developmental and environmental needs of present and future generations.

Principle 4

In order to achieve sustainable development, environmental protection shall constitute an integral part of the development process and cannot be considered in isolation from it.

Principle 5

All States and all people shall cooperate in the essential task of eradicating poverty as an indispensable requirement for sustainable development, in order to decrease the disparities in standards of living and better meet the needs of the majority of the people of the world.

Principle 6

The special situation and needs of developing countries, particularly the least developed and those most environmentally vulnerable, shall be given special priority. International actions in the field of environment and development should also address the interests and needs of all countries.

Principle 7

States shall cooperate in a spirit of global partnership to conserve, protect and restore the health and integrity of the Earth's ecosystem. In view of the different contributions to global environmental degradation, States have common but differentiated responsibilities. The developed countries acknowledge the responsibility that they bear in the international pursuit of sustainable development in view of the pressures their societies place on the global environment and of the technologies and financial resources they command.

Principle 8

To achieve sustainable development and a higher quality of life for all people, States should reduce and eliminate unsustainable patterns of production and consumption and promote appropriate demographic policies.

Principle 9

States should cooperate to strengthen endogenous capacity-building for sustainable development by improving scientific understanding through exchanges of scientific and technological knowledge, and by enhancing the development, adaptation, diffusion and transfer of technologies, including new and innovative technologies.

Principle 10

Environmental issues are best handled with the participation of all concerned citizens, at the relevant level. At the national level, each individual shall have appropriate access to information concerning the environment that is held by public authorities, including information on hazardous materials and activities in their communities, and the opportunity to participate in decision-making processes. States shall facilitate and encourage public awareness and participation by making information widely available. Effective access to judicial and administrative proceedings, including redress and remedy, shall be provided.

Principle 11

States shall enact effective environmental legislation. Environmental standards, management objectives and priorities should reflect the environmental and developmental context to which they apply. Standards applied by some countries may be inappropriate and of unwarranted economic and social cost to other countries, in particular developing countries.

Principle 12

States should cooperate to promote a supportive and open international economic system that would lead to economic growth and sustainable development in all countries, to better address the problems of environmental degradation. Trade policy measures for environmental purposes should not constitute a means of arbitrary or unjustifiable discrimination or a disguised restriction on international trade. Unilateral actions to deal with environmental challenges outside the jurisdiction of the importing country should be avoided. Environmental measures addressing transboundary or global environmental problems should, as far as possible, be based on an international consensus.

Principle 13

States shall develop national law regarding liability and compensation for the victims of pollution and other environmental damage. States shall also cooperate in an expeditious and more determined manner to develop further international law regarding liability and compensation for adverse effects of environmental damage caused by activities within their jurisdiction or control to areas beyond their jurisdiction.

Principle 14

States should effectively cooperate to discourage or prevent the relocation and transfer to other States of any activities and substances that cause severe environmental degradation or are found to be harmful to human health.

Principle 15

In order to protect the environment, the precautionary approach shall be widely applied by States according to their capabilities. Where there are threats of serious or irreversible damage, lack of full scientific certainty shall not be used as a reason for postponing cost-effective measures to prevent environmental degradation.

Principle 16

National authorities should endeavour to promote the internalization of environmental costs and the use of economic instruments, taking into account the approach that the polluter should, in principle, bear the cost of pollution, with due regard to the public interest and without distorting international trade and investment.

Principle 17

Environmental impact assessment, as a national instrument, shall be undertaken for proposed activities that are likely to have a significant adverse impact on the environment and are subject to a decision of a competent national authority.

Principle 18

States shall immediately notify other States of any natural disasters or other emergencies that are likely to produce sudden harmful effects on the environment of those States. Every effort shall be made by the international community to help States so afflicted.

Principle 19

States shall provide prior and timely notification and relevant information to potentially affected States on activities that may have a significant adverse transboundary environmental effect and shall consult with those States at an early stage and in good faith.

Principle 20

Women have a vital role in environmental management and development. Their full participation is therefore essential to achieve sustainable development.

Principle 21

The creativity, ideals and courage of the youth of the world should be mobilized to forge a global partnership in order to achieve sustainable development and ensure a better future for all.

Principle 22

Indigenous people and their communities and other local communities have a vital role in environmental management and development because of their knowledge and traditional practices. States should recognize and duly support their identity, culture and interests and enable their effective participation in the achievement of sustainable development.

Principle 23

The environment and natural resources of people under oppression, domination and occupation shall be protected.

Principle 24

Warfare is inherently destructive of sustainable development. States shall therefore respect international law providing protection for the environment in times of armed conflict and cooperate in its further development, as necessary.

Principle 25

Peace, development and environmental protection are interdependent and indivisible.

Principle 26

States shall resolve all their environmental disputes peacefully and by appropriate means in accordance with the Charter of the United Nations.

Principle 27

States and people shall cooperate in good faith and in a spirit of partnership in the fulfilment of the principles embodied in this Declaration and in the further development of international law in the field of sustainable development.

Report of the United Nations Conference on the Human Environment, Stockholm, 5-16 June 1972 (United Nations publication, Sales No. E.73.II.A.14 and corrigendum), Chap. I.

This document is posted online by the United Nations Department of Economic and Social Affairs (DESA). Reproduction and dissemination of the document - in electronic and/or printed format - is encouraged, provided acknowledgement is made of the role of the United Nations in making it available.

Date last updated: by DESA/DSD
Copyright © 1999 United Nations

(United Nations, 1992)

References

Cyprus Agrotourism Company (2004). *Welcome to agrotourism in Cyprus,* [on-line] available from: http://www.agrotourism.com.cy/, [accessed March 8th 2005].

Ecotourism Australia (2005). *What is ecotourism?* [on-line] available from: http://www.ecotourism.org.au/, [accessed March 2nd 2005).

Eurasia Foundation (2004). *The South Caucasus Cooperation Program (SCCP),* [on-line] available from: http://www.eurasia.am/page.php?id=004&s=02, [accessed March 8th 2005].

European Commission (1997a). Cooperation in the regional development in the EU. In *Studie Europa 2000*, Vol. 1, Ministry for Regional Development, Prague.

European Commission (1997b). Supra-national Prospects of European Regional Development. In *Studie Europa 2000*, Vol. 1, Ministry for Regional Development, Prague.

European Commission (1997c). Spatial Planning in the EU. In *Studie Europa 2000*, Vol. 2, Ministry for Regional Development, Prague.

European Commission (2002). *Using natural and cultural heritage to develop sustainable tourism,* [on-line] available from: http://europa.eu.int/comm/enterprise/services/tourism/studies/ecosystems/heritage.htm [accessed August 15th 2004], p. 2.

European Spatial Development Perspective (ESDP) (2000) *Towards the Balanced and Sustainable Regional Development in the EU*, Ministry for Regional Development (MMR), Prague.

Eustat (2005), *Survey on tourist establishments,* [on-line] available from: http://www.eustat.es/elem/ele0002800/not0002898_i.html. [accessed March 8th 2005].

http://www.coe.int.

http://www.czso.cz/eng/edicniplan.nsf/o/2001-03-2002-metodicke_vysvetlivky.

http://www.ebrd.com.

http://www-esd.worldbank.org.

http://europa.eu.int/comm/enterprise/services/tourism/studies/ecosystems/heritage.htm.

http://www.fao.org.

http://www.foei.org.

http://www.iaea.or.at.

http://www.iisd.org.

http://www.imf.org.

http://www.imo.org.

http://www.iucn.org.

http://www.nato.int.

http://www.ncsdnetwork.org.

http://www.nrdc.org.

http://www.oecd.org.

http://www.un.org/esa/sustdev.

http://www.undp.org.

http://www.unep.org.

http://www.unesco.org.

http://www.unido.org.

http://www.wmo.ch.

http://www.worldwatch.org.

http://www.wwf.org.

Iakovidou, O. and Turner, C. (1995). The female gender in Greek agrotourism, *Annals of Tourism Research,* Vol. 22, No. 2, pp. 481-484.

Indrová, J., Malá, V., Munzar, Z., Patočka, J., Petrů, Z., Ryšlavý, I., Slámová D. and Vaško, M. (1995*). Podpora podnikatelů začínajících v turistice na venkově* (The Support for Entrepreneurs Starting Country Tourism Operations), Inpro-Institut, University of Economics (VŠE), Praha.

Institute of Ecotourism (2004). *The travel and tourism industry: a global economic force,* [on-line] available from: http://www.ioet.org/iet_ecotourism.html, [accessed March 2nd 2005].

International Ecotourism Society (1991). *What is ecotourism?* [on-line] available from: http://www.ecotourism.org/index2.php?what-is-ecotourism, [accessed March 8th 2005].

Ministry of Environment of the Czech Republic (2002). *Sustainable development indicators,* [on-line] available from: http://indikatory.env.cz/?main_groline]rp=IUR [accessed August 15th 2004].

Novotný, J. (2000). *Hotelnictví a ekologie, diplomová práce(Hotel Management and Ecology),* University of Economics (VŠE), Praha.

Pásková, M. and Zelenka, J. (2002). *Cestovní ruch, výkladový slovník* (Tourism, a dictionary of tourism terminology), Ministry for Regional Development (MMR), Čzech Republic.

Stetina, V. and Lambojova, M. (2002). *Ecological Principles in Construction and Operation of Accommodation and Catering Facilities,* Collection of works/essays on sustainable development in the Czech Republic, Charles University in Prague, Centre for Environmental Studies, Prague, Volume III, pp. 363–368.

Project partners (2004). *Development of Eco-agrotourism in the Southern Caucasus* [on-line] available from: http://www.eatsc.com/for_all/about_project.html, [accessed March 8th 2005].

United Nations (1992). *Report of the United Nations conference on environment and development* (Rio de Janeiro, June 3rd-14th), Annex 1 Rio declaration on environment and development, [on-line] available from: http://www.un.org/documents/ga/conf151/aconf15126-1annex1.htm [accessed August 15th 2004].

United Nations (1996). *The Habitat Agenda Istanbul Declaration on Human Settlements,* [on-line] available from: http://www.unhabitat.org/istanbul+5/declaration.htm, [accessed August 15th 2004].

United Nations (2003). *Agenda 21,* Department of Economic and Social Affairs, Division for Sustainable Development, [on-line] available from: http://www.un.org/esa/sustdev/documents/agenda21/index.htm [accessed August 15th 2004].

Zidek, T. (2002). *Organic Farming in the Czech Republic 2001,* [on-line] available from: http://www.organic-europe.net/country_reports/czech_republic/default.asp [accessed August 15th 2004].

Suggested Further Reading

Balcer, P. (2003). *Možnosti rozvoje ekologického turismu v ČR,* University of Economics (VŠE), Prague.

Brundtland Commission (World Commission on Environment and Development) (1987). *Our Common Future,* Oxford University Press, Oxford/New York.

Dekoster, J. and Schollaert, U. (1999). *Cycling: the way ahead for towns and cities,* Office for Official Publications of the European Commission, Luxembourg.

Hassan, S. S. (2000). Determinants of Market Competitiveness in an Environmentally Sustainable Tourism Industry, *Journal of Travel Research,* Vol. 38, No. 3, pp. 239-246.

Hawkes, S. and Williams, P. W. (1993). *The Greening of Tourism: from Principles to Practices,* in Cooperation with Industry, Science and Technology, Canada Tourism, Simon Fraser University, Centre for Tourism Policy and Research, Burnaby, B.C.

Weaver, D.B. (1998). *Ecotourism in the Less Developed World,* CAB International, New York.

Indrová, J. (2002). *Vývojové trendy evropského cestovního ruchu a jejich projevy v cestovním ruchu České republiky,* University of Economics (VŠE), Prague.

Indrová, J., Petrů, Z. and Štěpanovská R. (2003). *Udržitelný rozvoj cestovního ruchu – důležitý předpoklad rozvoje cestovního ruchu v rámci sjednocené Evropy*, University of Economics (VŠE), Prague.

Ježková, L. (2003). *Analýza cestovního ruchu na Plzeňsku se zaměřením na možnosti rozvoje agroturistiky*, University of Economics (VŠE), Prague.

Juhászová, V. (2001). *Postavení agroturistiky v rámci cestovního ruchu Rakouska*, University of Economics (VŠE), Prague.

Middleton, V.T.C. (1998). *Sustainable Tourism a Marketing Perspective*, Butterworth Heinemann, London.

Nováková, R. (2001). *Vliv organizované turistiky na ekonomiku regionů a na národní hospodářství*, *diplomová práce*, University of Economics (VŠE), Prague.

Pourová, M. (2000). *Agroturistika, možnosti rozvoje a perspektiva v ČR*, Česká zemědělská universita, Prague.

Principy udržitelného územního rozvoje (Important principles for regional development) (2000). Ústav územního rozvoje (Institute for regional develpoment), Brno, Czech Republic.

Řezníčková, J. (1994*). Životní prostředí a cestovní ruch v rámci Severní, Západní a Jižní Evropy*, University of Economics (VŠE), Prague.

Růžičková, J. (2001). *Postavení a možnosti rozvoje cykloturistiky v ČR*, University of Economics (VŠE), Prague.

Sborník, K. (2002). *Udržitelnému rozvoji České republiky: vytváření podmínek*, Universita Karlova v Praze, Centrum pro otázky životního prostředí, Praha, svazek II a III.

Šlechtová, Z. (2002). *Podnikatelská činnost v agroturistice*, University of Economics (VŠE), Prague.

Stříbrná, M. (2002). *Venkovská turistika*, Agakcent, Prague.

Swarbrook, J. (1999). *Sustainable tourism management*, CAB International, Oxford.

The Eurasia Foundation (2005). *South Caucasus Cooperation Program* [on-line] available from: http://www.efsccp.org/, [accessed March 8th 2005].

World Tourism Organisation (1997). *International Tourism: A Global Perspective*, WTO, Madrid, Spain.

World Tourism Organisation (1998). *Guide for Local Authorities on Developing Sustainable Tourism*, WTO, Madrid, Spain.

Websites for Further Information

http://www.agakcent.cz.

http://www.cdv.cz.

http://www.eceat.cz.

http://www.ecn.cz/rosa/agroturistika/index.htm.

http://www.env.cz.

http://www.greenpeace.org.

http://www.iclei.org.

http://www.mmr.cz.

http://www.mze.cz.

http://www.panda.org.

http://www.sendme.cz/ca_kopretina/venkovsk.htm.

http://www.visitczechia.cz.

Chapter Nine

Risks and Responsibilities

John Hunter-Jones and Philippa Hunter-Jones

Overview

Holiday-taking carries with it a range of health and safety risks. Such risks can be classified into four inter-related categories: travel-related illness and disease; travel-related conditions; travel-related accidents and injuries; travel-related threats. Illnesses and diseases most prevalent include travellers' diarrhoea and communicable diseases, notably sexually transmitted infections; conditions arise most commonly within the travel stage of the holiday experience. They include motion sickness, deep vein thrombosis and the consequences of air rage. Accidents and injuries present the most common risk within the tourism environment. Whilst most are minor, slips, trips and falls, fatalities, which relate commonly to falling from balconies, drowning or road traffic accidents, do occur. Threats include both actual and perceived threats with international terrorist threats playing an increasingly significant role. Where the responsibility for managing risk and disseminating health information to the traveller lies is unclear. The tourism industry, governments and the tourist all have roles to play. However, such roles are impeded currently by a lack of comprehensive documentation detailing health and safety risks worldwide. The objective of this chapter is to consider the relationship between health, safety and holiday-taking. Chapter 7 considers the meaning of health and wellbeing. In particular it considers the beneficial relationship between holiday-taking and health within the context of health tourism. In contrast, this chapter examines the health consequences of travel.

Introduction

According to Reid (1995) travel has long been recognised as contributing in some way to health problems. The Grand Tour was riddled with periods of travellers illness prompting some destinations, Italy for instance, to require a health certificate of the traveller prior to entry: "The Italians, who gave us the word 'quarantine', implying 40 days' isolation, required a balletino di santi [certificate of health] as well as a passport at every frontier" (Trease, 1967, p.8). More recent interest in health and safety matters can be charted over the last decade, a period of increased research activity (see for instance Cook, 1995; Clift and Page, 1996; Cossar, 1996; Clift and Grabowski, 1997; Hunter-Jones, 2000; Dawood, 2002). Common themes covered during this period include tourism and health risks, sexual behaviour and sun-seeking among tourists, international tourism and the global diffusion of Human Immunodeficiency Virus/Acquired Immune Deficiency Syndrome (HIV/AIDS) and sex tourism. Whilst it would be misleading to suggest that each issue has received equal coverage, it is commonly acknowledged that the traveller may be exposed to four types of risk. Table 1 summarises these risk types.

Type	Examples
Travel-related illness and disease	Cholera, malaria, diarrhoea, food poisoning, communicable diseases
Travel-related conditions	Phobias, motion and altitude sickness, air rage
Travel-related accidents and injuries	Skiing injuries, swimming pool accidents, sprains and traumas
Travel-related threats	Perceived and actual threats, air rage

Table 1: Types of Risk (Ordered according to Frequency of Occurrence)
Source: adapted from Behrens and Barer (2002, p. 17-18)

Travel-Related Illness and Disease

Investigating the health problems experienced by British holidaymakers in Malta, Clark and Clift (1996) found diarrhoea, vomiting and an upset stomach to be the most prevalent illnesses. Diarrhoea is a particularly common travel-related illness, linked mainly to food, drink and poor hygiene. Most cases in the holiday environment, usually ingested, are "caused by micro-organisms that either damage the gut or interfere with the normal mechanisms that control water flow across the gut wall. Many different micro-organisms including bacteria, viruses and protozoa may be responsible" (Behrens and Barer, 2002, p.19). Three geographical areas of risk can be identified as shown in Table 2.

Level of Risk	Location
High Risk	Latin America, Africa and Southern Asia
Intermediate Risk	Northern Mediterranean, China, Eastern Europe and the former Soviet Union
Low Risk	United States, Canada, North Western Europe, Australia, New Zealand and Japan

Table 2: Geographical Areas of Risk
Source: adapted from Behrens and Barer (2002, p. 17-18)

Rudkin and Hall (1996) provide detail on some of the communicable diseases most common to tropical areas, specifically Australia and New Zealand. They focus in particular on malaria, dengue fever, cholera, diarrhoea and other diseases including HIV, other sexually transmitted infections (STIs), typhoid and tuberculosis. Literature considering many communicable diseases, particularly HIV and AIDS, is frequently referenced in the context of the sex tourism industry. Graburn (1983, p.64) describes sex tourism as "tourism whose main or major motivation is to consummate commercial sexual liaisons". The concept itself, whilst only formally acknowledged in the past two decades, has gained momentum in certain parts of Africa and many countries of Asia, for example, Philippines, Thailand and Sri Lanka. The view of the World Health Organisation (WHO) is that, "sex tourists contribute the highest risk group for catching [AIDS] and transmitting the disease" (Brown, 1988, p.94).

International tourism, most notably in third world/developing nations provides the reference point for a significant amount of literature on sex tourism (Harrison, 1992; Clift and Carter, 2000). A theme central to a number of papers is to consider sex tourism in association with prostitution literature. The relationship between tourism and prostitution is especially symbiotic in such countries where tourism is a relevant contributor to economic development. However there is considerable doubt over the true relationship between sex tourism and travel-related illnesses. For over a decade, studies (for example Cohen, 1982; 1988; Lenehy, 1995) have questioned whether sex tourism is the principal channel through which HIV and other such communicable diseases were introduced into various Asian countries. In Thailand for instance, Cohen (1988) suggested that foreign drug addicts were more likely than tourists to be the main source of AIDS infection. Therefore, whilst it is likely that a number of transmitted diseases, STIs in particular, are fuelled by the sex tourism industry, they are not exclusive to it, nor are they exclusively tourism illnesses, although they are often recognised as such. Much scaremongering during the 1980s has now receded to an acknowledgement that the spread of communicable diseases such as HIV may be *partly* related to sex tourism, in some areas more so than others. Notwithstanding this viewpoint, the role which tourism plays becomes more obvious through the realisation that tourists themselves may travel from countries where the incidence of such diseases has been increasing. Arrival in a foreign country followed by either participation in the sex industry or a non-commercial sexual encounter with an infected tourist allows disease to cross geographic spatial barriers.

Travel-Related Conditions

The travel stage of a holiday can induce a number of travel-related conditions. Research into this area is currently in its infancy. Studies which do exist have tended to concentrate upon the effects of long-haul travel upon health and wellbeing. Areas covered often include:

> Motion sickness including land, sea and air borne sickness

> Deep Vein Thrombosis (DVT) associated most commonly with long-haul economy class flights

> Jet lag, common particularly in long-haul travel, associated with the crossing of time zones

> Infections passed through close contact with fellow travellers, as exemplified by the recent outbreak of Severe Acute Respiratory Syndrome (SARS)

Travel-Related Accidents and Injuries

Accidents are the most common health and safety complication within the tourism environment (Page, 2002). Robens (1972) and Dawson, Willman, Clinton and Bamford, (1988) found workplace-related accidents often to be a consequence of apathy, low motivation and a failure to accept responsibility. Alcohol consumption provides an added complication within the holiday environment. Such accidents, often minor, commonly include road accidents, slips, trips and falls. According to the Federation of Tour Operators, when fatalities do occur, they are often the consequence of falls from balconies, drowning and road traffic accidents (Hunter-Jones, 2000). The incidence of accidents within the first week of travel is high. Jet Lag (Reilly, Atkinson and Waterhouse, 1997), motion sickness and unfamiliar surroundings all have a role to play. Key factors influencing the nature of accidents and injuries on holiday include: location; type of holiday; and the profile of tourists. Locations, such as New Zealand and Switzerland, are popular for adventure tourism based activities. Such activities may include air (for example, parachuting and paragliding), water (for example, rafting, wind surfing and canyoning) and land (for example, bungee jumping, rock climbing, glacier hiking and ski-jumping) based pursuits, often sports-related and classified to be high, intermediate or low risk with these classifications being linked to the cost of travel insurance premiums.

Sports-related injuries do themselves account for a significant area of accident research. Such activities carry with them an inherent risk, a situation often compounded by the 'novice' who attempts participation whilst on holiday. Harlow (1996), for example, reviews the cost of injuries in both health and financial terms. Harlow (1996) estimates that around 14,000 skiers sustain minor injuries abroad each year whilst approximately 6,000 skiers sustain sports injuries abroad which are serious enough to warrant medical treatment. Of the 6,000, approximately a third are thought to require operations upon their return. Quantifying both the health and financial implications of such accidents is shown to be complex, so much so that Harlow (1996) concludes the paper arguing for a case to be made for holiday insurance to cover medical treatment on return to the UK. The situation is exacerbated by the fact that, to date, "...there has been little research into the occurrence and impact of accidents among international visitors and that the scale of tourist accidents and injuries remains largely unknown in many countries" (Page and Meyer, 1996). Considering the findings from a nationwide survey of travel agents' provision of health advice in New Zealand, these authors suggested the most common range of accidents and injuries which may be sustained as a result of travel includes: "lacerations, sunburn and heat exhaustion, sprains, insect bites, extremity trauma and head trauma" (Lawton and Page, 1997, p.91).

Travel-Related Threats

In addition to recognising the *actual* health and safety costs of tourism, some researchers are now beginning to document the *perceived* and *potential* health and safety costs also. According to Page (2002, p.5) particular areas of concern include: "vehicle theft, handbag theft, currency exchange fraud, cash and credit card fraud ... over a third of European holidaymakers ... worried about personal safety on holiday". Tourists' perceptions of health and safety are often linked to the images they hold of different destinations. This linkage is illustrated by the work of Grabowski and Chatterjee (1997) who provide an account of the impact of the Indian plague scare in 1994 upon tourism to the area. Analysing UK national press coverage of the plague and investigating subsequent reactions to the outbreak (including the Indian Tourist Office, London, UK tour operators, airlines and the WHO), the authors conclude that, despite there being no reported cases of tourists contracting the plague, the outbreak had a negative impact upon the Indian tourism economy, although the magnitude of the impact they found difficult to determine. Given that it may take 18 months to two years for a destination to recover from a negative image, the impacts of such issues on the local tourist industry are a cause for grave concern.

An area of increasing concern relates to the rising incidence of air rage cases. Questioning why such incidents occur, Barrett (1999) reports the findings of research undertaken by Professor Bor (City University, UK) into the psychological causes of air rage. Lack of space, dry cabin air, low cabin pressure, noise and interaction between cabin crew and passengers are all suggested to contribute to increased levels of stress prompting potentially aggressive behaviour. The implications for health are summarised as, "...cramped conditions may exacerbate stress and trigger violence as passengers seek to claim their own territory" (p. T2). Given that reported cases of air rage are suggested to have increased by 400% over a five year period (Barrett, 1999), the health consequences of such actions may take on increasing significance in the future.

Reassuring potential travellers about the safety of travel destinations has taken on even greater significance today since the terrorist attacks of September 11th 2001. A recent paper by the World Tourism Organisation (WTO) (WTO, 2002) suggests that travellers are not only avoiding destinations associated with natural disasters, earthquakes or hurricanes for instance, but also destinations perceived to have problems with crime, terrorism and infectious diseases. Recognising the increasing need to counteract negative perceptions about a destination, Wilks, Pendergast and Wood, (2002, p.550) undertook a study of overseas visitors' deaths in Australia 1997-2000 "in order to maintain the country's reputation as a safe destination, and to identify potential areas where overseas visitors may experience health and safety problems". Examining the deaths of 1513 overseas visitors during this period the authors found that most deaths (76%) were due to natural causes including heart disease (29%), malignant neoplasms (15%), and cerebrovascular diseases (6%) as the main reasons cited. In mitigation the authors argued that some travellers visit Australia in the terminal stages of illness, both for specialist treatment and also wishing to complete a travel career. Death related to infectious diseases, in line with world trends, accounted for only 2.5% of fatalities. Here it was unclear whether the infection had been contracted in Australia or imported with the tourist. Arguing that the research provides a safety benchmark for worldwide destinations, the authors concluded by indicating that visitor deaths relating to preventable accidents (24%), road and water related particularly "must remain the focus of prevention and education initiatives" (Wilks et al., 2002, p.556).

Managing Risk

In determining where the responsibility for managing risk lies, it is first necessary to take account of two factors: the tourist; and the tourist experience.

> *The Tourist*: health and safety risks will vary from tourist to tourist. Dawood's (2002) text 'How to stay healthy abroad' for instance identifies seven high risk traveller typologies: pregnant women; children; the elderly; diabetics; the disabled; the HIV infected; and expedition travellers

> *The Tourist Experience*: Page (2002) suggests that tourist safety relates to every part of the travel experience including: pre-travel planning; the trip from the origin to the destination area; personal safety; and tourist health at the destination; and tourist health on their return to their home area

Roles and Responsibilities

Whose responsibility it should be to disseminate health information to the traveller, in what form, at what level and influenced by which objectives are contentious issues. Tables 3 and 4 provide guidance issued by the WHO on the matter. Conducting research for the Health Education Authority (HEA) in the UK, Evans and Smeding (1996) found that health information contained within travel brochures was seldom comprehensive and in some instances completely absent, a situation corroborated by Sharpley, Sharpley and Adams, (1996). To Dawood (2002) the Tourism Industry has a key role to play. Yet, as work by Hall and Brown (1996 p.46) has shown, the situation is less than clear-cut. Reviewing the implications and consequences of the European Community (EC) Directive on Package Travel, Package Holidays and Package Tours (90/314/EEC, 1990) these authors conclude that, "despite the EC Directive, there appears to be both a fragmentary and at best loosely co-ordinated provision of pre-holiday information upon which tourist and travellers can base realistic judgements on the likely welfare risks they might face". To Sharpley et al. (1996) the government is the key role-player. Adopting the Gambia as a case study these authors demonstrate how tourism, and the consequences of tourism, are inseparable from politics.

1. Advise the traveller to consult a travel medicine clinic preferably four to six weeks prior to departure.

2. Advise last-minute travellers to consult a travel medicine clinic even the day prior to departure.

3. Advise the traveller of particular hazards or threats to personal safety and security a destination may present.

4. Encourage travellers to take out comprehensive insurance.

5. Inform travellers of how to claim against insurance, particularly if the policy is arranged through themselves.

6. Provide information on:

   ➢ Mandatory yellow fever vaccination requirements.

   ➢ Malaria precautions.

   ➢ Health hazards in the destination.

   ➢ Availability/non-availability of good quality medical facilities at the destination.

Table 3: Risks and Responsibilities: The Role of the Tourism Industry
Source: World Health Organisation (2005, p.7).

1. The decision to travel.

2. Recognition and acceptance of any risks involved.

3. Seeking medical advice prior to departure, preferably four to six weeks prior to departure.

4. Obtaining appropriate vaccinations and/or medication relevant to the destination/s to be visited.

5. Planning pre-departure.

6. Equipping themselves with an appropriate medical kit and the knowledge of how to use it.

7. Obtaining appropriate and adequate insurance cover.

8. Health precautions prior to, during and post the travel activity.

9. Obtaining appropriate medical letter if carrying prescription medicines, syringes etc.

10. Health and wellbeing of accompanying children.

11. Precautions to avoid the transmission of infectious diseases during and post travel.

12. Careful reporting of any illness upon return from travel.

13. Respect for the host country and host population.

Table 4: Risks and Responsibilities: The Role of the Traveller
Source: World Health Organisation (2005, p.8).

Travel agents have the capacity to play a pivotal role in disseminating health and safety information to travellers. A study of British travel agents in 1992 found that one-third of respondents consulted newsletters and flyers produced by the Department of Health to update themselves on such matters (Gorman and Smyth, 1992). However as various other studies have shown (see for instance Lawlor, Burke and Bouskill, 2000; Provost, Gaulin and Piquet-Gauthier, 2002) the quality of information provided may not simply reflect the origins of the data, but rather how seriously the particular travel agency views such matters. In Quebec, in order to improve the quality of information available, a newsletter on travel health has been introduced by the public health authorities. Published six times a year, starting in 2000, the aim of the newsletter is to raise agents' awareness of health issues and to encourage them to recommend preventive action to potential travellers. Provost (2003) carried out an evaluation of the impact of the newsletter circulating a postal questionnaire to 950 travel agencies. Provost (2003 p.177) found that of those who responded (only 27%; n=252), satisfaction with, and interest in the contents of the newsletter was high "according to the respondents, the newsletter encouraged them, often or very often, to inform travellers about travel-related health problems (70%) or to recommend a consultation in a travel clinic (63%)". Whilst encouraging, the low response rate to the survey indicates that interest in this matter may not be widespread.

Risk Management and Prevention

To manage risk effectively the need to inform or educate the would-be traveller is paramount. How best to achieve this is not easily resolved as travel health and safety risks are poorly documented. Documentation problems are compounded by a lack of government information and limited access to travel sector information (due to commercial sensitivity) (Hunter-Jones, 2000). Table 5 provides an indication of information sources available in this area; travel insurance companies provide one of the key sources. Analysing the patient claim files between 1997 and 1998 of the largest Swiss Travel insurance company, ELVIA, Kniestedt and Steffen (2003) concluded that of the 242 claims received, 69.4% were illness-related (cerebrovascular, cardiovascular, vascular – particularly thrombosis, pulmonary gastrointestinal – particularly travellers diarrhoea, nephrology, obstetric/gynaecological, infectious, malignant, psychiatric and other) and 30.6% were accident-related (head, extremities, spine/pelvis, para-tetraplegia, thorax, burns, abdomen and other). Infections (often occurring late on in travel) and accidents (particularly within the first week of travel) related to extremities were the most significant problem areas. The illness to accident ratio for visitors to Northern Europe was six to four differing slightly from the seven to three ratio for Southern and Eastern Europe.

The status of the consumer in managing his/her own risk was enhanced significantly by the 1990 European Directive on Package Travel, Package Holidays and Package Tours (90/314/EEC). This Directive was incorporated into UK law by the Package Travel Regulations (1992) and "it provides civil rights to consumers and criminal enforcement against organisers who fail to comply with particular regulations. As with all implementation of directives, there is some freedom in the member country concerning its application" (Hunter-Jones, 2000 p.194). Health and safety matters for the package tourist are covered by Regulations 5, 7 and 9 which make reference to the need for information to be available in relation to health requirements, the destination, meals and accommodation.

Organisation	Type of Information
Public sector organisations, for example:	Offer practical advice on health and safety matters
Governments	
Health authorities	
Foreign Office	
Non-governmental organisations, for example:	Offer policy advice and suggests actions for member states
World Tourism Organisation (WTO)	
World Health Organisation (WHO)	
Journals and Consumer Magazines, for example:	Provide information on research studies conducted into various aspects of traveller health and safety
Journal of Travel Medicine	
Holiday Which?	
Tour Operators	Collect information on tourist health experiences but do not usually release the information for public consumption
Insurance Companies	Collect information on claims lodged and reasons for such claims, for example, accidents, injuries sustained. Requires the consumer to provide notification of existing conditions prior to insurance agreement
Interactive Sources for example:	Offer practical advice on health and safety matters including immunisations and disease control
National Centre for Infectious Diseases, Centre for Disease Control and Prevention (http://www.cdc.gov/travel)	
Travel Health Online (US based) (http://www.tripprep.com)	
International Society for Travel Medicine (http://www.istm.org)	

Table 5: Information Sources
Source: Adapted from Page (2002).

From an industry perspective, prevention and the management of risk have taken on increasing significance in the international tourism arena since the events of September 11th 2001. The terrorist activities witnessed that day were not the first of their kind. They followed, for example, the Lockerbie bombing of 15 years earlier plus other hijacking events. Such atrocities have prompted the need for a worldwide response to terrorism. Considering specifically the reaction of the aviation industry, Reid (2003) outlines the measures being introduced to improve passenger safety. Such measures include:

> The 35 member states of the European Civil Aviation Conference (ECAC http://www.ecac-ceac.org/uk/) agreeing to screen all hold baggage from January 2003

➤ The introduction (end of 2003) of European Union (EU) legislation setting common standards for passenger, luggage, staff and cargo screening, supported by perimeter patrols

➤ The establishment in the United States (US) of the Transportation Security Administration (TSA)

➤ The introduction of a mandatory airport inspection scheme by the United Nations (UN) agency for international aviation (ICAO http://www.icao.org/) with Bulgaria and Uganda being the first countries to be audited

Such measures alone are unlikely to be enough. Continuing cooperation between such agencies is necessary particularly in order to assist the ongoing collection of detailed intelligence. Table 6 provides an indication of the range of agencies involved in tourist health and safety matters.

International
United Nations
International Civil Aviation Authority (ICAO)
International Air Transport Association (IATA)
Global Aviation Security Action Group
International Maritime Organisation
World Health Organisation (WHO)
World Customs Organisation (WCO)
World Tourism Organisation (WTO)
The European Union
National
Government
National tourism boards
Airport authorities
Police
Customs
Transport operators
Health departments (including Health Education Authority in the UK)
Accommodation providers
Tourism industry associations (including professional membership organisations)
Local and regional tourism associations
Insurers
Tourism victim support services
Tourism educators
Trainers

Table 6: Agencies involved in Tourist Health and Safety
Source: Adapted from Page (2002).

Other organisations playing a valuable role in risk management today include: *The Tourist Victim Support Service*, a voluntary organisation set up in Dublin, Ireland in 1994. To date this service has dealt with in excess of 5000 incidents, providing assistance in a number of areas (Page, 2002):

- ➢ Replacement of travel and identity documents
- ➢ Contacting insurers
- ➢ Contacting banks
- ➢ Contacting embassies
- ➢ Contacting airlines
- ➢ Advice on the provision of legal support

Other specific advice centres also exist such as the Aviation Health Institute (http://www.aviation-health.org/) which provides advice both on how to prepare to travel most comfortably and also on how to minimise any side-effects of pressurised aircraft travel. Aviation travel is an increasingly popular area for research with the issues covered including stress, so called 'air rage' situations and the more recent economy class syndrome or "travellers' thrombosis" (Pain and Derbyshire, 2001, p.9).

Conclusions

This chapter has examined the relationship between health, safety and holiday-taking. Risks commonly associated with travel have been outlined and the issue of whose responsibility it should be to manage such risks have been considered. Page (2002 p.5) argues that much of the existing tourism health and safety research is focused narrowly upon tourist satisfaction with the holiday. Such an approach fails to appreciate: "what motivates the tourist to travel on holiday, why they select certain destinations, where they stay, how they spend their time and the broad range of risks they may encounter". The fact that tourists may elect to engage in risk-taking behaviour on holiday, or indeed select destinations because of their risk image is often not appreciated. Consequently one key to managing risk may ultimately lie with the tourism industry's need to gain a deeper insight into and understanding of the wider expectations of the tourist experience.

Student Activities

Table 3 outlines the role of the tourism industry in managing health and safety risks whilst Table 4 outlines the role of the traveller in this area.

Select a tourist destination in your chosen country.

1. Name and locate your destination.

2. Identify the type of tourism activity predominant in the destination, for example, coastal resort; skiing resort.

3. Devise a health and safety checklist to be completed by a travel agent when advising international tourists on travelling to this destination.

4. Consider how this checklist might need to be modified to accommodate (for example):

    ➢ The needs of a family with two children under 10 years of age

    ➢ The needs of elderly travellers

References

Barrett, P. (1999). Raging Over Loss of Space, *Telegraph Travel*, Saturday June 12th , p. T2.

Behrens, R. and Barer, M. (2002). Diarrhoea and Intestinal Infections, In Dawood, R. (2002). *Travellers' Health. How To Stay Healthy Abroad*, Oxford University Press, Oxford, Fourth Edition, pp. 17-40.

Brown, F. (1988). Sex Tourism a Cause for Concern, *Tourism Management*, Vol. 9, No. 2, pp. 94-95.

Clark, N. and Clift, S. (1996). Dimensions of Holiday Experience and Their Health Implications. A Study of British Tourists in Malta. In Clift, S. and Page, S. J. (eds.) *Health and the International Tourist*, Routledge, London, pp. 108-133.

Clift, S. and Page, S. J. (eds.) (1996). *Health and the International Tourist*, Routledge, London.

Clift, S. and Grabowski, P. (eds.) (1997). *Tourism and Health. Risks, Research and Responses*, Pinter, London.

Clift, S. and Carter, S. (2000). *Sex and Tourism. Culture, Commerce and Coercion*, Continuum, London.

Cohen, E. (1982). Thai Girls and Farang Men: The Edge of Ambiguity, *Annals of Tourism Research*, Vol. 9, No. 3, pp. 403-428.

Cohen, E. (1988). Tourism and AIDS in Thailand, *Annals of Tourism Research*, Vol. 15, No.9, pp. 467-486.

Cook, G. C. (ed.) (1995). *Travel Associated Disease*, Royal College of Physicians of London, London, pp. 1-8.

Cossar, J. H. (1996). Travellers' Health: A Medical Perspective. In Clift, S. and Page, S. J. (eds.) *Health and the International Tourist*, Routledge, London.

Dawood, R. (2002). *Travellers' Health. How To Stay Healthy Abroad*, 4th edn. Oxford University Press, Oxford.

Dawson, S. Willman, P. Clinton, A. and Bamford, M. (1988). *Safety at Work: The Limits of Self Regulation*, Cambridge University Press, Cambridge.

Evans, G. and Smeding, S. (1996). *Health Travel and Tourism. A Research Report for the Health Education Authority*, Centre for Leisure and Tourism Studies, University of North London (UK).

Gorman, D. Smyth, B. (1992). Travel Agents and the Health Advice Given to Holidaymakers, *Travel Medicine International*, Vol. 10, pp. 111-115.

Grabowski, P. and Chatterjee, S. (1997). The Indian Plague Scare of 1994: A Case Study. In Clift, S. and Grabowski, P. (eds.) (1997). *Tourism and Health. Risks, Research and Responses*, Pinter, London, pp. 80-96.

Graburn, N. H. H. (1983). Tourism and Prostitution, *Annals of Tourism Research*, Vol. 10, No. 3, pp. 437-443.

Hall, D. and Brown, F. (1996). Towards a Welfare Focus for Tourism Research, *Progress in Tourism and Hospitality Research*, Vol. 2, pp. 41-57.

Harlow, T. (1996). Factors Predisposing to Skiing Injuries in Britons, *Injury*, Vol. 27, No. 10, pp. 691-693.

Harrison, D. (ed.) (1992). *Tourism and the Less Developed Countries*, Belhaven Press, London.

Hunter-Jones, J. (2000). Identifying the Responsibility for Risk at Tourism Destinations: The UK Experience, *Tourism Economics*, Vol. 6, No 2, June, pp. 187-198.

Kniestedt, R. A. S. and Steffen, R. (2003). Travel Health Insurance: Indicator of Serious Travel Heath Risks, *Journal of Travel Medicine*, Vol. 10, pp. 185-188.

Lawlor, D. A., Burke, J. and Bouskill, E. (2000). Do British Travel Agents Provide Adequate Health Advice for Travellers? *British Journal of General Practice*, Vol. 50, pp. 567-568.

Lawton, G. and Page, S. (1997). Evaluating Travel Agents' Provision of Health Advice to Travellers, *Tourism Management*, Vol. 18, No. 2, pp. 89-104.

Lenehy, D. (1995) A Political Economy of Asian Sex Tourism, *Annals of Tourism Research*, Vol. 22, pp. 367-384.

Package Travel Regulations (1992) European Community (EC) Directive on Package Travel, Package Holidays and Package Tours (90/314/EEC) SI 1992 No 3288. [on-line] available from: http://www.dti.gov.uk/ccp/topics1/guide/packtravel.htm [accessed February 14th 2005].

Page, S. and Meyer, D. (1996). Tourist Accidents: An Exploratory Analysis, *Annals of Tourism Research*, Vol. 23, No. 3, pp. 666-690.

Page, S. (2002). Tourist Health and Safety, *Mintel*, Mintel International Group Limited, October.

Pain, B. and Derbyshire, D. (2001). Blood Clots Risk For Any Journey Over Four Hours, *The Daily Telegraph*, Monday April 9th, p.9.

Provost, S., Gaulin, C. and Piquet-Gauthier, B. (2002). Travel Agents and the Prevention of Health Problems Among Travellers in Quebec, *Journal of Travel Medicine*, Vol. 9, pp. 3-9.

Provost, S. (2003). Evaluation of a Public Health Newsletter Intended for Travel Agents, *Journal of Travel Medicine*, Vol. 10, pp. 177-184.

Reid, D. (1995). Epidemiology of Travel Related Diseases. In Cook, G. C. (ed.) (1995). *Travel Associated Disease*, Royal College of Physicians of London, London, pp. 1-8.

Reid, R. (2003). Airport Security, *Holiday Which?* Summer, pp. 146-149.

Reilly, T. Atkinson, G. and Waterhouse, J. (1997). Travel Fatigue and Jet Lag, *Journal of Sports Sciences*, Vol. 15, No. 3, pp. 369-379.

Robens Committee Report (1972). *Safety and Health at Work*, Cm 5034, HMSO, London.

Rudkin, B. and Hall, C. M. (1996). Health and Tourism in the Pacific. In Hall, C.M. Page, S. J. (eds.) (1996). *Tourism in the Pacific. Issues and Cases*, International Thomson Business Press, London, pp. 130-145.

Sharpley, R. Sharpley, J. and Adams, J. (1996). Travel Advice or Trade Embargo? The Impacts and Implications of Official Travel Advice, *Tourism Management*, Vol. 17, No. 1, pp. 1-7.

Trease, G. (1967). *The Grand Tour*, Heinemann, London.

Wilks, J., Pendergast, D. L. and Wood, M. T. (2002). Commentary. Overseas Visitor Deaths in Australia: 1997-2000, *Current Issues in Tourism*, Vol. 5, No. 6, pp. 550-557.

World Health Organisation (WHO) (2005). *International Travel and Health*, World Health Organisation, Geneva.

World Tourism Organisation (WTO) (2002). Safety and Security in Tourism: Partnerships and Practical Guidelines for Destinations, World Tourism Organisation, Madrid.

Suggested Further Reading

Page, S. (2003). *Managing Tourist Health and Safety*, Elsevier, London.

http://www.who/int/en/.

Chapter Ten

Perspectives on the Economic Impact of Tourism

Paul Connellan

Overview

Tourism is the largest industry in the world and the largest employer. For many countries it is the major source of employment and foreign exchange earnings. It brings both direct and indirect benefits but there can be economic disadvantages and there is increasing concern about the balance between economic advantages and environmental impacts. In this chapter, an overview of both global and Central and Eastern European travel and tourism related economic issues are examined in the context of employment, exports, contribution to Gross Domestic Products (GDPs) and expected annualised real growth in the next 10 years.

Introduction: The world industry

Studies by the World Travel and Tourism Council (WTTC, 2004) indicate that tourism is the world's largest generator of jobs. They estimated that tourism would account for over 10% of total employment in 2004 with over 214 million people engaged in varying aspects of the industry and by 2014, they expect this figure to reach 347 million. The travel and tourism industry accounts for over $5 trillion (approx. €3.86 trillion) worth of economic activity worldwide and "industry analysts confirm [that] online travel bookings currently generate more sales than any other product or service sold on the Internet – and conservative estimates have online travel bookings increasing 280% from 1999 to 2004" (Travel Action, 2005, p. 2). There is virtually no country in the world where tourism is not a major factor in creating employment, contributing to the balance of payments and determining infrastructure developments. For 83% of countries in the world, tourism is one of the top five sources of foreign exchange (World Tourism Organisation, 2002).

Even Saudi Arabia, which for religious and cultural reasons has not issued tourist visas, announced in 2004 that it would begin to allow tourists into the country. Although it is the largest oil producer in the world, Prince Sultan, the Secretary General of the Supreme Commission for Tourism indicated that the Government perceived tourism to be the industry of the future (Abdul Ghafour, 2003). However, "tourism demand depends strongly on the economic conditions in major generating markets. When economies grow, levels of disposable income will usually also rise. A relatively large part of discretionary income will typically be spent on tourism, in particular in the case of emerging economies. A tightening of the economic situation on the other hand, will often result in a decrease or trading down of tourism spending". (World Tourism Organisation, 2003, p.1).

Economic Impact of Tourism

The impact on the industry can be seen on a local basis by looking at specific industries. Each hotel room creates up to 2 jobs (Cain, 1997). In Western Countries the traditional ratio of direct jobs at an airport has been circa 1000 posts for each 1 million passengers (Airports Council International (ACI) Europe, 1998; Parry Lewis, 2001), known as the jobs/million passengers per year ratio (mppy). Although in developing countries, even when labour is less expensive, based on the lower productivity in such countries, it is estimated that the ratio could be anything up to 2000 jobs per 1 million passengers; in Europe, it is claimed that the ratio is reducing (on average about 1:950 in 2004) due to the development of 'no-frills' carriers and success of the airports' measures to reduce costs and increase productivity, despite increased security costs (ACI Europe, 2004). Examples are provided of low density on-site employment with ratios from 1:350 to 1:500 mppy, including Edinburgh, Gothenburg, Malaga and Nice, through to very high density ratios (over 1:1200) of Cardiff, Hamburg, Shannon and, Tallinn. Notably, Budapest is operating at relatively low density due to the high volume of international traffic and low cost carriers (ACI Europe, 2004, p. 8).

As may be seen from Table 1, the percentage of a country's workforce directly and indirectly engaged in tourism and related areas varies considerably depending on the extent of the development of the tourism industry. One should bear in mind that, initially, the proportion of domestic tourists (residents visiting destinations within their own country) is likely to be greater than that of international tourists. However, as the tourism potential of a country is realised and developed, the greater its potential becomes for attracting international tourists. Therefore in developed countries, whose residents have relatively high disposable incomes and longer holidays, a much greater percentage of the workforce tends to be engaged in travel and tourism industries than in developing countries. Generally, travel and tourism industry (T&T industry) employment includes those jobs where employees have face-to-face contact with visitors. It encompasses transport services, accommodation providers, food and beverage suppliers, retailers, attraction, entertainment and recreation providers etc. (WTTC, 2004). However, the travel and tourism economy (T&T economy) has a wider base and embraces industry suppliers (for example, caterers, laundries, food suppliers, wholesalers, professional service personnel, government agencies, manufacturers and constructors associated with the export, provision and supply of goods and commodities to the T&T industry (WTTC, 2004)). In the United Kingdom (See Table 2), the total employment figure for tourism 2004 was estimated at 9.5% of the workforce. Contrasting global sample data (See Table 1) include: China (8.3%); USA (11.9); Switzerland (17.6%); New Zealand (18%); Spain (22.2%); Maldives (64.4%); Seychelles (70.2%); and British Virgin Islands and Antigua and Barbuda top the list with 95% (WTTC, 2004).

Estimated % of total in 2004	Direct impact T&T industry		Total impact T&T economy (Direct and indirect)			Expected annualised real growth (real decline) in next 10 years			
Country/Area	Employ-ment	GDP	Employ-ment	GDP	Exports	Employ-ment	GDP	Exports	Demand
World	2.8	3.8	8.1	10.4	12.2	1.7	3.3	5.8	4.5
British Virgin Islands	38.3	37.3	95.0	95.2	63.7	1.2	5.2	5.0	4.9
Antigua and Barbuda	34.8	24.9	95.0	82.1	72.3	2.2	4.7	4.6	4.3
Maldives	36.6	41.8	64.4	74.1	68.2	2.7	4.1	4.1	4.5
Seychelles	38.2	28.6	70.2	56.7	52.4	3.9	3.4	3.6	3.3
Mauritius	16.2	14.0	33.1	31.0	33.4	-0.4	15.1	3.7	19.6
Dominican Republic	7.7	8.8	22.2	25.5	34.2	1.7	2.0	1.8	2.5
New Zealand	8.5	7.6	18.0	15.7	25.2	0.2	3.1	5.7	4.3
Egypt	6.7	7.9	12.9	15.3	36.1	0.7	2.5	1.7	3.4
Australia	5.6	5.5	12.9	12.3	18.0	1.8	4.8	8.6	5.3
Thailand	4.3	5.4	8.9	12.2	12.3	1.4	5.3	5.5	5.8
China	2.0	2.5	8.3	11.4	8.4	1.7	8.3	7.7	8.7
USA	4.7	4.1	11.9	10.7	14.9	1.7	3.6	4.9	4.1
Lybia	2.2	1.5	9.4	9.9	12.8	9.8	15.1	1.4	6.4
Venezuela	2.1	2.0	8.7	9.5	19.5	4.6	4.0	4.5	3.3
Mexico	2.4	2.7	10.0	9.4	13.8	3.1	5.0	7.9	7.1
Uruguay	3.8	3.2	8.8	8.1	16.1	2.0	4.4	4.6	4.7
South Africa	3.0	3.0	6.8	7.4	14.0	3.4	5.3	7.2	5.9
India	2.6	2.0	5.6	4.9	6.7	0.9	7.1	9.0	8.8

Table 1: Comparative Economic Data for the Travel and Tourism Business by Country for 2004 and the next 10 years (ordered by estimated total contribution of T&T to GDP in 2004)
Compiled from data available from WTTC (2004)

Proportionally, tourism can often be the largest export earner for a country. Globally, tourism was expected to account for 12.2% of exports of services and merchandise [goods] (WTTC, 2004). Tourism in Antigua and Barbuda accounts for 72.3% of the total exports and 68.2% in the Maldives. High figures can also be found for the British Virgin Islands (63.7%) and the Seychelles (52.4%). See Table 1 for further global examples including the Dominican Republic (34.2%), New Zealand (25.2%), Uruguay (16.1%.) and South Africa (14.0%). Even in Venezuela, with its huge oil exports, the figure is 19.5% (WTTC, 2004).

Tourism can also be a major contributor to the Gross Domestic Product (GDP) which, in very simple terms, is the "the total value of goods and services produced by a nation within that nation" (Marie Curie Glossary, p. 1). Numerous definitions of GDP may be found at: http://www.google.co.uk/search?hl=en&lr=&oi=defmore&q=define:Gross+Domestic+Product+(G DP). The total contribution of travel and tourism to the GDP is very variable. Example data (See Tables 1 and 2) are India (4.9%); Uruguay (8.1%); Mexico (9.4%); United Kingdom (10.2%); World-wide (10.4%); United States of America (10.7%); European Union (11.5%); Switzerland (13.5%); Spain (19.9%); Seychelles (56.7%) and British Virgin Islands (95.2%)(WTTC, 2004).

The economic impact of random events such as political and natural disasters on countries whose existence and survival depends on the tourism industry is clearly evident and therefore all countries are advised to have in place crisis management strategies within their tourism development plans. Within days of the 2004 Tsunami, the following statement was issued: "Right now, cleanup is the major order of business and they expect that to take about a week; a bit longer for the more major [severe] damage. We have had nobody cancel their plans and, indeed, that is not necessary. Seychelles depends on its tourism and one of the best ways to support the country is to visit" (Carta, 2004, p. 2).

The Economic Impacts of Tourism in Europe

Using the WTTC (2004) Country Reports data, Table 2 was compiled, indicating membership of the EU from May 1st 2004.

Estimated % of total in 2004	Direct impact T&T industry		Total impact T&T economy (Direct and indirect)			Expected annualised real growth (real decline) in next 10 years			
Country/Area	Employ- ment	GDP	Employ- ment	GDP	Exports	Employ- ment	GDP	Exports	Demand
European Union**	4.8	4.3	12.9	11.5	13.0	1.0	2.4	5.5	3.8
Central & Eastern Europe*	2.2	2.6	8.9	10.1	13.7	1.2	5.6	6.4	6.3
Malta+	19.9	14.2	34.7	28.5	26.3	1.7	5.3	5.4	5.1
Cyprus+	18.6	13.3	35.9	27.6	54.1	1.1	4.4	4.5	4.6
Croatia*	13.8	11.5	28.9	24.2	47.7	3.2	6.6	6.6	6.4
Estonia*+	4.9	5.4	20.7	23.8	16.2	0.6	6.2	6.7	6.0
Spain**	8.7	7.7	22.2	19.9	25.7	2.2	3.4	4.3	4.1
Bulgaria*	4.3	5.0	14.4	16.8	26.5	-0.4	3.8	3.8	4.6
Ukraine*	3.2	4.1	13.1	16.2	29.7	1.7	5.9	6.0	5.2
Montenegro*	8.1	8.1	14.9	14.8	33.2	5.7	9.0	12.1	10.3
Czech Republic*+	3.0	2.9	13.8	14.5	15.0	2.2	6.3	7.6	7.0
Slovenia*+	4.9	3.6	16.7	14.1	14.7	0.6	4.5	5.8	5.7
Switzerland	8.0	5.8	17.6	13.5	10.2	2.9	2.9	6.0	3.3
Albania*	3.2	3.9	10.0	12.3	37.4	0.5	3.8	3.6	4.2
Slovakia*+	2.4	2.5	10.5	11.5	9.4	2.4	5.6	7.1	5.4
UK**	3.5	3.9	9.5	10.2	12.0	-0.7	1.6	6.1	3.2
Hungary*+	6.0	4.7	9.8	10.1	10.0	1.2	6.3	7.8	6.6
Turkey	3.1	4.9	6.3	10.0	15.8	0.6	2.5	6.1	5.4
Lithuania*+	1.7	1.9	8.5	10.0	13.3	0.4	5.9	6.5	6.8
Poland*+	2.2	2.1	8.3	8.8	19.0	1.4	5.3	5.5	5.4
Russia*	1.5	1.7	7.3	8.6	10.0	0.8	5.4	6.9	6.8
Bosnia & Herzegovina*	1.1	1.4	5.8	7.1	6.0	0.1	4.0	5.7	5.4
Macedonia*	1.7	1.8	6.5	7.0	7.9	1.7	4.9	6.4	5.4
Belarus*	1.2	1.4	5.6	6.9	7.4	0.2	4.5	5.0	4.9
Latvia*+	1.2	1.4	5.7	6.7	6.6	0.0	5.6	6.3	6.8
Romania*	1.2	1.4	5.0	5.9	6.4	1.1	5.5	6.8	5.4

Table 2: Comparative Economic Data for the Travel and Tourism Business by Country for 2004 and the next 10 years (ordered by estimated total contribution of T&T to GDP in 2004)
Compiled from data available from WTTC (2004)
Notes: Regional memberships are denoted by * (Central and Eastern Europe); * *(EU prior to 01.05.04); Turkey and Switzerland (Other Western Europe); Cyprus (Middle East); Malta (North Africa); + EU from 01.05.04.

It is evident from Table 2 that Malta and Cyprus are very dependent on the T&T economy with GDP contributions of 28.5% and 27.6% and, with exports of 26.3% and 54.1% respectively. In each case, over one third of the workforce is employed directly and indirectly in travel and tourism. Examples of European respective contributions to GDPs, employment and exports are: Central and Eastern Europe (10.1%; 8.9% and 13.7%); UK (10.2%, 9.5% and 12.0%);, Switzerland (13.5%, 17.6% and 10.2%); and Spain (19.9%, 22.2% and 25.7%). Regarding specific Central and Eastern European countries, the economic dependence of Croatia and Estonia on their travel and tourism industries is outstanding. In contrast, it appears that the development of tourism in Romania, Latvia and other lower ranked countries could benefit their national economies in particular. It is interesting to note the differences in the position of the Baltic States, with Estonia's position probably due to political history, close geographical link with Scandinavia and its many visiting cruise liners.

Direct and Indirect Benefits

Tourism can contribute either directly or indirectly not only to the national but also to the local economy. Direct benefits are a direct consequence of travel activity in the area. Visitor expenditures become business receipts which in turn are used to pay wages and salaries and then returned to capital and taxes. Examples include visitor expenditure on local services and recreation, that is benefits related directly to the tourists' travel activity. With respect to indirect benefits, business operators spend part of their receipts on the goods and services that they need to serve their customers, including supplies, as well as capital costs such as interest on debt and profits to owners. In turn, their suppliers must purchase certain items from other sources. As this chain continues, locally and within a country, income and employment are generated indirectly (Organisation of American States, 1997). Furthermore, there are 'induced' benefits which result from tracking the consumption spending of the wage, salary, and other labour income generated directly by visitor expenditures in the area. "As tourism industry employees and operators purchase goods and services for personal use, they generate business receipts which, in turn, are used to purchase supplies, pay employees and pay capital costs" (Organisation of American States, 1997, p. 7).

Direct Benefits

To examine the direct benefits of tourism to a local economy, it is usual to undertake an economic impact study. "In its simplest form, the economic impact of tourism can be measured as the difference in economic well-being between the incomes that would have existed without tourism activity and the income levels after tourism activity" (Economic and Social Commission for Asia and the Pacific, 2001, p. 4). Impact studies have been conducted in a variety of tourist destinations. In a report for the New York State Senate (Bruno and Stafford, 2002) the contrasting expenditures of domestic and international tourists were broken down as follows:

Type	Percentage Expenditure Domestic visitors	Percentage Expenditure International visitors
Lodging (accommodation)	38%	38%
Eating	22%	18%
Public transport	14%	11%
Entertainment	14%	9%
Shopping	7%	23%
Car transport	5%	1%

In contrast, a similar study conducted in the North East of England by the regional investment bureau (Trends Business Research and Cogentsi, 2002) of overseas visitors found the following percentages: accommodation (31%); shopping (27%); food, including eating and drinking (21%); UK transport (9%), entertainment (3%) and other, including services, (10%). Both of these destinations are in Western developed countries but it is clear from the data that the tourists are visiting for differing reasons. Although the contributory elements tend to be very similar, the concentration and spread of the expenditure is dependent on the nature and type of the particular local attractions. For example, entertainment (theatres) figures quite prominently in London and New York but not in the North East of England. It is also important to look in more detail at the tourist flows in order to understand how spending patterns can vary. At first sight it may seem odd that the percentage of expenditure devoted to shopping is higher in a region of England which cannot compare with New York for the number and variety of shops. In this case, however, large numbers of visitors arrive on cheap ferry trips from Scandinavia with the main purpose of shopping because the prices in England are much lower than in Scandinavia. More recently, since their entry to the European Union, the Baltic states of Estonia, Latvia and Lithuania are popular destinations for Scandinavians who wish to purchase large quantities of alcohol at discounted prices, as Hungary has been for increasing numbers of Germans and Austrians since the early 1990s.

In other destinations, the level of local employment and the balance of tourist expenditure by activity can vary quite dramatically. For example, if one includes under the 'Entertainment' heading such things as Scuba Diving on the Great Barrier Reef in Australia, Rock Climbing or Glacier Walking in Switzerland, Deep Sea Fishing in the Caribbean or Museums and Art Galleries in Florence then one can see the various sectors which generate employment and provide economic benefits for the local communities.

Indirect Benefits

The indirect benefits of tourism fall into two categories: (i) Those which flow directly from the impact of the spending in the tourism sector and (ii) Those which cannot be quantified directly but which are seen to be producing positive changes in the local economy as a result of tourism related activities. This latter group can be very wide reaching but it is possible for them to provide greater financial benefit to local communities and to countries than the direct tourism sector. The clearest examples are usually associated with the airports through which the tourists pass. For both production and service industries wishing to compete on a global basis, it appears that easy access (within two hours drive) to a major airport can be crucial in persuading companies to locate factories or offices. Many airports arose initially to serve tourism but subsequently their existence created a demand for other business. Alongside the airports, in terms of initiating, maintaining and increasing demand, is the image which an area projects. To persuade multinational companies to locate in a region, it must have a positive image so that expatriate managers will want to live there, companies will feel confident that the infrastructure will support their industry and customers will feel positive about products that are made in the area. A strong tourism image provides all those benefits and encourages companies to relocate in what is, by its definition 'a tourist destination', a desirable place to be.

Without doubt, the aeroplanes that bring the tourists can enable a business to start, which would be very difficult otherwise. In Southern Spain there are millions of hectares of greenhouses, polytunnels and general agriculture that have grown up because of the easy access to Northern European markets that tourist flights provide. Most modern aircraft have considerable amounts of cargo space that is not used to carry passengers' luggage. This space is now utilised by this enormous agricultural industry to transport fruits and vegetables to the markets of Northern Europe. To transport them to such markets by previously accessible methods of road or rail would be much slower, generally more expensive and might not meet the time limits associated with fresh produce.

A further indirect benefit of tourism to the economy comes from the spending by the tourists. In most countries there is a spending or value added tax (sometimes referred to as VAT) on goods and services. This percentage of the tourist expenditure, which varies across the European Union from 15% in Cyprus and Luxemburg to 25% in Denmark, Hungary and Sweden (European Commission, 2004, p.3), goes directly to fund either local or national government services. Extra demand flows directly from what the tourists do. Hoteliers may buy their food from local suppliers or may send their linen to be cleaned at local laundries. Such activities create revenue for local companies and employment for the locals, thus boosting the economy.

What tourists eat and buy while they are visiting destinations can impact on their spending patterns when they return home; changes in 'home' eating patterns may be related to visits to new countries (Keynote Publications Ltd., 2003) (See also Chapter 1, p. 11-12). The consequent changes in purchasing habits can in turn impact on local production. For example, in Australia, the demand by Asian visitors and immigrants for locally grown Asian vegetables has been driven not only by the increasing number of Asian immigrants but also by the changes in eating patterns of native Australians because of their tourist visits to Asia where they pick up a taste for different foods. (Rural Industries Research and Development Corporation, 2005).

Transportation services are often highly dependent on the use that tourists make of them. In most major cities tourist travel, particularly off-peak, makes a major contribution to the revenues of the transport companies. In London the figure could be as high as 10% (author's estimate) based on number of tourist arrivals (http://www.visitlondon.com/ems/ downloads/5823londonstatscontents.pdf) and number of journeys listed by Transport for London (2004). Given that a high percentage of expenditure in any destination is on eating and drinking, it is clear that there would be fewer restaurants and other food outlets if there were not a demand from tourists and it is probable that many restaurants in city centres would be obliged to close. In both cases the residents would then lose some or all of the facilities which the tourists make possible.

In some destinations, the survival and/or success of whole industries, events, attractions and even local communities depends on the tourist market. For example, the theatre sector in London and New York is highly dependent on tourist spending. In London the figure is estimated to be over 20% of total income (Society of London Theatres, 2002). They note that after the steep decline in arrival numbers to London following the events of September 11th 2001, there was a 14% decline in cash takings at London theatres. If it had happened in the peak months of July and August it is estimated that this figure could have been as high as 50%. In Central and Eastern Europe, spa tourism has benefited greatly from the recent tourist boom with the consequent development of health destination resorts (See Chapter 7 for further details).

Induced Effects

Part of the money which is spent by the tourists provides salaries for hotel, restaurant and tourist attraction employees. This money becomes part of employees' household income and they spend it on their housing, food and transport et al. When this money is spent it is classified as an 'induced effect' with respect to the total economy. The size of this induced effect has been measured in differing countries but a good example is Hawaii, which is highly dependent on tourism. "The direct and indirect impact of tourism supports about 21% of the GDP. However, when the induced effect is accounted for, the total rises to almost 33%" (State Government of Hawaii, 1998, p. 4).

Multipliers

The combined effects of the direct, indirect and induced economic activities resulting from visitor spending are termed the 'multiplier'. "This is the arithmetic ratio of total impact, measured in sales, personal and capital income, or employment, to the initial visitor expenditure. While difficult to estimate reliably, the sales, income, or employment multiplier is a useful tool for quickly estimating the total economic benefits generated by an increment of visitor expenditures" (Organisation of American States, 1997, p. 7). In short, tourism multipliers are used to measure [estimate] the effect that tourist spending has on economies. Their magnitude is based on the extent to which the direct tourist spend is multiplied through the economy via the indirect and induced effects. They are used to "determine the changes in output, income, employment, business and government receipts and balance of payments due to a change in the level of tourism expenditures in an area" (Economic and Social Commission for Asia and the Pacific, 2001, p. 7). Students who require further details are referred to the bibliography compiled by Wen Huei-Chang (2000). Multipliers are subject to wide interpretation because of the uncertainty of what might happen if the tourists did not visit. The multiplier can vary between 0.5 and 1.5 of the amounts produced by measuring the direct or induced spending. To avoid overestimating its magnitude, the figure of 1 is usually used unless there is strong evidence to support a higher or lower figure. The use of the multiplier should be shown clearly as "it can introduce complexities that most users of the results do not fully understand" (Stynes, 1999, p. 16).

Leakage

As tourism brings money into a country, it is also associated with money leaving a local economy or country, the latter effect being referred to as leakage (Benavides, 2001). All of the money that tourists spend does not stay in the local or even national economy. For example, "in most all-inclusive package tours, 80% of travellers' expenditures goes to the airlines, hotels and other international companies that often have their headquarters in the travellers' home countries, and not to local businesses or workers" (United Nations Environment Programme, 2001, p.1). The percentage that remains in the local economy can vary considerably, with the lowest amount being retained in the least developed countries that frequently are obliged to import relatively costly foodstuffs, alcohol and other goods specifically to satisfy the [cultural] needs of the visiting tourists.

A study in the Annapurna region of Nepal (World Resources Institute, 1993) found that only 10% of the cost of visitors' holidays remained in the local area. It has been estimated (World Bank Study, 1996) that 55% of international tourism income in the developing countries leaves those countries via foreign-owned airlines, hotels and tour operators, or payments for imported food, drink and supplies. Studies in individual countries have put the figure for leakage even higher, for example at 70 % in Sri Lanka (Ecotourism and Conservation Society of Sikkim, 2001) and 75% in the Caribbean (Mann, 2005). Two-thirds of the income from tourism in the Mediterranean went to fewer than 10 tour operators from Northern Europe who owned the airlines that brought the tourists, the hotels where they slept and eat, and the buses which took them on excursions (World Wild Life Fund, 2004).

As economies develop the percentage of leakage decreases generally, but in the early stages of tourism growth, local developments can be almost counter-productive. Work undertaken by the author (Connellan, 1988) demonstrated that setting up tourism projects from scratch (ab initio), not only with total reliance on foreign made equipment and materials but also with operational dependence on imported food, can be so expensive that the cost of borrowing the money to fund them can be greater than the net return. New tourism projects will usually create local employment but, because of the many potential aspects which send money out of the country, they may not make a very positive contribution to the national balance of payments. A further example is evident when the 'local' workforce comprises mostly foreigners who choose to remit their earnings to their home countries to support their families. Whenever a tourist project is suggested by a developer to the government, either local or national in under-developed countries it is on the basis of the large number of jobs it will create. Whilst there may be high initial employment in the development phase, this increase can be followed by redundancies and disappointment as the need for trained operational and managerial personnel might demand non-local labour to be brought in, especially for all attractive and well paid work.

Types of Employment

Tourism is generally very seasonal. In the European Alps, for example, there is almost no access to skiing in the summer months, although artificial snow is now extending the season in some resorts. The South of France hosts 70% of its tourist nights in July and August (French Government Tourist Office, 1998). Even major cities, unless highly dependent on business tourism, have a very high peak of arrivals in the summer months. This uneven seasonal and monthly demand can mean that all aspects of the tourist experience including hotels, restaurants, transport facilities, must either close down completely during the quieter months or operate on reduced staffing levels. For many staff this means that their income can drop dramatically during certain months of the year. Arrivals at hotels in Blackpool (Northern England) can drop by half in the 'off-season', that is, after the main tourist (seaside and autumn illuminations) and conference months, from November until Easter. The hotels need to cut their staff numbers accordingly when the wages they pay are already much less per hour than those in most other industries. Remuneration for positions in tourism companies is universally below the national average (International Labour Organization, 2001), except in developing countries where the comparison is with a largely agricultural workforce. The reasons for such low wages are generally in the nature of the job requirements. The posts tend to demand low levels of skill, are 'easy' to recruit to and attract people who will not have long-term careers. They also have a high concentration of female workers (73%) who begin from a lower wage base than their male counterparts (European Foundation for the Improvement of Living and Working Conditions, 2000). In order to mitigate the effects of seasonality, some tourism providers attempt to attract other market segments. For example in mountainous areas where winter sports are popular, summer hiking, hang-gliding and parachuting may be promoted, year-round wet weather attractions may be developed in seaside or centres with an arts, craft or historical focus in country locations.

Other Negative Factors Relating to Tourism

Although there are many positive economic aspects derived from tourism there are also factors which can diminish its economic importance. In most countries tourism has an inflationary impact on local prices. This impact has two economic causes. Firstly, tourists create additional demand which pushes the price demand curve in an upward direction as in any standard economic scenario of supply and demand. Secondly, the tourists tend to overpay for most of the things they buy because they are not aware of local prices and can only make comparisons with the prices of the items in their home country. The flow of tourism is generally to lower cost countries but even when tourists visit a destination that is more expensive than their own country, they tend not to be aware of the predominant local price and so they pay whatever is asked for a particular 'necessary' product or service.

The attraction of creating extra jobs can often cause central governments to spend large sums of money on infrastructure projects which may not be appropriate for the country. Many environmental groups are now campaigning against new tourism projects because of this. They maintain that the negative aspects of tourism such as pollution, prostitution and water supply problems can outweigh the monetary inflows which tourists bring. For example tourists often use much more water than the local people. In areas where water is scarce, such as Cyprus or the parts of the Mediterranean coast, this problem can divert water resources away not only from native agriculture but also from the basic needs of the locals.

The Future

It might be assumed that if tourism is the reason for substantial income generation in a country, income from tourism will continue to grow. This may not always be the case. In order to make some predictions for the future, the data representing expected annualised real growth (real decline) in the next 10 years (See Tables 1 and 2) may be examined. Firstly, taking the global figures, without doubt it is anticipated that world tourism will continue to grow, with Mauritius appearing as the clear leader in terms of demand followed by Montenegro with India, China, Mexico and the Czech Republic in close contention; the presence of two Central and Eastern European countries in this list is extremely encouraging in terms of tourism developments. Examples of countries likely to be seeking tourism employees are Libya, Venezuela and the Seychelles and, in Central and Eastern Europe: Montenegro; Croatia; and Slovakia. It should be noted that there are projected annualised real declines in employment for Mauritius and Bulgaria. Montenegro seems best placed to benefit from growth in travel and tourism exports in the next 10 years with India, Australia, Mexico, China and South Africa also well placed. Other high ranked contenders within Central and Eastern Europe are Hungary, the Czech Republic and Slovakia. Finally according to the WTTC data (2004), the contribution of travel and tourism to the GDP (annualised real growth) is forecasted to rise spectacularly in Mauritius and Libya. From a global perspective, tourism developments in Montenegro, China and India also look very promising with strong growth anticipated also in Croatia, the Czech Republic, Hungary and Estonia.

Conclusion

In assessing economic impact the most important factor is the accuracy of the statistics. For example, if one examines the national employment data, taking into account the total (direct and indirect) impacts of the travel and tourism sector on employment and the national economies then the figures quoted above increase substantially (See WTTC, 2004 for details). Without a solid foundation and a clear explanation of the nature and source data including the conditions under which they were collected, any assumptions on which decisions are based can be flawed. Secondly the overall impact of tourism must be taken into account. Increased employment is only one thing to be considered. What changes will be made to the society by an increase in tourist numbers? The answer to this question requires tourism impact studies and the development of the concept of tourism capacity if the distribution is not to be irrevocably altered. Tourism can bring economic prosperity when no other industry is available. It can also mean increased crime, environmental problems and social disharmony. However, although impact studies are fairly well developed in terms of criteria for measuring economic benefits, difficulties arise when trying to measure (quantify) some of the negative aspects and impacts of tourism (See Chapter 9 p. 160 and Chapter 11 pp. 194/5; 197/198).

Whether the current popularity of the Central and Eastern European cities for short breaks will continue remains to be seen. Having attracted tourists to the cities, one way forward is to move them on to the rural, mountain and coastal regions, bearing in mind that continuous expansion of accommodation stock can be an economic disbenefit to regions. Tourists are fickle; they seek new experiences. The proportion of independent travellers is growing and as they move about a country, lesser known areas suddenly become more important and require not only marketing but also access with internal and external transport. Most of the countries have developed their infrastructures very quickly and put local and international services in place to cope with the huge increase in demand generated since the political constraints were removed. To some extent the 'no-frills' airline carriers have spotted potential destinations and aided such developments. Without doubt, Central and Eastern Europe look set to provide many competitive and interesting tourism development projects in the future.

Student Activities

1. Contact a local hotel and find out how many full time equivalent staff they employ. See what numbers other local industries employ. How do the wages compare? Is the percentage of female workers the same?

2. Examine the figures for the balance of payments for your country. Make a list of all the things that the country imports which it needs mainly for tourists. What percentage of total imports do you estimate this is?

3. Prepare a report on the industries which depend on tourists for part of their existence. Do not include the direct ones such as hotels, charter buses (but you can include local buses if tourists use these a lot) or tour guides. Estimate how

much of their turnover is related to tourists, if possible making a distinction between local and international visitors.

4. Choose a local facility, such as an amusement park, which is at least two years old and which was built for tourists. How much use of it is now made by local people?

5. Choose an attraction which is special to your area or country. Prepare a report on the economic impact to the country if something were to happen to it, for example a serious fire in an historic building or long-term drought which might cause a river level to fall significantly.

6. Compare tourists on beach holidays, city breaks and golfing holidays. Estimate their expenditure on the following items: hotels, eating out, souvenirs, visiting local attractions, car hire and cultural visits. Which type of tourist would be best to attract?

7. Find out the *average* wage for the following positions, for example from a series of job advertisements: assess perks/benefits?

    (a) A chamber maid in a local hotel

    (b) A cleaner in a local office block

    (c) A technical position in a local tourist attraction (e.g. Engineer, Electrician)

    (d) A semi-skilled position in a local factory

    (e) A duty manager in a local hotel

    (f) A middle manager in a local bus company

How do the salaries compare between Tourism and Other Industries?

References

Abdul Ghafour, P. K. (2003). Ideal Climate for Investment in Kingdom: SAGIA *Arab News*, September 29th, [on-line] available from: http://www.mafhoum.com/press6/161E61.htm [accessed, March 30th 2005].

Airports Council International (ACI) Europe (1998). *Creating Employment and Prosperity in Europe*, A study on the social and economic impact of airports, [on-line] available from: www.aci-europe.org/[accessed March 26th 2005].

Airports Council International (ACI) Europe (2004). *The Social and Economic Impact of Airports in Europe*, [on-line] available from: www.aci-europe.org/[accessed March 26th 2005].

Benavides, D.D. (2001). Is the socio-economic sustainability of International Tourism assured under hyper-competitive conditions? *Tourism, a source of employment and revenue for the population*, Third summit conference of The Association Les Sommets du Tourisme, Chamonix, Mont-Blanc, December.

Bruno, J. L. and Stafford, R. B. (2002). *Financial Impact of the World Trade Centre Attack*, [on-line] available from: http://www.senate.state.ny.us/Docs/sfc0102.pdf [accessed March 30th 2005].

Cain, C. (1997). *World Bank Review*, International Finance Corporation (IFC), [on-line] available from:
http://www.ifc.org/ifcext/spiwebsite1.nsf/0/99378c64cc153f0085256fb90076555d?OpenDocument [accessed March 30th 2005].

Carta, P. (2004). Status of Seychelles and Mauritius after Tsunami, *New Adventures Newsletter*, Vol. 7, No. 5, [on-line] available from:
http://www.newadventures.com/newsletters/NL0412A.htm [accessed March 30th 2005].

Connellan, P. (1988). *Catering development in Khartoum*, Unpublished research.

Economic and Social Commission for Asia and the Pacific (ESCAP) (2001). *Promotion of Investment in Tourism Infrastructure*, United Nations ESCAP, [on-line] available from:
http://www.unescap.org/tctd/pubs/pubs_chron.htm#2001 [accessed March 26th 2005].

Ecotourism and Conservation Society of Sikkim (ECOSS) (2001) *Policies governing Ecotourism and Tourism in Nepal*, [on-line] available from:
http://www.sikkiminfo.net/ecoss/sarce/country_report.htm [accessed March 30th 2005].

European Commission (2004). *VAT rates applied in th member state of the European Community*, [on-line] available from: http://europa.eu.int/comm/taxation_customs/ taxation/vat/how_vat_works/rates/index_en.htm [accessed March 28th 2005].

European Foundation for the Improvement of Living and Working Conditions (2005). *Working Conditions*, [on-line] available from: http://www.eurofound.eu.int/working/working.htm [accessed March 30th 2005].

French Government Tourist Office (1998). *Statistics Abstract*, [on-line] available from:
http://www.franceguide.com/prehome.asp?

http://www.google.co.uk/search?hl=en&lr=&oi=defmore&q=define:Gross+Domestic+Product+(GDP).

http://www.visitlondon.com/ems/ downloads/5823londonstatscontents.pdf.

International Labour Organization (2001). *Human resources development, employment and globalization in the hotel, catering and tourism sector*, [on-line] available from:
http://www.ilo.org/public/english/dialogue/sector/techmeet/tmhct01/tmhctr2.htm [accessed March 30th 2005].

Keynote Publications Ltd. (2003). *Ethnic Foods Market Report Plus 2003*, Description, [on-line] available from: http://www.researchandmarkets.com/reports/35282 [accessed March 30th 2005].

Mann, M. (2005). *Tourism and people*, p. 2, Data taken from Caribbean Development Bank, Study (1996). [on-line] available from: http://www.peopleandplanet.net/doc.php?id=1113dbsa [accessed March 30th 2005].

Marie Curie Glossary (2004) [on-line] available from:
europa.eu.int/comm/research/fp6/mariecurie-actions/glossary/glossary_en.html [accessed March 25th 2005].

Organisation of American States (1997). *Sustaining Tourism by Managing Financial and Human Resources*, p. 7 [on-line] available from: http://www.oas.org/TOURISM/docnet/Iatc1en.htm [accessed March 30th 2005].

Parry Lewis, J. (2001). *Comments on Thanet Local Plan*, [on-line] available from: http://www.planet-thanet.fsnet.co.uk/local_plan/jplewis.htm [accessed March 26th 2005].

Rural Industries Research and Development Corporation (2005). *Research and development plan for Asian foods 2005-2010*, [online] available from: http://www.rirdc.gov.au/ [accessed March 30th 2005].

Society of London Theatres (2002). *Report on Tourists*, Society of London Theatres, London

State Government of Hawaii (1998). *The Economic Impact of Tourism: An Update*, [on-line] available from: www.state.hi.us/dbedt/hecon/he7-99/impact.html [accessed March 30th 2005].

Stynes, D. J. (1999). Economic impacts of tourism in Michigan's Eastern Upper Peninsula. In M. McDonough, J. Fried, K. Potter-Witter, J. Stevens and D. Stynes, *The Role of Natural Resources in Community and Regional Economic Stability in the Eastern Upper Peninsula*, East Lansing, Michigan, Research Report 568.

Transport for London (2004) *London Travel Report, 2004*, [on-line] available from: http://www.tfl.gov.uk/tfl/reports_library_stats.shtml [accessed March 30th 2005].

Trends Business Research and Cogentsi (2002). *Tourism Impact; A pilot study for the North East, Part 2 – Results*, One NorthEast, Newcastle-upon-Tyne, [on-line] available from: http://www.onenortheast.co.uk/page/reports/cat2.cfm [accessed March 29th 2005].

Travel Action (2005) *Travel action 1994-2005*, [on-line] available from: http://www.travelaction.com/pages/2/index.htm [accessed March 26th 2005].

World Resources Institute (1993) *Research Paper*, [on-line] available from: www.wri.org [accessed June 24th 2004].

World Bank (1996). *Reports 1995-2000*, World Bank, Paris.

United Nations Environment Programme (UNEP) (2001) *Economic impacts of tourism*, [on-line] available from: http://www.uneptie.org/pc/tourism/sust-tourism/economic.htm [accessed March 30th 2005].

World Tourism Organisation (WTO) (2002). *Document S/C51, Background Paper on Tourism Services*, Para.12, WTO, Madrid.

World Travel and Tourism Council (WTTC) (1997). *Travel & Tourism - Jobs for the Millennium*, [on-line] available from: http://www.wttc.org [accessed March 17th 2005].

World Travel and Tourism Council (WTTC) (2004). *Country reports*, [on-line] available from: http://www.wttc.org/ [accessed March 26th 2005].

World Wild Life Fund (2004) *News Article*, August, [on-line] available from: www.panda.org [accessed June 14th 2004].

World Tourism Organisation (2003). *Tourism and the world economy*, [on-line] available from: http://www.world-tourism.org/facts/tmt.html [accessed March 26th 2005].

Suggested Further Reading

Airports Council International (ACI) Europe (2000). *Creating Employment and Prosperity in Europe* - Economic Impact Study Kit, ACI EUROPE follow-up study, [on-line] available from: www.aci-europe.org/[accessed March 26th 2005].

At http://www.onenortheast.co.uk/page/reports/cat2.cfm a number of useful economic studies can be located.

Wen Huei-Chang (2000). *Bibliography of Economic Impacts of Parks, Recreation and Tourism,* [online] available from: http://www.msu.edu/user/changwe4/bibli.htm [accessed March 28th 2005].

This bibliography lists numerous diverse economic impact studies in the recreation and tourism field, varying from classic texts to contemporary research. Most of the contemporary studies on economic impacts of recreation and tourism use input-output models; however, other approaches such as economic base models, econometric techniques, hybrid models and non-survey methods are also included.

Chapter Eleven

Cultural Factors in Tourism Development

Gianfranco Nobis

Overview

The purpose of this chapter is to increase awareness of the relevance of culture in tourism activities. It is proposed that the established cultural practices of different societies arose as a balancing influence, aligned to maximise the benefits of local communities in relation to the prevailing social and environmental conditions. Over time members of these communities have converted their cultural practices into norms of behaviour which have moulded their perceptions and influenced their beliefs. The way of life in one society is a phenomenon that may be totally unsuitable and alien in a different societal environment. Consequentially any destination that aims to attract tourism from other regions or continents must make an effort to prepare and develop the local human capital, that is, both the workforce and the local residents. By adapting their understanding and modes of interaction to meet the needs of the tourists, various forms of ethical and ideological conflict could be avoided hence promote the long-term opportunity of success for the destination in question. In turn, potential problems might be alleviated substantially if the tourists took more responsibility for self-preparation.

Introduction

Tourism, technology and telecommunications were identified by McRae (1995) as the three 'super industries', which by the turn of the century would drive the world's economy in the new millennium. In the context of tourism, McRae's vision has turned into reality, confirmed by the fact that, in 2001, tourism was firmly established as the world's largest industry (Mastny, 2001). Economies tend to follow a developmental progression beginning with a heavy reliance on agriculture, followed by industrial growth leading to a more service-based structure. LaborLawTalk.com (2004) states that the first economy to follow this path in the modern world was the United Kingdom (UK) but the speed at which other economies have made the transition to service-based, sometimes called post-industrial, economies has accelerated over time. As standards of living continue to increase in such post-industrial economies, in general, more disposable income is available to a wider proportion of the population. Traditionally, the 'annual vacation' was devoted to rest or relaxation over a maximum period of two weeks. New patterns of occupational leave (for example, maternity and paternity benefits), reduced working hours, innovative working practices such as flexitime and the many labour saving appliances in the home have not only increased consumers' leisure time but also encouraged women [with children] to continue [return to] working. Consequently there is even more disposable income, while international travel has become relatively very cheap.

In recent times, the need to satisfy the natural instincts of curiosity has added a new dimension to travel. This, aided by the last half century's progress in transportation technology, which has caused the world to shrink figuratively; in consequence, new global vacation patterns have emerged. In a few hours travellers can find themselves in new continents not only with different climatic environments but also amongst different cultures with their own languages, beliefs, religions, traditions and legal systems. It has been mooted that environmental conditions determine the selection of strategies that groups or societies adopt for their survival and for the well-being of the community concerned (Brown Weiss, 1989). Thus local and regional practices are reinforced over time so becoming the basis for the organised life of the community.

In addition to survival strategies, communities develop their own languages, codes of communication and rules for orderly co-existence and the regulation of community affairs in relation to kinship, property and the role of individuals. Furthermore, 'official' religious practices may be invoked to support the rule of law and social behaviour within the community or even the whole country and, it might be argued that 'local' people are products of their own cultural identity. The method that different cultures use to retain their identity is to project to their members the positive and valued aspects of their society. In turn, culture tends to form mental templates in individuals who consequentially perceive the external world from their cultural perspective and who tend to apply their own cultural norms regardless of where they are placed geographically or in whose company they find themselves. This chapter examines the potential impact of some of these issues on international tourism development and tourists' destination choices.

The Concept of Culture

In the last century, Tylor (1913) identified the component parts of culture as arts, beliefs and values, knowledge, law, morals and manners and any other competences and habits acquired by people through membership of their society (community). Subsequently a plethora of definitions and descriptions of culture has evolved (See Kroeber and Kluckhohn, 1952 and Gerring and Baressi, 2002). The more one attempts to look at the origins of cultural practices, the more it becomes apparent that they are determined by environmental conditions, as indeed are the characteristics of humans whose survival is dependent on their intrinsic ability to adapt to the surrounding environmental conditions. Throughout the world, indigenous people demonstrate dramatic changes in their characteristics which permit such successful adaptation. For example, in extremely hot sunny climates, light clothing is required to maintain coolness and natives tend to be tall, slender and dark skinned, qualities that promote optimal performance in such conditions. In contrast, locals in severely cold climates tend to be relatively short and stocky, hence releasing minimal body heat. People living in the equatorial belt appear to perform efficiently on an almost totally vegetarian diet, taken at frequent intervals, which provides much needed fluids and minerals. It is of low calorific value so as to prevent perspiration by raising the metabolic rate during the digestive process. In contrast, in the polar regions, the diet comprises of animals and birds, including seal, whale and caribou meat, to produce heat-giving fat. Even climate would seem to have an influence on culture (cf. Usunier and Lee, 2005). It can create problems of physical adaptation for non-local tourists in terms of their skin, energy levels and digestive systems should they try to exist solely on the 'local' diet.

Terpstra and David (1985, p. 5) defined culture as "a learned, shared, compelling, interrelated set of symbols whose meanings provide a set of orientations for members of society. These orientations, taken together, provide solutions to problems that all societies must solve if they are to remain viable". Twenty years later, Usunier and Lee (2005, p. 10-11) discussed the sources of culture at the individual level. They include: sex; family; group (ethnicity); language(s); nationality; religion; social class; general and professional (specialised) education; and corporate or organisational culture. It might be argued that the primary functions of culture are the acquisition of food, clothing and shelter and provision of protection from human enemies and natural disasters. Therefore, although it is evident that environmental adaptation is essential for man's survival, it is apparent that cultural practices are the consequence of people's adaptation to the local environment. The adoption of these practices by members of a community was, in the past, essential for the survival of the group. If one attempts to examine the concept of culture in the context of attracting tourists to new environments, examples include the provision of:

➤ sustenance, that is food and drink which should be purchased, and ideally, grown locally;

➤ comfortable accommodation of an acceptable quality and temperature, with adequate facilities;

➤ advice regarding style of dress and general patterns of expected behaviour;

➤ attractions based on local developments, crafts, and folkloristic traditions;

➤ galleries, theatres, concert halls, traditional local buildings and architecture.

➤ information centres, museums, libraries and archives where knowledge might be acquired;

➤ places of worship, a low risk environment marinated by law-enforcers with enforced regulations against crime and health care; and

➤ opportunities to make close contact with the local people and to learn about their lifestyles, way of thinking etc.

The concept of national culture is one which has been examined by various academics following the realisation that although work practices and worker behaviour differed across the units within global companies, there appeared to be some commonality within units across a country in particular when the workers were from a local cultural environment. Led by Hofstede (1984 then 1991 and 2001), research by Chinese Culture Connection (1987), Schwartz and Bilsky (1990), Fiske (1991) Schwartz (1992) and Trompenaars (1995 and 2000) sought to identify profiles and patterns by which cultural differences could be determined. Although their sample sizes, compositions (ranging from employees in international companies to students), sampling methods and data analytical techniques were very diverse, their findings displayed commonalities which provide a fascinating insight into national cultural differences. However, "national culture reflects the culture of a nation and, as such, relies on the concept of within-country homogeneity and between country differences" (Usunier and Lee, 2005, p. 12). As people travel, immigrate and emigrate, the distinctive nationalities are merging into a global melting pot. Usunier and Lee (2005, p. 13) argue that the concept of national culture which was evident in the last century now suffers "a systematic lack of coherence ... cultures do not often correspond to nation-states but to linguistic, ethnic, religious or even organisational entities". From a tourist's perspective, in Benidorm (Spain) for example, one might expect to meet 'local' people who display the indigenous culture and then be surprised to find the hotels are staffed by foreigners and restaurants are not run by natives but by UK ex-patriots. Of course, this might be exactly the reason why some tourists have chosen such a multicultural destination.

Usunier and Lee (2005) have concluded that culture is a process, as opposed to a distinctive whole, and that its elements are organically interrelated and work as a coherent set. If culture is a process that is concerned with those extrinsic features of human society which are acquired by exposure rather than being constituted by the inherited characteristics of individuals then it is evident that, when tourists are exposed to new environments, they are automatically exposed to the processes of new cultures which, if they work as a coherent whole, provide the visitor with more confidence in the destination. It might be of interest, therefore, to examine the relationship between these cultural processes and their destination choices in the context of the tourists' cultural norms.

Enculturation and Acculturation

From the moment of birth each person is exposed to, and enveloped within, the boundaries of his/her society. Thus the language that individuals learn as their initial mean of communication and the patterns of behaviour that they adopt reflect the accumulation of knowledge and standards of their ancestors (Cracknell and Nobis, 1985). This knowledge is then codified by individuals and is reflected in the social institutions which guide their personal patterns of interaction within the values and wills of the majority. In complying with these principles individuals enter into a social contract with their fellow citizens, any deviation from which incurs not only the disfavour of others but also creates a sense of dissonance which can affect the individual's well being. The system of beliefs and values that guide a particular group may be referred to as their 'ideology', a term which seeks to explain why a specific group acts in a particular way (for further discussion of this concept see Scollon and Wong Scollon, 2001, p.131-2). Accordingly, as individuals undergo the process of enculturation (a socialisation process within their own group, which is elaborated on in Scollon and Wong Scollon, 2001, p.163-4), a template becomes superimposed on their instinctual human behaviour which determines the form of their actions in different situations within the confines of the community and the new environment. This is the reason why culture is more powerful than instincts. In fact, although man may be a product of his cultural identity, Usunier and Lee (2005) describe it as a 'collective fingerprint' and point out that, although cultural differences exist, there is no reason to judge specific cultural groups as inferior or superior to others. They note that the strength of a culture is in its distinction, although coherence is needed at the highest level.

Enculturation can give rise to the phenomenon of 'Ethnocentrism', "an idea that one's own cultural, national, racial or religious group is superior to or more deserving than that of others" (Carlson and Buskist, 1997, p. 78). Fundamentally, because individuals have acquired the norms and value of the culture in which they grew up, they tend, often without any knowledge basis for comparison, to form a belief that their own cultural rituals and practices are superior to those of others. Whilst this concept may assist in maintaining group cohesion and sustain the fabric of a nation or a community, it can also become a source of ideological conflict. Forms or rules of human behaviour vary considerably from one society to another, as may be noticed from the simplest modes of human interaction such as: body posture; bodily proximity; eye contact; forms of expressions and gestures and modes of social communication including simple signals of approval and disapproval. For example, even within the confines of European culture the vertical up and down movement of the head in most countries is taken to mean 'yes', but in some countries it means 'no', whilst in the latter the horizontal head movement from left to right and vice versa actually means 'yes'. Such signals are also evident in social etiquette and business practices (See Axtell, 1990, 1991, 1993, 1994 and 1997 and McGrath, 2005 for comprehensive further information and advice regarding the above and many other cultural dimensions of international business and leisure travel).

Cultural assumptions are basic responses to human problems which provide members of a particular cultural community with a framework for evaluation of solutions to these problems

(Giddens, 2004). They provide a 'cognitive dimension' (people think that it works that way), an 'affective dimension' (people like it that way) and a 'directive dimension' (people will do it that way). Both tourists and hosts can form prejudiced perceptions of people from other cultures, maybe due to social or economic barriers, and as a consequence show disregard for them, known as cultural blindness or cultural ignorance. It is imperative that tourism employees who deal with international visitors should avoid such feelings and displays of ignorance. In fact, it might be argued that both the hosts and the visitors have an obligation to make the effort to understand each others' cultural rites and traditions. They need to appreciate that all international visitors might arrive at the host destination with a mental template constructed by their own cultural backgrounds. Such personal cultural rites can assume a deep importance in all aspects of social interaction, especially in an insecure environment, and so an apparent lack of understanding by the 'local' people might alienate them or even become a source of conflict through lack of knowledge and understanding. Equally conflict can arise from within the mainstream culture by the action of subcultures or countercultures, resulting from groups who choose to reject the established values of their own societies and tourists may be exposed to, or even caught up in, such local disturbances. Interestingly, the abandonment of certain social rituals or established forms of etiquette by the younger generation can effectively become the source of conflict across similar or different generations of their own or their host communities.

In fact, the representation of any culture is necessarily selective. The process involves the appropriation, analysis and re-presentation of that culture and runs the inherent risk of creating cultural stereotypes (Teague, 1997), of which nationality may be used as a predictor (Dann, 1993). Stereotyping or national character has been referred to as the relatively fixed psychological traits shared by most of the people who originated in one community or country (Giddens, 2004) and represents the predominant attitudes, beliefs, values and dominant behaviour (Burns, Myers and Kakbadse, 1995). Heterostereotypes, preconceived images of one another's nationality, can influence perceptions, behaviours and reactions and lead to cultural hostility. A series of illustrative scenarios based on Italians' views of English tourists (from Ineson and Nicholls, 2002, pp. 5-6) follow: Italian police were reported to have a negative view of English football fans, stereotyping them as being 'violent hooligans', particularly when they are not on their 'home' ground. Consequently, Italians may judge *all* English Football supporters to be hooligans so, in their presence, a hostile, unpleasant, disrespectful and fearful atmosphere is generated. Luca (an Italian music student) had a stereotypical idea of British people – they drink large quantities of alcohol from early in the day – that was reinforced by encounters with 'football' tourists visiting his home town near Rome. "Alcohol, especially beer and wine, is very cheap in Italy relative to the UK, and is enjoyed at meal times and social events by Italians, 'enjoyed' being the operative word". He maintained it is uncommon and unacceptable to drink excessively but claimed drunkenness to be responsible for the violent and rude behaviour of some British tourists. "They leave a negative impression with Italians, who cannot accept or understand why these tourists choose to disregard the consequences of their excessive drinking". In contrast, John, an English lorry driver commented that Italian people were less law abiding and considerate than English people, especially when driving. "Lack of patience with other drivers is evident with consistent beeping of the horns and offensive gestures. Why there are traffic lights in Italy is questionable as every other Italian jumps a red light, also very few Italians wear the seat belt when travelling". In 2004, the introduction of penalty points on the driving licence for such offences appears to have curbed the latter cultural habits.

However although it is important that tourists and hosts should try to offer mutual consideration and the needs of the visitors should ideally be met and satisfied, this process should not be at the expense of the local cultural traditions. The latter almost certainly have their values in the local situation and environment, since alternative behavioural patterns and attitudes may not be capable of sustaining the existing social framework in the long term. Equally if a country makes a pledge to enter the tourist market and attract tourists from other cultures some background preparation in terms of cross-cultural learning and training is required.

Cultural Pychology

Because of the brain's role in controlling human activities, some practitioners of psychology assume that people in all cultures experience the same psychological processes (See Atkinson, Atkinson, Smith, Bern, Nolen-Hoeksema and Smith, 2005 for further details). However, they note that this proposition has been challenged by various exponents of cultural psychology and from different branches of the humane sciences including anthropologists and social psychologists. They presume that cultural psychology is intent on explaining how the culture in which individuals live influences their mental representation and the psychological processes which guide their actions and claim that it is during the maturational and enculturation process that individuals internalise their constructs (images) on the external world. In simple terms, people's experiences become the basis for their interpretation of the world.

Perception, Attitudes, Behaviour and Culture

Attitudes towards the provision for raising children, the regulation of sexuality, the division of labour and sharing and exchanging tend to be functions of the birth environment and the parental home. It seems that cultural background has an influence in perceptual and cognitive skills (Segall, Dasen, Berry and Poortinga, 1990). Perceptions regarding social controls, incentives for motivation, distribution and legitimisation of power, and priorities and values in daily conduct, although they might be initiated in the home, may be considered to be relatively fragile when people are exposed to the influences of the 'external' environment in their own culture. In turn, tourists' perceptions are likely to be coloured and influenced by what they see, hear and experience in other cultures. An interesting aspect of perception is found in the phenomenon of 'perceptual constancy' which may explain why security and comfort reside with people's own familiar environment, culture, knowledge and professional experience.

From the above brief overview of cultural and psychological aspects, it is apparent that tourists are products of their own cultures and environments. Wherever they travel, they take with them not only their cultural norms but also their accumulated experiences; they react to circumstances according to their perceptions of the situations within which they have internalised their accumulated knowledge and experiences. Lack of familiarity with foreign environments and habits, in addition to difficulties with communication, can initiate stress and fear. Strangers in new environments like to be understood and find comfort in familiar symbols and patterns of life. That is one of the reasons why many holiday-makers, given an opportunity and similar conditions, prefer to visit destinations in which their language is the official one and also where a comparative social order to that of their mother country is apparent.

Issues Influencing Tourists' Destination Choices

Current tourism trends indicate the increasing popularity of air travel as more and more Europeans, Britons and Germans in particular, travel further and further to reach their chosen tourist destinations. One aspect in the organisation of these journeys that may be overlooked consists of devoting sufficient time to evaluating the social and cultural environment of the destination. The provision of food and drink, accommodation, local facilities, sustainable and health issues, safety, security and ethics can all impact not only on tourists' satisfaction but also their initial choice of destination.

The Provision of Food and Drink

One of the most distinctive and powerful cultural and traditional elements of a society which can attract tourists resides in its food habits which have evolved over centuries and are based on local climatic conditions, the fertility of the land, religious prescriptions and the traditional culinary practices handed down from one generation to another. An interesting feature of supplying food to travellers is the fact that the most important point does not rest with the need to make good the depletion of nourishment within individuals, but with the capacity to provide them with a combination of food products which will meet the cultural, psychological and physiological needs of that specific group. The role of food in maintaining the well-being of international consumers needs to be appreciated fully by tourism operators. Although food may be considered as a form of body fuel, it can not only prevent but also create a variety of health problems. Over 2000 years ago Lucretius, pronounced his famous dictum "What is food to one man is bitter poison to others" (http://www.quotationspage.com/quote/1559.html). The clearest example of this dictum comes from milk, which is the most popular nourishment of the Alpine races, but a form of nourishment which to most native Asian and Africans in its natural state is indigestible (Nobis, 1993) and can act as a laxative, taking nourishment out of their systems.

Cultural differences are immediately evident in the provision and consumption of food and drink. For example, Jewish people do not eat pork, Hindus do not eat beef, Horsemeat is avoided in the UK and in some parts of the world young dogs and cats are considered to be a delicacy (Giddens, 2004). When the food is consumed as a main meal, in 'westernised establishments' guests sit round the table. In some cultures they kneel and in others they squat. Meat and fish may be eaten raw or cooked; food may be cold or hot depending on the culture; it may be conveyed to the mouth with cutlery, chop-sticks or fingers, in the latter instance ranging from the formation of a neat, one inch wide, rice ball, which may be dipped in sauce then consumed, to the tearing apart of meat from the bones or the crunching of fish bones, eyes and heads. There are also cultures in which men and women do not eat together; it is because of these cultural differences some large international hotels, which specialise in receiving officials and missions from distant countries, have special dining areas for different cultures. For example, the Crescent Village Muslim Restaurant in the Yin Du Hotel, Urumqi, China has 8 private dining rooms and a Muslim master chef (See http://www.yinduhotel.com/e_dining.htm) and the King's Kosher Hotel in Budapest's Jewish quarter where the dining room offers Glatt Kosher Mehadrin food kept under the local Rabbi's observation (See http://www.totallyjewishtravel.com/features/?disp_feature=xenYJz). It is interesting to note at this point that because of its kosher status, such food can be attractive to Muslims (Kosher Today, 2005).

In relation to the nutritional needs of visitors, an understanding of the requirements of individuals in the host environment is a necessity for tourism providers, as is an understanding of the potential effect on other cultures of different forms of nutrients. This is particularly true in relation to the food preferences of different cultural groups. Even in a period of resource depletion or starvation some people would refuse to eat otherwise nourishing food which is abhorred and rejected by their culture. It is an established fact that in many parts of the industrialised world people suffer not from under nourishment but from malnutrition caused by over-eating resulting in obesity, cardiovascular disorders and high cholesterol levels. Patterns of food consumption appear to be deteriorating due to the high proportion of fat and salt present in the diet (Bosely and Radford, 2004). Salt is a more of a problem for the older generation. In terms of ethics and ensuring customers' well being, the amount of salt should be limited to six grams per day but for professional chefs flavour is the overriding guide. In fact, salt content can even be increased by dedicated chefs who smoke; such practice lowers the sensitivity of the taste buds.

There are two important areas to be considered in the safe provision of food: Nutrition and Hygiene. The negative publicity that can follow a food poisoning outbreak is clearly counterproductive in international destination marketing. It is imperative, therefore, that some form of governmental control should be exercised regarding hygienic practices in all food outlets. According to the Food and Agriculture Organisation of the United Nations, problems have become apparent with the opening up of Central and Eastern European markets including misleading advertising, unsafe and poor quality goods, bad services and lack of redress. "In terms of food issues there is a great deal of similarity in the challenges each country faces, such as regional and international harmonisation alongside adherence to their national regulations. The prominent issues that consumer organisations are trying to tackle are, food hygiene, food labelling, lack of regulation and enforcement, additives, safety of products, GM [genetically modified] foods, food contamination and identification/traceability" (Sutton, 2002, p. 1). Hospitality operators have a duty to update their knowledge in relation to the changing needs of their customers and there should be some means of ensuring that all involved comply with this responsibility.

The World Tourism Organisation (WTO, 1999) Global Code of Ethics for Tourism, (available in 26 languages including Czech, Hungarian, Polish, Romanian, Russian, Serbian, Slovak and Slovenian) provides guidelines for the role of professionals in the Industry. Familiarity with the 10 articles of the Global Code of Ethics is imperative for all industry personnel responsible for providing food and beverages to consumers. Article 1, Section 3 states: "The host community on the one hand, and local professionals on the other, should acquaint themselves with and respect the tourists who visit them and find out about their lifestyles, tastes and expectations" (WTO, 1999, p. 4). Only when the consumers' needs are understood is it possible to formulate an operational policy intent on providing international tourist satisfaction. It is the culture of the society from which the tourist originates that determines what is acceptable and what is not acceptable as nourishment by the members of that cultural group. Article 2, Section 6 states: "Tourism professionals, insofar as it depends on them, should show concern with public authorities for the security and safety, accident prevention, health protection and food safety for those who seek their services" (WTO, 1999, pp. 5-6).

Examples of Central and Eastern European consumer organisation research and campaigning on food standards include:

> Bulgaria: Research on food labelling has found that enforcement must urgently be improved to protect consumers against fraudulent foods. They have also been running a high profile media campaign on food product safety and quality

> Lithuania: National Consumer Federation is carrying out quality and safety testing on a range of foods and surveying consumers' food complaints

> Romania: A consumer information campaign has been launched with extensive consumer surveying on labelling needs, particularly for GM Foods; they are lobbying for the setting up of a National Consultative Codex Committee in Romania

> ➤ Ukraine: Banned the growth of GM crops in 2001. Implementing systems for imports, state testing, registration and use of GM products in the Ukraine and provided educational material to farmers, young people and those in rural areas

> ➤ Croatia: Working on the problem of meat hygiene by holding seminars for small meat producers hosting 'round tables' with producers and enforcement agencies. They are also providing advice to consumers about consumer redress after purchasing or consuming harmful products

However, "enforcement of food standards is a major problem in their countries. The inspection bodies do not have the capacity to cope with the need. This is compounded by the fact that much fresh food is bought from stalls at food markets, for example in Macedonia this is estimated to be 40-50%, which are more difficult to regulate" (Sutton, 2002, p. 1). Another major problem is the lack of a formal consultation system between government and consumer organisations. One example of the formal structure which should be in place is a National Consultative Codex Committee (NCCC). There are National Consultative Codex Points (NCCP) in all but a few of the Central and Eastern European countries ... but [consultation with consumer groups in Central and Eastern Europe has been low] ... Of a survey in 2000 of Consumers International members in Bulgaria, Macedonia, Bosnia, Romania, Slovenia and Slovakia, only one was represented on their national food standards body (Sutton, 2002, p.1-2).

Recommendations for Central and Eastern European countries include:

> ➤ Governments consulting with consumer organisations to inform them of consumer needs, perceptions and information related to issues under discussion in order to develop national policy; the establishment of links and stronger co-operation between government departments and consumer organisations.

> ➤ Training, ideally facilitated by the Food and Agriculture Organisation (FAO) of the United Nations and the World Health Organisation (WHO) in consultation with consumers, is necessary to improve the credibility and the effectiveness of the codex process so that locals can more effectively participate in the national policy making process, manage food safety concerns and strengthen food safety control systems in their countries.

"Governments face many problems which are closer in similarity to developing countries compared with developed countries". They are under-represented in the codex process and must be included, ideally funded by FAO and WHO in consultation with consumer organisations and other interested parties to enable them to "more effectively manage food safety risks, improving quality management, the quality and safety of products in the domestic market and will increase the confidence and trust of consumers" (Sutton, 2002, p. 2).

Accommodation

Western Europeans on package tours prefer to arrive at destinations where they are greeted by company representatives who speak their own language and/or local officials who project a feeling of welcome. They desire organised modes of transportation and advice on reliable local transport with regulated tariffs. Independent travel is increasing and such visitors are unlikely to choose to be accommodated and segregated within residential compounds, preferring to benefit from local amenities which form part of the destination's attraction. Such tourists seek 'official' and fair prices for accommodation, via guide books, visitor information centres or websites; international guests have a strong preference for en-suite facilities not just in hotels and self-catering accommodation but increasingly in guest houses. Yet such 'luxuries' may not be available in many parts of Central and Eastern Europe, which can be a source of dissatisfaction for tourists. The descriptions and grading of hotels should conform to internationally agreed facility and quality standards in relation to price, space and amenities (See Chapter 4 for further details). Modern hotels created for the international clientele should conform to internationally approved standards of building construction providing comfort, security and safety. Due to climatic variations, it may be physiologically difficult for foreign tourists to adapt to the conditions of certain indigenous cultures and so they might require and expect air-conditioning or central heating for their comfort. At the very least, all amenities should include at least minimal services such as water and electricity available for 24 hours a day.

Facilities

New destinations entering the tourism market almost invariably seek to attract tourists from wealthy post industrial economies. However, as indicated above, there may be great differences amongst the cultural practices and across individuals' perceptions of different continents and countries. Within Europe, for example, there are apparent and considerable differences not only between the East and the West but also the North and the South. There are also commonalities such as natives of adjacent countries speaking different languages but with the ability to understand one another (for example Czech and Slovak or Spanish and Portuguese). There are increasing efforts worldwide to ensure that facilities at major tourist destinations conform to international consumers' expectations. One such study is the heritage and urban tourism project in Conwy, Chepstow, Naarden and Alcudia (Bruce, Jackson and Cantallops, 2000). A much larger example was prepared by Rambøll Water and Environment on behalf of The European Commission (2003) incorporating 'QUALITEST' to evaluate the quality performance of tourist destinations and services in Helsinki, Toulouse, Cork, El Vendrell, Odsherred, Lesbos, Lech, Lillehammer, Söderslätt and the Isle of Man; 16 quality themes, each giving rise to three quality indicators have been developed. Further details may be found at their websites listed in the references at the end of this chapter. Both studies rely on creating 'measurement tools' for monitoring the quality of tourist destinations and local services and products based upon the 'quality perceptions' of the tourists. However, this task is complicated by the fact that tourists originating from different localities, with different cultural backgrounds, tend to interpret quality according to their own cultural norms and travel experiences.

Sustainability and Health Issues

Whilst good practices of the past ought to be preserved, tourism and hospitality operators must move with the times. Although efforts may be made by destination marketers to project the destination's image and identity, the provision of products and services for the incoming tourists should be matched to their needs and expectations. Generally, reasonable care is taken in this context in the provision of information, transportation, banking and local folklore. A further feature of a destination's success originates from its capacity as a host to integrate visitors into the existing community. This is often a complex task which requires a sensitive approach, in particular trying to avoid conflict with the local residents as in the sombre warning of Krippendorf (1987), who refer to ecologists and conservationists as those people who "want to get at the tourist landscape eaters"; he specified a number of problems arising from tourist development including:

> ➢   economic imbalance;

> ➤ lack of planning resulting in overcapacity;

> ➤ loss of local identity; and

> ➤ the gravest problems, those of the physical environment including disturbance and destruction of flora and fauna, soil erosion, air and water pollution, waste disposal problems, ground water depletion and degradation of the landscape.

Hence the success of a tourist destinations depends on how the increasing numbers of visitors can be integrated into the life of the local subculture. By necessity, this process requires those destinations which intend to attract a large number of tourists in rural, suburban and even urban areas to adapt not only their infrastructure to cope with larger numbers of people making additional demands on the physical surroundings, but also to provide the range of amenities, products and services which comply with the nature of visitors' requirements. Frequently, the latter demands a departure from local traditions and involves new directives and training for the local human capital resources. Human understanding requires not only an understanding of the language that the foreign visitors speak but also an understanding of their cultural practices and expectations which vary according to the state of development and sophistication of different societies in specific periods. However, it is not always easy to integrate oneself with the locals as demonstrated by the following true story reported on English television: "A 61 year old man who spent six days sleeping rough in Italy after getting separated from a coach tour has returned to his home in the UK. He got lost on a visit to Sorrento with his partner. He struggled to explain his situation to people because he is Spanish and speaks little English or Italian. He was eventually helped by police and Spanish consular authorities to return to his home in the UK" (British Broadcasting Corporation, 2002).

Environmental issues are given considerable importance by many groups of tourists. Members of industrialised countries are well aware of the effects of industrial pollution. Citizens of post-industrial economies may be disinclined, or even afraid, to holiday in districts where there are concentrations of: fossil fuel power stations; chemical and smelting plants; manufacturing industry; traffic with consequent air pollution; and acid rain which is of considerable worry to asthmatics and aged visitors who suffer from respiratory disorders. The acceleration of the phenomenon of global warming is a further issue. Girardet (1992) refers to a number of cities, particularly in Eastern Europe, as 'cities of death', where life expectancy is about five years lower than in the cleaner areas. These cities had an uphill struggle to revitalise their image since the communism schism. Although standards of health care can also be a cause for concern in Central and Eastern Europe, certain cities and resorts are attractive destinations for health tourism (See Chapter 7, p.123). All professionals within the industry have the solemn responsibility to apply ethical principles to all their business activities, and implement operational practices and procedures which are environmentally responsible and protect the well being of consumers.

Safety, Security and Ethics

Although it might be considered essential to have guaranteed aspects of safety and security for all tourists, such guarantees are not always possible. Nevertheless, hosts should do their utmost to create an awareness of the impending visitors' cultural and psychological requirements and to promote their confidence in unfamiliar environments. As international travellers gain experience they become more discerning regarding destination choices with a consequent impact on the success of destinations. The importance of good public relations in service industries is gradually taking hold, at least on the 'surface structure' (Giddens, 2004). He explains that in Greenland, the

Inuit ('translated' as 'real people', that is Eskimos) do not smile or exchange pleasantries with strangers but, with training, this practice is becoming more accepted particularly in the work place. Training for all concerned in providing customer comfort and satisfaction is essential.

Once operational, the running and maintenance of the buildings and the welfare of the visitors is the responsibility of the unit management team who should be aware that customers have the right to be protected from injuries, diseases, or illness arising from their stay in the establishment. It is the duty of the management team to ensure that they have the requisite up-to-date knowledge to guarantee that every customer leaves the premises in better physical and psychological condition than s/he entered them. Within the accommodation sector, safe drinking water and air purity constitute an essential part of this responsibility. Contaminated drinking water and contaminated ice cubes have been an historic problem for the Industry, but more recently serious problems have arisen with the advent of the potentially fatal Legionnaires' disease (Ricketts and Joseph, 2003). Outbreaks have been linked to air conditioning and hot and cold water systems resulting from poor maintenance programmes, frequently caused by lack of technical understanding or training and poor or outdated professional preparation for the maintenance duties involved.

Corruption and petty crime even by officials is embedded in the culture of many exotic destinations. In time these undesirable practices will be subjected to more official control, but in the meantime travellers, must be prepared to deal with a completely new environment totally alien to their culture which more often than not is not conducive to repeat business.

What is actually required by the industry at national and international level is the establishment of a minimal level of professional competences and the inculcation of 'ethical standards' for all involved from the executive director to the lower operatives. These competences should include every aspect of the operation which affects customers' comfort, safety and security supported by frequent statutory updating programmes. This obligation applies to all aspects of tourism activities but recent examples in hotels and cruise liners have demonstrated that it is more acute in the area of food supply, particularly in relation to food preparation and production where the provision of food to a variety of foreign visitors from different ethnic backgrounds requires sound knowledge of nutrition and broader understanding of their specific needs.

Conclusion

Tourists have the absolute right to expect, from all cultures involved in the supply of transport, food and accommodations, not only professionalism and value for money but also safety, honesty and ethical practices and security. Cultural dimensions are present throughout daily individual and collective activities and, although culture may be learned, it may also be forgotten. For example, people who are brought up to speak a language may move permanently to a location where another language is spoken and lose their linguistic facility through lack of practice. As culture is oriented towards adaptation to reality, both in terms of constraints and opportunities, it is important that tourists should try to consider the perspectives of the 'the natives', that is, what the people living in the culture consider to be significant about the way in which they live in terms of the language (semiotics) and symbols required to understand a given social system and then respond to the 'other culture' accordingly. Although some visitors prepare themselves for 'new' cultural experiences, others can be shocked and upset when they reach unfamiliar destinations. However, all societies engage in cultural rituals and patterns of behaviour. International tourists, service sector employees and managers alike can all learn a substantial amount about their own prejudices, rules, codes of behaviour etc. if they examine their own societies as if they are 'anthropologically strange' (cf. Miner, 1956) and therefore come to realise that they should not be surprised but fascinated by the 'strange' and 'exotic' customs they encounter but see them as valuable learning experiences.

Student Activities

The following questions suggest topics for class discussion. Students are requested to prepare their stances in advance so that they can improve their learning experiences in the debate.

1. Discuss the concept that different cultures result from the prevailing environmental conditions.

2. To what extent can it be said that the process of enculturation moulds individuals as members of a society.

3. Review the importance of familiarising local tourism employees with the cultural practices of visitors.

   Practical exercise: Students are divided into groups of three or four and asked to research the cultural practices of a pre-allocated (agreed) country. They should prepare a fact sheet for visitors from other cultures (i) providing general advice and guidance and (ii) providing specialist advice and guidance for business travellers. In addition to a series of discussions, each group of students can be required also to make presentation to the rest of the groups. Consideration should be given as to whether the country of choice should be the home country of at least one of the students in each group or whether students should examine the procedures in countries with which they are not familiar.

4. Debate the importance of sound ethical practices in the business activities of any [local] organisations involved in the provision of food and beverages, accommodation and/or transport for locals and tourists.

References

Atkinson, R.L., Atkinson, R.C., Smith, E. Bern, D. Nolen-Hoeksema and Smith, C.D. (eds.) (2005) *Hilgard's Introduction to Psychology*, 14th edn., Wadsworth, Belmont, CA.

Axtell, R.E. (1990). *The dos and taboos of hosting international visitors*, Wiley, Chichester.

Axtell, R.E. (1991). *Gestures : The do's and taboos of body language around the world*, John Wiley and Sons, New York.

Axtell, R.E. (ed.) (1993). *Dos and taboos around the world*, 3rd. edn., Wiley, Chichester.

Axtell, R.E (1994). *The dos and taboos of international trade: a small business primer*, Wiley, Chichester.

Axtell, R.E. (1997). *Dos and taboos around the world for women in business*, Wiley, Chichester.

Bosely, S. and Radford, T. (2004). Against the Grain, *The Guardian*, September 15th, Manchester.

British Broadcasting Corporation (2002). *British tourist lost in Italy,* Ceefax, October 23rd .

Brown Weiss, E. (1989) *In Fairness to Future Generations: International Law, Common Patrimony, and Intergenerational Equity,* Transnational/United Nations University, pp. 297-327.

Bruce, D.M., Jackson, M.J. and Cantallops, A.S. (2000). PREPARe: a model to aid the development of policies for less unsustainable tourism in historic towns, *Tourism and Hospitality Research,* Vol. 3, No. 1, pp. 21-36.

Burns, P., Myers, A, and Kakabadse, A. (1995). Are national stereotypes discriminating? *European Management Journal,* Vol. 13, No. 12, pp. 212-217.

Carlson, N.R. and Buskist, W. (1997). *Psychology: The science of behaviour,* 5th edn. Allyn and Bacon, London.

Chinese Culture Connection (1987). Chinese values and the search for culture-free dimensions of culture, *Journal of cross cultural psychology,* Vol. 18, p. 143-164.

Cracknell, H. and Nobis, G. (1985). *Practical Professional Gastronomy,* Macmillan, London.

Dann, G. (1993). Limitation in the use of "Nationality" and "Country of Residence" variables. In D. Pearce and R. Butler (eds.). *Tourism Research: Critiques and Challenges.* London, Routledge.

Fiske, A. P. (1991). *Structures of social life: the four elementary forms of human relations: communal sharing, authority ranking, equality matching, market pricing,* Free Press, New York.

Gerring, J. and Baressi, P.A. (2002). *A selection of definitions and descriptions of culture from the 'social science' literature,* [on-line] available from: www.concepts-methods.org/xtras/culturedef.pdf [accesseed March 18th 2005].

Giddens, A. (2004). *Sociology* 4th edn., Cambridge Polity Press, Cambridge.

Girardet H. (1992). *The Gaia Atlas of Cities,* Gaia Books, London.

Hofstede, G. (1984). *Culture's consequences: international differences in work-related values,* London, Sage.

Hofstede, G. (1991). *Cultures and organizations: software of the mind,* London, McGraw-Hill.

Hofstede, G. (2001). *Culture's consequences: comparing values, behaviours, institutions and organisations across nations,* London, Sage.

http://www.totallyjewishtravel.com/features/?disp_feature=xenYJz.

http://www.quotationspage.com/quote/1559.html.

http://www.yinduhotel.com/e_dining.htm.

Ineson, E.M. and Nicholls, M. (2002). United Kingdom visitors to Italy: intercultural encounters, In ESADE (Ed.) *Cross-cultural challenges in the tourism industry: the educational answers,* Conference prodeedings, EuroCHRIE congress, ESADE, Barcelona, October-Nov.

Kosher Today (2005). *The Impact of the Sharm el-Sheikh Meeting on Israeli Kosher Food: Two Views,* [on-line] available from: http://www.koshertodaymagazine.com/archives/newsletter_2005/02_14_05.htm [accessed March 21st 2005].

Krippendorf, J. (1987). *The Holiday Makers; Understanding the Impact of Leisure and Travel,* Butterworth Heinemann, Oxford.

Kroeber, A. L. and Kluckhohn, C. (1952). Culture: A critical review of concepts and definitions, Anthropological Papers, No. 4 Peabody Museum.

LaborLawTalk.com (2004). [on-line] available from: http://encyclopedia.laborlawtalk.com/Service_sector [accessed March 18th 2005].

Mastny, L. (2001). *Worldwatch Paper #159: Traveling Light: New Paths for International Tourism,* December, Worldwatch Institute, [on-line] available from: http://www.worldwatch.org/pubs/paper/159/ [accessed March 18th 2005].

McGrath, G. (2005). (ed.) *City Guides,* [on-line] available from: http://www.businesstraveller.com/default.asp [accessed March 21st 2005].

McRae H. (1995). The World in 2020, Power Culture and Prosperity: A Vision of the Future, Harper Collins, London.

Miner, H. (1956). Body rituals amongst the Nacerima, *American Anthropologist,* Vol. 58, No.3, pp. 503-507.

Nobis. G. (1993). Trends and Integration in Food Processing, *International Journal of Hospitality Management* , Vol. 5, No. 3, pp. 26-31.

Rambøll Water and Environment on behalf of The European Commission (2003) *A Manual for Evaluating the Quality Performance of Tourist Destinations and Services,* Enterprise DG Publication II, [on-line] available from: http://europa.eu.int/comm/enterprise/services/tourism/index_en.htm [accessed April 2nd 2005].

Ricketts, K. and Joseph, C. on behalf of the European Working Group for Legionella Infections (2003). *Travel Associated Legionnaires' Disease in Europe: 2003* Health Protection Agency, CDSC, London, [on-line] available from: http://www.eurosurveillance.org/em/v09n10/0910-223.asp [accessed April 2nd 2005].

Schwatrz, S.H. and Bilsky, W. (1990). Toward a theory of the universal content and structure of values: extensions of cross-cultural replications, *Journal of personality and social psychology,* Vol. 58, pp. 878-891.

Schwartz, S.H. (1992). Universals in the content and structure of values: Theoretical advances and empirical tests in 20 countries. In M.P. Zanna (Ed.), Advances in Experimental Social Psychology, Academic Press, Inc. , San Diego, pp. 1-65.

Scollon, R. and Scollon, S.W. (1999). *Intercultural communication,* Blackwell, Oxford.

Segall, M.H., Dasen, P.R., Berry, J.W., and Poortinga, Y.H. (1990). *Human Behavior in Global Perspective: An Introduction to Cross-Cultural Psychology,* Pergamon, New York.

Sutton, R. (2002) Report on behalf of Food and Agriculture Organisation of the United Nations/World Health Organisation, Consumer activities related to food safety and quality in Central and Eastern Europe, by Consumers International. FAO/WHO Pan-European Conference on Food Safety and Quality, Budapest, Hungary. Conference room document PEC/CRD 12, [on-line] available from: http://www.fao.org/docrep/meeting/004/ab505e.htm [accessed March 31st 2005].

Teague, K. (1997) Representations of Nepal. In Abram, S. J., Waldren, J. & Macleod, L, V. *Tourists and Tourism: Identifying with people and places.* Berg Educational Offices, Oxford.

Terpstra, V. and David, K. (1985). *The cultural environment of international business,* 2nd edn. South-Western Publishing Company, Dallas.

Trompenaars, F. (1995). Worldwide vision in the workplace, *People Management,* May 18th, pp. 20-25.

Trompenaars, F. (2000). *Riding the waves of culture: understanding cultural diversity in business,* 2nd. edn., Brealey Publishing, London.

Tylor, E. B. (1913). *Primitive Cultures,* John Murray, London.

Usunier, J-C. and Lee, .A. (2005). *Marketing across cultures,* 4th edn. Pearson Education Ltd., Harlow.

World Tourism Organisation (1999). *Global Code of Ethics for Tourism,* [on-line] available from: http://www.world-tourism.org/code_ethics/eng.html [accessed March 29th 2005].

Suggested Further Reading

Bareham, J. R. (1995).*Consumer behaviour in the food industry: a European Perspective,* Butterworth-Heinemann, Oxford.

Barnard G. (1999). *Cross-cultural communication: a practical guide,* Cassell, London.

David M Kennedy Centre (1995). *Culturegrams,* Brigham Young University, Vol. 1, The Americas and Europe; Vol. 2, Africa, Asia and Oceania.

Jafari, J. and Way, W. (1994) Multicultural strategies in tourism, *The Cornell Hotel and Restaurant Quarterly,* Vol. 36, No. 3, pp. 80-85.

Jandt, E. F. (1995). *Intercultural communication,* Sage Publications Ltd., London.

Pizam, A. and Sussman, S. (1995). Does nationality affect tourist behaviour? *Annals of Tourism Research,* Vol. 22, No. 4, pp. 901-917.

Reisinger, Y. and Turner, L. (2003). *Cross cultural behaviour in tourism: concepts and analysis,* Butterworth-Heinemann, Oxford.

Ward, C., Bochner, S. & Furnham, A. (2001), *The psychology of culture shock,* 2nd edn., Routledge, Sussex.

Index

A

Aalborg Chart, 133
Accommodation, 23, 33, 34, 43, 44, 45, 46, 47,
    48, 49, 50, 51, 52, 53, 62, 63, 64, 65, 66,
    67, 68, 69, 70, 86, 96, 110, 111, 124, 127,
    135, 136, 137, 138, 139, 140, 141, 142,
    143, 163, 165, 172, 176, 181, 189, 193,
    195, 198
Accommodation preferences, 34
Acculturation, 190
Affective dimension', 191
Agrotourism, 135, 151
Air conditioning, 198
Airports, 50, 172, 176, 182
Airports Council International (ACI) Europe,
    172
Alcudia, 196
Alternative, 36, 112, 120, 144, 192
American (USA), 8
Animatronics, 105
Annapurna, 179
Antigua and Barbuda, 172, 173
Armenia, 13, 31, 52, 136
Art galleries, 33, 103
Arts, 76, 77, 80, 98, 102, 109
Asia, 17, 158, 175, 177, 178
Athletic, 111
Attitudes, 7, 15, 56, 122, 127, 136, 142, 191,
    192
Attraction, 12, 96, 102, 103, 104, 105, 108, 110,
    111, 112, 172, 178, 180, 195
    built, 103, 111, 112
    free, 103
    paid, 103, 106, 112
Attraction types, 102
Audiovisuals, 75, 92, 93
Audit, 78, 95
Australia, 29, 32, 33, 34, 35, 41, 96, 158, 161,
    173, 176, 177, 180
Australian wine, 34
Australian wine tourism, 32, 41
Austria, 12, 30, 48, 52, 120, 124
Automatic switches, 137
Automobile Association (AA), 18, 61, 63, 64, 65
Aviation industry, 164
Azerbaijan, 31, 52, 136

B

Bank Holidays, 46
Barriers to wine tourism, 35
Beaches, 104
Beatles, 105

Bed and breakfast accommodation, 34
Behaviour, 192
Belgium, 11, 12, 31, 48, 52, 119, 124
Benchmarking, 3, 5
Benefits, 2, 3, 9, 32, 33, 35, 36, 37, 41, 44, 45,
    76, 77, 79, 80, 81, 82, 86, 90, 97, 107, 108,
    134, 135, 171, 175, 176, 182, 187
Benefits of wine tourism, 32
Benidorm (Spain), 189
Bermuda, 104
Best Practice Forum, 1, 2, 5, 6
BIO trademark, 135
Biodiversity, 134
Blackpool, 102, 179
Boosterists tendency, 53
Bosnia, 31, 174, 195
Brand identity, 110, 111
British, 2, 3, 8, 9, 10, 13, 19, 20, 21, 46, 102,
    122, 158, 163, 167, 168, 173, 191, 197
British Hospitality Association, 2, 3
British Olympic Association, 79
British Tourist Authority, 67
British Virgin Islands, 172, 173
Buckingham Palace, 105
Budapest, 109, 123, 172, 193
Budget, 51, 52, 62, 86, 89, 103
Building, 2, 3, 78, 137, 143
    disabled access, 137
Built, 18, 29, 51, 88, 103, 111, 112, 135
Bulgaria, 30, 32, 47, 51, 52, 53, 107, 109,
    117, 123, 165, 174, 180, 194, 195
Bulls, 106
Business practices, 190
Business strategies, 29
Business tourists, 43
Buxton, 45

C

California, 35, 36, 104
Canary Islands, 110
Cannock Chase, 103
Cardiff, 172
Caribbean, 11, 20, 117, 122, 176, 179
Case studies, 121
Case study, 18, 136, 140
Cash flow, 89
Catering, 1, 4, 19, 51, 75, 90, 92, 93, 94, 103,
    135, 136, 137, 196
Cellar door, 32, 34, 41
Cellar door sales, 32, 33
Cellar door services, 33

Central and Eastern Europe, 13, 22, 32, 40, 43,
    47, 48, 49, 51, 52, 53, 54, 75, 101, 106,
    107, 108, 109, 111, 117, 118, 123, 124,
    174, 175, 178, 189, 181, 195, 196, 197
Central and Eastern European, 11, 14, 15, 47,
    49, 50, 51, 52, 53, 97, 101, 107, 108, 110,
    111, 171, 175, 180, 181, 194, 195
Cheese, 13, 135
Chepstow, 196
China, 8, 19, 30, 158, 172, 173, 180, 193
Chinese, 8, 10, 19, 20, 21
Chinese Culture Connection, 189
Cities of death, 197
Climatic variations, 196
Coastal regions, 181
Cognitive dimension, 191
Collectivisation, 107
Commonwealth Games, 18, 79, 86, 88, 96
Communicable diseases, 157, 158, 159
Communication, 5, 76, 85, 90, 91, 92, 93, 94,
    131, 188, 190, 192
Communist ideology, 108
Concept of culture, 188, 189
Concessions, 90, 93
Conservation, 103, 131, 134
Conservation of natural resources, 132
Consumer, 7, 8, 16, 17, 18, 19, 20, 21, 22, 23,
    33, 36, 37, 43, 44, 47, 51, 61, 63, 64, 69,
    70, 71, 87, 88, 91, 101, 104, 118, 120, 123,
    124, 163, 164, 194, 195
Consumer awareness, 7, 16, 22, 43
Consumption, 22, 29, 91, 101, 120, 122, 131,
    134, 139, 144, 145, 146, 147, 148, 159,
    164, 175, 193, 194
Contingency plans, 93, 94
Contract, 82, 88, 90, 190
Contracts, 82, 93, 123
Conwy, 196
Cork, 196
Corporate hospitality, 75, 77, 80, 90
Corporate identity, 88
Costing, 89
Council of Europe, 129
Country Tourism, 135
Courtesy of choice, 137
Creative product, 96
Creolisation, 9, 20
Crime, 49, 161, 181, 189, 198
Critical path analysis, 84, 92
Croatia, 30, 32, 109, 174, 175, 180, 195
Cruise liners, 175, 198
CSA Czech Airlines, 50
Cultural, 7, 8, 9, 11, 14, 16, 18, 19, 20, 21, 29,
    33, 45, 47, 54, 55, 56, 75, 76, 77, 78, 80,
    87, 97, 102, 106, 107, 108, 110, 111, 128,
    132, 133, 134, 136, 171, 179, 187, 188,
    189, 190, 191, 192, 193, 194, 196, 197, 198
Cultural and social aims, 76
Cultural activities, 33

Cultural assumptions, 190
Cultural differences, 193
Cultural dimensions, 198
Cultural facilities and events, 97
Cultural heritage, 132
Cultural identity, 7, 188, 190
Cultural legal and ethical principles, 127
Cultural norms, 188, 190, 192, 196
Cultural practices, 187, 189, 196, 197
Cultural processes, 190
Cultural pychology, 192
Cultural rites, 191
Cultural rituals, 190, 198
Culture, 7, 8, 9, 13, 15, 17, 18, 19, 22, 44, 46,
    55, 79, 84, 98, 109, 111, 148, 187, 188,
    189, 190, 191, 192, 193, 194, 198
Currency, 49, 62, 107, 160
Customer spend, 2, 3, 43
Customer volume, 2, 3
Cyprus, 11, 12, 30, 48, 135, 174, 175, 177, 180
Cyprus Agrotourism Company, 135
Cyprus Tourism Organisation, 135
Czech Republic, 12, 31, 32, 47, 48, 49, 51, 52,
    54, 62, 107, 108, 109, 117, 123, 127, 131,
    135, 141, 142, 174, 180
Czechoslovakia, 47, 49

D

Debriefing, 96, 97
Deep Vein Thrombosis (DVT), 159
Defined culture, 188
Defining health, 117
Definition, 29, 33, 37, 63, 75, 84, 108, 117,
    118, 119, 132, 133, 134, 177
Demand, 171, 177, 179, 180, 181
Demographic profile of overnight visitors to
    wineries, 35
Denmark, 12, 48, 52, 124, 177
Design, 2, 34, 45, 65, 66, 90, 92, 107, 137, 138,
    139, 140, 142
Destination, 11,119, 121
Destination marketing, 14, 194
Developing events, 77
Direct, 51, 89, 131, 173, 174
Direct benefits, 175
Directive dimension, 191
Directive for Sustainable Development Planning
    and Management (1996), 132
Disability Discrimination Act, 21
Disabled access, 93, 137, 138
Disease, 117, 118, 122, 158, 159, 161, 164, 198
Disney, 103, 104, 105
Disrupting the harvest, 35, 36
Distribution, 13, 56, 87, 91, 181, 192
Distribution techniques, 45
Docklands, 104
Domestic tourists, 32, 172
Dominican Republic, 173
Due diligence, 83

Duty of care, 83

E

Eastern Block, 49
Eco-agrotourism, 135
Ecological audit framework, 142
Economic, 8, 9, 13, 29, 32, 36, 44, 45, 48, 49,
50, 51, 52, 54, 55, 62, 67, 75, 76, 78, 80,
97, 101, 104, 106, 107, 108, 110, 111, 122,
127, 129, 130,131, 132, 133, 134, 136, 148,
171, 173, 174, 175, 176, 178, 180, 181,
191, 196
Economic benefits, 29, 36, 97, 134, 176, 178,
181
Economic development, 159
Economic environmental and social aspects, 127
Economic impacts, 174
Economic impact of tourism, 171, 172
Economic viability, 76
Economist Intelligence Unit, 50
Ecotourism, 134, 135, 179
Ecotourism Australia, 134
Eden Project, 104
Edinburgh, 18, 77, 105, 172
Education, 49, 120, 135, 161, 188
Egon Ronay, 18
El Vendrell, 196
Emergency services, 82, 84
Employed, 2, 33, 47, 86, 140, 142, 143, 175
Employment, 173, 174
Empowerment, 84
Enculturation, 190
Energy consumption, 131, 138, 139, 141, 142,
147
Energy management, 144
Enforcement of food, 195
English Tourism Board, 67
English Tourism Council, 69, 70
English Tourist Board, 67
Entertainment, 95, 101, 102, 105, 109, 176
Environmental, 35, 78, 95, 129, 131, 148, 197
    adaptation, 189
    assessment, 95
    conditions, 130, 187, 188, 199
    cultural awareness, 134
    impact, 35, 78, 133, 134, 141
    indicators, 130
    issues, 35, 148, 197
    protection, 127, 132, 136, 137, 139, 140,
    141, 148
    social aspects, 127
Environmentally Friendly, 134
Estonia, 12, 14, 31, 48, 52, 53, 54, 109, 111,
174, 175, 176, 181
Ethical, 127
Ethical standards, 198
Ethnic food, 8, 9, 10
Ethnocentrism, 190
Eurasia Foundation, 136

Europe, 1, 7, 8, 16, 17, 19, 21, 43, 44, 45, 46,
47, 48, 50, 52, 53, 54, 102, 106, 107, 108,
110, 112, 117, 121, 123, 158, 163, 174,
177, 179, 180, 196, 197
European Bank for Reconstruction and
Development, 129
European Campaign for Sustainable Towns and
Cities, 133
European City of Culture, 105
European Commission, 1, 13, 52, 128, 132, 177,
183, 196
European Community, 48
European Community (EC) Directive on
Package Travel, Package Holidays and
Package Tours, 161
European Foundation for the Improvement of
Living and Working Conditions, 2000, 180
European Monetary Union, 49
European Spatial Development Perspective, 132
European Union, 11, 48, 49, 51, 54, 101, 108,
165, 173, 174, 176, 177
Evaluation, 84, 87, 96
Event, 75, 77, 78, 80, 81, 85, 89, 92, 94, 95, 96
Event Development Matrix, 78
Event evaluation, 95
Event generators, 80, 81
Event shut down, 94
Events' industry, 75, 76
Experience, 7, 11, 13, 14, 18, 19, 21, 22, 29, 33,
34, 36, 37, 45, 47, 64, 66, 75, 77, 78, 79,
84, 85, 87, 88, 90, 96, 101, 103, 104, 106,
117, 120, 135, 157, 161, 166, 179, 192, 197
Exports, 171, 173, 174, 175, 180

F

Facilities, 50, 122, 196
familiar symbols, 192
Fast food, 7, 9, 15, 16, 17, 18, 22, 23, 90
Fast food culture, 15
Feasibility study, 78, 82, 89, 91, 93
Federation of Tour Operators, 159
Festivals, 7, 10, 14, 23, 33, 75, 76, 77, 80, 87,
96, 97, 109
Financial aspects, 89
Financial benefits, 134, 135
Financial control, 89
Financial management, 75, 89
Finland, 12, 48, 52
Fiscal, 33, 112
Five star, 63, 65, 66, 69
Flight catering, 4
Florence, 45, 176
Food, 3, 5, 7, 8, 9, 10, 12, 13, 14, 15, 16, 17,
18, 19, 20, 21, 22, 23, 29, 33, 39, 41, 44,
46, 64, 66, 69, 70, 82, 86, 90, 93, 135, 146,
158, 172, 176, 177, 178, 179, 189, 193,
194, 195, 198
Food and Agriculture Organisation, 128, 194

Food and Agriculture Organisation (FAO) of the
    United Nations, 195
Food and beverage, 90, 146
Food and drink, 189, 193
Food culture, 7, 8, 9, 10, 15, 16, 17, 22, 23
Food events and festivals, 14
Food habits, 193
Food preparation, 198
Food quality, 18
Food Standards Agency (FSA), 17
Food tourism, 7, 10, 13, 14, 22, 23
Food type, 9
Football, 111, 191
Forecasting, 5, 85, 86
Foreign exchange, 171
Four star, 62, 64, 66, 69
France, 7, 8, 11, 12, 16, 30, 32, 48, 52, 61, 102,
    117, 120, 124, 179
Franchised, 19, 142
Free, 47, 48, 50, 77, 79, 86, 88, 103, 111, 112
French, 8, 9, 19, 20, 21, 121, 122
French Government Tourist Office, 179
Friends of the Earth International, 130
Funding, 51, 52, 75, 76, 81, 82, 84, 89, 96, 100,
    103, 112, 124

G

Galleries, 102
Gantt charts, 84, 92
Geographical areas of risk, 158
Georgia, 13, 30, 52, 136
Germany, 11, 12, 30, 47, 48, 52, 62, 102, 117,
    120, 121, 122, 124
Glasnost, 107
Global, 7, 8, 9, 13, 15, 16, 17, 20, 22, 29, 32,
    44, 47, 50, 51, 76, 77, 101, 102, 110, 121,
    129, 130, 132, 134, 139, 148, 157, 171,
    172, 173, 176, 180, 187, 189, 197
Global destinations, 105, 106
Global problem, 127
Global wine production, 29
Globesity, 17
Gothenburg, 172
Government, 1, 2, 17, 21, 53, 55, 61, 68, 79, 80,
    81, 82, 95, 103, 110, 123, 124, 127, 133,
    141, 161, 163, 165, 171, 172, 177, 178,
    179, 195
Government information, 163
Government sector, 80
Grading of hotels, 196
Grading systems, 61, 62, 63, 67, 68, 69
Grand inspiration, 104, 111
Grand Tour, 45, 157
Greece, 11, 12, 30, 44, 48, 49, 135
Greek, 8, 9, 10, 20, 44, 45, 48
Green activities, 145
Green Hotelier & Restaurateur, 137
Greenland, 197
Greenpeace, 130

Gross Domestic Product (GDP), 1, 55, 171,
    173, 174, 175, 178, 180

H

Hallmark 97
Hallmark-events, 76, 88, 97
Hamburg, 172
Harmony, 132, 134, 148
Harrogate, 45
Hawaii, 178
Health, 5, 9, 17, 22, 45, 47, 83, 93, 118, 119,
    120, 121, 122, 123, 124, 141, 148, 157,
    158, 159, 160, 161, 163, 164, 165, 166,
    178, 189, 193, 194, 197
Health and Safety, 83, 93, 163, 165
Health and Safety Executive, 83
Health consequences of travel, 157
Health information, 157, 161
Health issues, 196
Health tourism, 107, 117, 118, 119, 120, 121,
    122, 123, 124, 125, 157
Health tourism consumer, 120
Health tourism product, 117, 118
Health tourist, 117, 120
Health-care tourism, 117, 118, 121
Healthy eating, 7, 16, 17, 22, 23, 119
Helsinki, 196
Heritage tourism, 7
Heterostereotypes, 191
Hi-life diners club, 20
Historical, 14, 33, 46, 49, 77, 94, 102, 105, 106,
    108, 111, 180
Hofstede, 189
Holiday environment, 120, 158, 159
Holiday experiences, 29
Holiday insurance, 160
Hospitality, 1, 2, 3, 4, 7, 9, 21, 23, 43, 44, 45,
    46, 53, 54, 64, 65, 66, 68, 75, 77, 80, 90,
    92, 94, 110, 196
Hospitality packages, 94
Host community, 75, 81, 194
Hotel classification, 61, 67
Hotel facilities, 63, 65
Hotel management and offices, 147
Hotel rating system, 62
Hotels, 1, 4, 5, 14, 18, 19, 20, 22, 29, 46, 48,
    50, 52, 61, 62, 63, 64, 65, 66, 67, 68, 70,
    71, 108, 123, 124, 137, 138, 140, 141, 142,
    178, 179, 181, 189, 193, 196, 198
Housekeeping, 146
Human capital resources, 197
Human Immunodeficiency Virus (HIV)/Acquired
    Immune Deficiency Syndrome (AIDS), 157
Human resource, 53, 86, 91
Human resource management, 75, 85, 86
Hungary, 12, 30, 32, 38, 47, 48, 51, 52, 53, 54,
    107, 109, 117, 123, 174, 176, 177, 180

I

Ideology', 190
Ill-health, 118
Imagescape, 104, 111, 112
Impact studies, 181
Impacts of events, 78
Incidental, 117, 120
Income, 9, 21, 32, 33, 48, 51, 81, 88, 90, 93, 94,
    97, 103, 133, 171, 175, 178, 179, 180, 187
Independent travel, 195
India, 8, 173, 180
Indian, 8, 10, 20, 160
Indirect benefits, 175, 176
Indoor facilities, 143
Induced effects, 178
Induction, 86
Industrial impacts, 45
Industrial pollution, 197
Infrastructure, 13, 18, 33, 36, 41, 43, 44, 46, 47,
    48, 49, 50, 53, 76, 77, 81, 91, 106, 108,
    110, 111, 131, 134, 171, 177, 180, 197
Infrastructure requirements, 33, 34
Injuries, 158, 159, 160, 164, 198
Inns, 45, 46
Instinctual human behaviour, 190
Intangible, 88, 105
International Atomic Energy Agency, 128
International Council for Local Environmental
    Initiatives, 133
International Ecotourism Society, 134, 135
International foods, 8, 33
International Hotel & Restaurant Association,
    137
International Institute for Sustainable
    Development, 130
International Labour Organization, 179
International Maritime Organisation, 128, 165
International Monetary Fund, 129
International tourism, 159
International Union for Protection of Nature,
    129
International visitors, 33, 47, 48, 97, 160, 182,
    191
Interviews, 140
Ireland, 11, 48, 52, 106, 111, 166
Iron curtain, 49, 57, 106
Isle of Man, 196
Israel, 31, 102, 117, 122, 124
Italian, 8, 9, 19, 20, 21, 134, 191, 197
Italy, 7, 11, 12, 17, 30, 32, 48, 102, 117, 120,
124, 157, 191, 197

J

Jet lag, 159
Jewish, 121, 193
Jorvik Viking Centre, 105

L

Labour, 1, 2, 3, 4, 5, 46, 51, 135, 172, 175, 179,
    187, 192
Labour costs, 2, 3, 4, 5
Lake District, 103
Language, 47, 56, 71, 188, 190, 192, 195, 197,
    198
Languages, 188, 194, 196
Las Vegas, 105, 106, 110
Latitudes, 32
Latvia, 12, 31, 48, 52, 54, 109, 111, 174, 175,
    176
Laundry, 146
Leadership, 5, 85, 86, 88
Leakage, 178
Leamington Spa, 45
Learning experience, 134
Learning experiences, 199
Lech, 196
Legal, 127
Legal considerations, 82
Legislation, 82, 83, 121, 127, 142, 148, 165
Leisure, 1, 3, 4, 7, 9, 10, 18, 21, 43, 44, 46, 56,
    75, 77, 80, 85, 118, 119, 143, 187, 190
Lesbos, 196
Libya, 180
Licences, 82, 90, 93
Licensed trade, 5
Life style diseases, 118
Lights, 75, 92, 93
Lillehammer, 196
Lithuania, 12, 31, 48, 52, 54, 109, 174, 176, 194
Liverpool, 102, 105, 106
Local, 3, 7, 9, 12, 13, 14, 15, 16, 17, 20, 22, 23,
    29, 32, 34, 36, 41, 44, 46, 47, 49, 51, 53,
    71, 75, 76, 77, 79, 80, 81, 82, 86, 87, 91,
    92, 93, 94, 96, 97, 103, 106, 110, 111, 112,
    123, 124, 130, 133, 134, 135, 141, 143,
    145, 146, 148, 160, 172, 175, 176, 177,
    178, 179, 180, 181, 187, 188, 189, 191,
    192, 193, 194, 195, 196, 197, 199
Local economy, 32, 36, 175, 176, 178
Local government agencies, 133
Local population, 82, 123, 133
Local traditions, 197
Location, 13, 14, 18, 44, 45, 50, 53, 54, 82, 90,
    93, 97, 104, 112, 120, 137, 159, 198
Logistical plan, 92
Logistics, 75, 91, 92, 98
Logistic's plan, 91
London, 8, 14, 18, 46, 54, 63, 102, 103, 104,
    105, 160, 176, 177, 178
Long trip tourists, 32
Lottery, 62, 103
Lowry Hotel, 20
Luxembourg, 12, 31, 48, 52
Luxemburg, 177
Luxury hotels, 140, 142

M

Macedonia, 30, 174, 195
Maintenance and garages, 147
Malaga, 172
Maldives, 172, 173
Malta, 12, 31, 48, 158, 174, 175
Management, 2, 4, 5, 29, 40, 54, 56, 65, 75, 76, 79, 81, 82, 83, 84, 85, 86, 89, 90, 92, 93, 94, 95, 96, 103, 107, 108, 110, 112, 127, 128, 130, 133, 137, 139, 140, 141, 142, 143, 144, 145, 147, 148, 154, 164, 174, 195, 198
Managing risk, 161
Manchester, 7, 14, 18, 19, 20, 21, 46, 79, 86, 88, 96
Man-made, 101, 103
Marching bands, 104
Maritime, 105
Marketing, 1, 3, 13, 14, 15, 18, 22, 27, 40, 41, 51, 54, 55, 64, 71, 75, 82, 87, 88, 94, 95, 97, 103, 110, 111, 112, 118, 147, 181
Marketing formula, 87
Material costs, 3
Mauritius, 173, 180
McDonaldisation, 15
McDonalds, 15, 16, 17, 22
Medical treatment, 120, 160
Mediterranean coast, 180
Mega-event, 77, 82, 88
Mega-events, 76, 86, 90, 91, 96, 97
Mental template, 191
Mental templates, 188
Merchandise, 32, 93, 173
Merchandising, 3, 75, 87, 88, 94
Mexican, 8, 10, 20
Mexico, 30, 173, 180
Michelin, 14, 18, 19
Micro-climates, 29
Midland Hotel, 46
Million passengers per year ratio (mppy), 172
Mineral springs, 117, 118, 119, 120, 122, 123, 124
Mode of transport, 35
Models, 78, 101, 185
Moldova, 30, 32, 52
Montenegro, 109, 174, 180
Moscow, 49, 61, 72, 107
Motion sickness, 159
Mountain regions, 181
Multinational companies, 177
Multi-skilling, 4, 5
Multiplier, 133, 178
Multipliers, 178
Museums, 33, 102, 103, 189
Muslims, 193

N

Naarden, 196

National Consultative Codex Committee, 194, 195
National Councils for Sustainable Development, 130
National cultural differences, 189
National economy, 130, 178
National Mining Museum, 104
Natural, 9, 52, 88, 101, 103, 104, 112, 117, 118, 119, 120, 121, 123, 128, 130, 132, 134, 135, 141, 142, 146, 148, 161, 174, 187, 189, 193
Natural resources, 130, 133, 148
Natural Resources Defence Council, 130
Nautical, 106
Negative effects of tourism, 133
Negative impacts, 78, 79
Nepal, 179
Netherlands, 11, 12, 48, 52, 105, 124
Networking, 3, 5, 84
New York, 121, 122, 137, 175, 176, 178
New Zealand, 30, 158, 159, 160, 172, 173
Nice, 172
No-frills carriers, 172
Non-governmental, 108
Non-governmental organisations, 129
North Atlantic Treaty Organisation, 129
Northern, 52, 111, 158, 177, 179
Northern Europe, 163
Northern Ireland, 48
Numerical terms, 33

O

Obesity, 7, 17, 118, 193
Odsherred, 196
Olympic, 76, 79, 81, 83, 86, 87, 88, 93, 96
Olympic Games, 44, 76, 81, 83, 87, 93, 96, 100
One star, 62, 64, 66, 69
Operational, 75, 76, 83, 84, 86, 89, 90, 91
Operational management techniques, 2
Operational planning, 84
Organic, 131, 135, 146
Organic food, 135
Organisation for Economic Cooperation and Development, 129
Organisation of events, 84
Organisational culture, 189
Orientation, 51, 86, 87
Origins of cultural practices, 188
Outbound tourism, 11
Owned, 103, 112

P

Package, 14, 33, 94, 122, 135, 163, 178, 195
Paid, 33, 86, 90, 94, 103, 106, 112, 179
Pakistani, 8
Pamplona, 106
Paris, 45, 102, 104
Partnerships, 53, 79, 81, 82, 107
Perception, 192

Perceptual constancy, 192
Performers, 75, 82, 92, 93
PEST analysis, 54
Philippines, 158
PIECE, 87
Planning exercise, 29
Planning strategies, 84
Poland, 12, 47, 48, 51, 52, 53, 54, 107, 109,
    117, 123, 174
Political history, 175
Pollution, 36, 50, 128, 132, 133, 138, 148, 180,
    197
Portugal, 11, 12, 30, 48
Positive experiences, 134
Post-industrial, economies, 187
Power, 75, 92, 93
Prevention, 93, 117, 120, 143, 147, 161, 164,
    194
Price demand curve, 180
Primary functions of culture, 189
Principles,
    cultural, 127, 128, 132, 133, 134, 136, 151
    ethical, 127
    legal, 127
Private enterprise, 136
Privately owned, 103, 112
Procurement, 89
Production, 4, 11, 13, 14, 31, 32, 35, 36, 39, 45,
    46, 75, 91, 92, 107, 108, 132, 135, 138,
    139, 144, 146, 148, 176, 177, 198
Production areas, 139
Production schedule, 75, 92, 94
Productivity, 1, 2, 4, 5, 6, 172
Professional competences, 198
Programming, 87, 95
Project management, 94
Promotion, 3, 13, 18, 33, 35, 37, 41, 78, 88, 94,
    98, 107, 111, 112, 117, 123, 124
Prostitution, 159, 180
Provision, 43, 44, 45, 46, 47, 49, 50, 53, 66, 67,
    70, 71, 82, 86, 88, 90, 93, 96, 101, 104,
    105, 106, 108, 111, 118, 135, 147, 160,
    161, 166, 172, 189, 192, 193, 194, 196,
    198, 199
Psychological requirements, 197
Pub, 10
Public/private sector partnership, 110
Publicly, 68, 72, 103, 112, 124
Publicly owned, 103

Q

Quality, 1, 2, 5, 9, 17, 18, 33, 37, 41, 50, 51, 56,
    61, 62, 63, 64, 65, 66, 67, 68, 69, 70, 71,
    86, 90, 93, 106, 110, 111, 112, 130, 131,
    142, 148, 162, 163, 189, 194, 195, 196
Quality indicator, 61, 71
Quality perceptions, 196
Quality wine, 32
Queensland, 32, 38, 41

Questionnaire, 140, 163

R

Radium Hot Springs, 122, 124, 126
Rating systems, 61
Reception, 64, 66, 147
Recuperation, 117, 120, 144
Recycling, 131, 139, 144
Red Square, 107
Regional climate, 29
Regional development, 133
Regional food, 9, 15, 22
Regional practices, 188
Religious practices, 188
Reporting, 96
Respite, 117, 120
Responsibility for managing risk, 157, 161
Responsible business, 134
Restaurant and food services, 33
Restaurants, 1, 5, 9, 10, 14, 16, 18, 19, 20, 21,
    22, 29, 33, 50, 63, 66, 68, 108, 135, 137,
    143, 177, 179, 189
Retail operations, 33
Retention, 5, 14
Revenue, 4, 77, 78, 87, 88, 89, 90, 103, 106,
    177, 182
Ribbon Awards, 65
Risk, 21, 32, 35, 83, 84, 93, 94, 104, 157, 158,
    160, 161, 163, 164, 166, 189, 191
Risk assessment, 83, 84
Risk management, 75, 83, 84, 94, 166
Risk management and prevention, 163
Roads are congested, 35
Roles and responsibilities, 161
Roman Empire, 44, 45
Romania, 30, 32, 47, 51, 52, 53, 109, 174, 175,
    194, 195
Rome, 45, 191
Royal Automobile Club, 18, 61, 63, 65, 73
Rules, 129, 188, 198
Rules of human behaviour, 190
Rural, 35, 36, 38, 46, 51, 52, 76, 135, 181, 195,
    197
Russia, 30, 32, 47, 107, 113, 174

S

Safe drinking water, 198
Safety, 50, 63, 82, 83, 84, 90, 93, 141, 157, 159,
    160, 161, 162, 163, 164, 165, 166, 193,
    194, 195, 196, 197, 198
Safety risks, 157, 161, 163, 166
Saratoga Springs, USA, 121
Satisfaction, 32, 101, 163, 166, 193, 194, 198
Saudi Arabia, 171
Scandinavia, 175, 176
Scarborough, 45
Scotch Whisky Heritage Centre, 105
Scottish, 67, 69, 70, 71
Scottish Tourist Boards, 40, 67, 69, 70, 71

Seasonal, 9, 111, 179
Security screening, 91
Service areas, 139
Service industry, 4, 44
Service-based, 187
Severe Acute Respiratory Syndrome (SARS), 159
Sex tourism, 157, 158, 159
Sexually transmitted infections, 157, 158
Seychelles, 172, 173, 180
Shannon, 172
Short breaks market, 110
Short trip tourists, 32
Shrinking market, 32
Skilling, 4, 5
Slovakia, 12, 30, 32, 48, 49, 51, 52, 53, 54, 97,
    109, 117, 123, 174, 180, 195
Slovenia, 12, 30, 48, 54, 109, 174, 195
Slow food, 7, 15, 17
Small and medium sized enterprises (SMEs), 51
Social, 8, 27, 49, 78, 100, 107, 129, 131, 175,
    178
Social aims, 76, 79
Social benefits, 32
Social etiquette, 190
Social skills, 65
Social tourism, 107
Socialism, 47, 107
Söderslätt, 196
Soil, 29, 197
Sound, 75, 92, 93
Sources of culture, 188
South Africa, 30, 173, 180
South Australia, 32
South Australian Tourism Commission, 32
South Caucasus Cooperation Program, 136
Souvenir, 40, 108
Souvenirs, 32
Soviet Union, 47, 107, 117, 123, 158
Spa tourism, 117, 118, 125
    definition, 117
Spain, 8, 11, 12, 30, 32, 48, 52, 73, 76, 102,
    106, 135, 154, 172, 173, 174, 175, 177, 189
Spanish, 8, 9, 19, 20, 106, 196, 197
Special effects, 75, 92, 93
Special event, 77
Special events, 9, 77, 99, 101, 104
Sponsors, 79, 81, 82, 90, 94, 95
Sponsorship, 75, 81, 82
Sporting events, 77, 80, 102
Sri Lanka, 158, 179
Staffing, 86
Staging, 92, 95, 97
Stakeholders, 75, 76, 77, 79, 80, 81, 83, 84, 85,
    87, 90, 91, 92, 98
Stereotyping, 191
Strategic, 2, 33, 37, 53, 64, 76, 83, 84, 89, 112
Strategic planning, 87
Strategies, 12, 22, 29, 33, 37, 50, 54, 76, 93,
    111, 122, 129, 130, 147, 174, 188

Studie Europa 2000+, 132
Subculture, 197
Subcultures, 191
Superstructure, 43, 47, 49, 105, 106, 107, 108
Supply, 1, 43, 50, 51, 52, 81, 82, 90, 91, 118,
    121, 145, 147, 172, 180, 198
Supportive therapies, 118
Sustainability, 146, 196
Sustainable development, 108, 127, 128, 129,
    130, 132, 133, 135, 136, 137, 139, 140,
    141, 142, 145, 148
Sustainable development indicators, 131
Sustainable development of tourism, 127, 137,
    142
Sustainable tourism, 137
Sustainable tourism, 40, 127, 134, 142
Sustainable tourism development, 133
Sweden, 12, 48, 52, 177
Switzerland, 30, 52, 120, 159, 172, 173, 174,
    175, 176
SWOT analysis, 112

T

T&T (Travel and Tourism) economy, 172, 173,
    174, 175
T&T (Travel and Tourism) industry, 172, 173,
    174
Takeaway, 10
Tallinn, 172
Tangibilise, 105
Target market, 13, 23, 87, 103
Technological impacts, 46
Technology, 2, 46, 55, 56, 122, 139, 187
Temperature, 138, 189
Template, 190, 191
Tex-Mex, 8
Thai, 8, 9, 10, 20
Thailand, 158, 159, 173
The Worldwatch Institute, 130
Theatre, 80, 87, 105, 178
Theme park, 103, 104
Theming, 75, 92
Therapies,
    alternative, 118
    complementary, 118
Thermal tourism, 117, 118, 119
Three super industries, 187
Three star, 62, 64, 66, 69
Ticketing system, 87
Tickets, 56, 79, 81, 87
Tokyo, 104
Toulouse, 196
Tour operators, 35, 110, 160, 179
Tourism, 1, 3, 4, 7, 8, 11, 12, 13, 14, 18, 20, 21,
    22, 23, 29, 32, 33, 35, 36, 37, 43, 44, 47,
    48, 49, 51, 52, 54, 61, 62, 67, 68, 69, 70,
    75, 77, 78, 80, 87, 96, 97, 01, 102, 104,
    105, 106, 107, 108, 110, 111, 117, 118,
    119, 120, 121, 122, 123, 124, 128, 131,

132, 133, 134, 135, 136, 137, 140, 141, 142, 145, 157, 158, 159, 160, 161, 162, 164, 165, 166, 171, 172, 173, 174, 175, 176, 177, 178, 179, 180, 181, 187, 188, 191, 192, 193, 194, 196, 197, 198, 199
Tourism activities, 187, 198
Tourism development, 132, 187
Tourism economy, 106
Tourism industry, 12, 22, 29, 32, 33, 43, 49, 53, 101, 102, 106, 110, 111, 121, 122, 123, 124, 127, 136, 140, 142, 157, 158, 159, 166, 171, 172, 174, 175
Tourism legacy, 108
Tourism marketing, 12
Tourism strategies, 12, 13, 14, 22, 36
Tourist attraction, 104
Tourist attractions, 101, 104, 105, 108, 110
Tourist Boards, 63, 67, 68, 69
Tourist destination choices, 192
Tourist expenditure, 176, 177
Tourist experience, 161
Tourist flow, 32, 107
Trade unions, 107
Training, 3, 4, 5, 41, 48, 49, 52, 53, 67, 77, 80, 86, 88, 119, 137, 141, 145, 146, 192, 195, 197, 198
Training programme, 86
Trains, 51
Transport, 21, 35, 46, 47, 48, 50, 51, 78, 79, 86, 89, 93, 95, 106, 110, 111, 131, 134, 135, 136, 137, 141, 145, 146, 147, 165, 172, 176, 177, 178, 179, 181, 184, 195, 198, 199
Transport links, 50, 51, 111
Transportation links, 108
Travel agents, 163
Travel brochures, 161
Travellers' diarrhoea, 157
Travel-related accidents, 157
Travel-related conditions, 157, 159
Travel-related disease, 157
Travel-related illness, 157, 158
Travel-related injuries, 157
Travel-related threats, 157, 160
Trompenaars, 189
Tsunami, 174
Tuscany, 134
Two star, 62, 64, 66, 69
Types of employment, 179
Types of events, 80
Types of risk, 158
Typical nature of travel party, 34
Typology, 80, 101

U

U.S.S.R. (Union of Soviet Socialist Republics), 52
UK vineyards, 32
Ukraine, 30, 52, 174, 195
Umbria, 134

United Kingdom, 1, 7, 31, 32, 45, 48, 52, 61, 63, 72, 77, 79, 172, 173, 187
United Kingdom of Great Britain and Northern Ireland, 48
United Nations, 126, 128, 129, 132, 148, 165, 194, 195
United Nations Commission on Sustainable Development, 129
United Nations Conference on Environment and Development, 132, 148
United Nations Development Programme, 129
United Nations Economic Commission for Europe, 129
United Nations Educational, Scientific and Cultural Organisation, 128
United Nations Environment Programme, 129, 179
United Nations Industrial Development Organisation, 129
United Nations Istanbul Declaration, 132
United States of America, 32, 173
Uruguay, 30, 173

V

Varieties and blend of grapes, 29
Vegetarian, 10, 16, 19, 20, 21, 23, 146, 188
Velvet revolution, 49
Venezuela, 173, 180
Venice, 45, 77
Venue, 75, 76, 78, 82, 87, 91, 92, 93, 94, 95, 96
Venues, 96
Vinification, 29
VIP (Very Important Person) area, 90
Visit to the vineyard, 29
VisitBritain, 61, 69, 70
Visitor attraction, 104
Visitor attractions, 103, 112
Visitor services, 33
Visitors, 34, 46, 161, 179, 197
Volunteers, 79, 86, 88, 90

W

Walt Disney, 104
Waste, 4, 128, 131, 133, 139, 141, 142, 144, 146, 197
Waste management, 144
   recycling, 139
Water consumption, 133, 138, 141, 145
Water consumption management, 145
Water supply problems, 180
Wedding organiser/facilitator, 76
Welsh Tourist Board, 67
West Germany, 120, 124
Western Europe, 43, 47, 48, 50, 51, 52, 110, 121, 123, 158, 174
Western Europeans, 195
Wine, 12, 13, 29, 32, 33, 34, 35, 36, 37, 41, 64, 135, 146, 191
Wine consumption, 29, 32

Wine industry, 29, 32
Wine production, 31
Wine tourism, 12, 29, 32, 33, 36, 37
    definition, 29
Winemakers' Federation of Australia, 29, 32, 37,
    40
Winter sports, 180
Work breakdown schedules, 84, 92
World Bank, 129, 179
World conservation Union, 134
World cup, 87
World Health Organisation, 17, 117, 158, 162,
    164, 165, 195

World Meteorological Organisation, 128
World Resources Institute, 179, 184
World Tourism Organisation, 52, 61, 118, 132,
    133, 154, 161, 164, 165, 171, 194
World Travel and Tourism Council, 171
World War II, 47, 106
World Wide Fund for Nature, 130
World wine production, 32

Y

Yugoslavia, 30, 32, 47, 109